THE PROMISE OF HUMAN AUTONOMY

WALTER GRUEN, PH.D.

Copyright © 2017 by Walter Gruen, Ph.D.

ISBN: Softcover   978-1-4771-2775-9
       eBook   978-1-4771-2776-6

All rights reserved. No part of this book may be reproduced or transmitted in any form or by any means, electronic or mechanical, including photocopying, recording, or by any information storage and retrieval system, without permission in writing from the copyright owner.

Reviewed, edited and clarified by Mrs. Walter Gruen

Any people depicted in stock imagery provided by Thinkstock are models, and such images are being used for illustrative purposes only.
Certain stock imagery © Thinkstock.

Print information available on the last page.

Rev. date: 06/21/2017

To order additional copies of this book, contact:
Xlibris
1-888-795-4274
www.Xlibris.com
Orders@Xlibris.com
537308

Acknowledgments to our daughter, Marion Gruen Anderson, who researched, completed and arranged the bibliography. I wish it were possible to thank those who helped Walter as he wrote his book. I am sure he shared his appreciation with you. I would also like to thank those who have since helped Marion and me with the final touches.

Mrs. Walter Gruen

Walter Gruen, Ph. D.

Walter Gruen (1920-1980) was, in his last professional positions, Research Psychologist, Rhode Island Hospital, Providence, Rhode Island 1966-1980) and Clinical Assistant/Associate Professor of Psychiatry 1974/77-1980), Brown University Medical School. His academic degrees included: M.B., University of London, 1938; B.A.,

University of California at Los Angeles, 1942; M.A., Ph. D., University of California, Berkeley, 1949, 1950. He was a Diplomat in Clinical Psychology, American Board of Professional Psychology, and a Fellow of the American Psychological Association in Divisions 8 (Social and Personality Psychology), 9 (S.P.S.S.I.) and 29 (Psychotherapy). He was also a Fellow of the American Group Psychotherapy Association. Dr. Gruen was a former President of the Rhode Island Psychological Association (1972-1974) and of the Rhode Island Citizens for Better Mental Health, Inc. (1975-1977). Throughout his professional career as a clinical psychologist and teacher, Dr. Gruen held a number of research and teaching appointments in such institutions as: University of Illinois; University of Chicago; University of Buffalo; Harvard University and Tufts University. His publications and presentations included 9 chapters in a variety of books, 41 articles in scientific and professional journals, and 24 papers and other presentations at scientific conferences in the areas of personality psychology, group dynamics and group therapy.

CONTENTS

Synopsis xiii

Chapter I   Adam's Soliloquy: Humanity's Dilemma with
Autonomy 1

A fictional hour of leisure and solitude in the life of Adam during the adolescence of Cain and Abel, in which Adam wrestles with the common existential questions which have since been shared by mankind, and which are related to freedom versus dependency, faith in oneself versus faith in authority, and creativity versus the encapsulation of one's needs. These questions are also the ones which an autonomously functioning adult may have to face and solve in some fashion.

Chapter II   Early Technology and Economic Development as Deterrents to the Concept of Autonomy 13

This and the next two chapters examine different perspectives by which we can understand how the emphasis on human autonomy is only a recent phenomenon and was not generally accepted or understood 100 years ago. In this chapter we examine the technology, resources, technical know-how, and the economic organization of primitive and ancient civilizations of the western world, including the Middle Ages up to the Renaissance and the beginning of the industrial revolution. Man's tenuous foothold on his fate, and his lack of control and understanding of nature produced terror, uncertainty, and great hardships, so that there was neither time nor the stimulation to think about autonomy, nor the opportunity to accept it.

Chapter III   Religious Doctrine as an Obstacle to Self-Fulfillment 28

Here we connect the predominant ideologies with the physical realities described in the previous chapter by concentrating on the predominant religions of the past. We see how their definition of Man as a creature dependent on a powerful and merciful God filled in the existential void created by the struggle between one's own consciousness or reason, and the realities of a dangerous and capricious world. Hence the doctrines coming from the religions helped to both explain and sugarcoat various existential dilemmas, and therewith insured the status quo and a certain peace of mind. However, these principles also denied the existence of a "free will" and encouraged dependence on authority and conformity.

Chapter IV   Experiences of Autonomy as Illusions Prior to the Science of Psychology 60

A final reason for the lack of concern with autonomy was the great confusion that existed about the functioning of the human mind. Various philosophers are quoted who tried to examine and explain mental functioning prior to the development of psychology as a science. The confusion and the fallacies of their initial efforts are examined, and were seen to be rooted in the structuralistic approach, which compartmentalized and mechanized the mind and blinded them from recognizing the process characteristics of human personality. An overemphasis on general laws also blinded them from an understanding of individual differences and stages of development. Hence they missed the clues that might have led them to self-definition and self-involvement as legitimate stages in human maturation.

Chapter V   Definitions of Autonomy and its Beginnings in History and Philosophy..87

Various definition and labels of self-actualization and autonomy are examined to distil the essence of autonomous functioning as discussed in representative psychological theories. The first tender beginnings of these concepts are then traced back both to some ancient philosophers and to the more recent thinkers from the Renaissance on.

Chapter VI   The Anchorage of Human Autonomy in Contemporary Personality Theory 109

The personality theories of Maslow, Erikson, Fromm, and Rogers are examined to show that self-actualization is a valid and recognizable human process and a stage in development. It is further supported by clinical and empirical observations (e.g. from Angyal, Loevinger, Levinson, Shostrom, etc.). Autonomous functioning can then be defined objectively, even though it may be identified through slightly different processes, or in different developmental stages.

Chapter VII Psychotherapy as a Successful Program to Isolate and Activate Autonomous Behavior............. 141

An examination of some contemporary systems of psychotherapy show how selected theories of personality can become successful prescriptions for the achievement and practice of autonomous behavior. Some schools of therapy, especially those which magnify a concept of the self, encourage the patient to trust himself and to step out to new learning, new experience and new experimentation. Some recent research is summarized to show the common denominators in the therapeutic alliance that become the successful ingredients towards more autonomous behavior, regardless of the theoretical base of the therapist. These processes are further proof that humans can practice some self-fulfillment and that we know something about the ingredients and the antecedents.

Chapter VIII   General Systems Theory as a Scientific Base for Autonomous Behavior.. 153

The major concepts of general systems theory are presented in popular terms in order to reveal their power in helping us to understand any living process as distinct from movement and action in non-living machines and systems. These principles create an even firmer scientific base for: 1. the definition of an organizing force in the personality, such as an ego or a self; 2. the existence of a process towards self-definition and self-expansion, or autonomy. Various definitions of the ego are also examined and consolidated under general systems concepts. General systems theory even explains and legitimizes human faith and hope and a belief in values that cannot be proven. The criticisms of some existentialist and Zen writers against the legitimacy of an ego are examined and refuted with general systems principles. Their call for transcendental experiences are legitimized instead as a creative, but temporary, stage in the well-functioning ego operating in the peak of autonomous behavior.

Chapter IX　　Democracy as the Political Base of Human Autonomy 179

An examination of the democratic principles of contemporary western governments and of their Rights of Men reveals that this new emphasis on the worth of Man triggered the very discovery of autonomy as a psychological process and guaranteed its general acceptance. The uniqueness of the personality was then recognized as a cornerstone of human values and was rooted in a social system of enablements and opportunities. Democracy also provided a system of checks and balances which can prevent repressive power from exercising too much authority.

Chapter X　　The Failure of Communism as a Further Proof of the Process of Autonomy 205

An examination of the theoretical basis of communism with its so-called scientific theory of history reveals a disastrous omission of the facts of human motivation. There is in communism the insistence on an elite who claim that only "experts" can put the theory into practice and become permanent watchdogs. Thus the whole base of society is changed, so that power is again centralized and abused. Communism therefore invites its own failure to guarantee important human needs. This failure allows us to make further observations about corruption of power and its inhibiting effects on self-enhancement. The necessity of checks on personal power is therefore reinforced.

Chapter XI　　The Problems around Human Autonomy 221

The excesses of autonomous behavior or the misinterpretations of autonomy as license may result in irresponsible behavior, lack of trust, compulsive and destructive non-conformity, a cancerous lack of concern and even in anarchy. Often problems arise from the frustrations of being autonomous in a large and impersonal society which advertises its advantages, and these problems may result in alienation and apathy. Most of these problems seem tied up with the deficiencies in human development. They are magnified by the misunderstanding that autonomy is an achievement rather than an instant gift. In this way genuine autonomous functioning is short-circuited and becomes an artificial exercise. Or it results in a loss of hope which may be destructive to the self or to others. In either case further development to higher stages of mental functioning are inhibited.

Chapter XII   Autonomy and Responsibility: Towards a Scientific Morality..242

An examination of stages of personal development leads to such systems as Kohlberg's presentation of maturational stages in human morality and similar observations in Loevinger and others. Further evidence of the fact that responsible behavior is a necessary forerunner of independent behavior comes from a variety of recent research. This evidence provides support that we can achieve a balance between self-actualization and conformity, and between self-development and responsibilities. Also newer emphasis on the power and use of rational thinking in some of the contemporary schools of psychotherapy (cognitive therapy, rational-emotive therapy, etc.) give us hope that we can solve existing and future problems inherent in our encouragement of autonomous behavior.

Chapter XIII Suggestions for the Future 263

    A number of suggestions are advanced that would alert us to the dangers of ideologies and practices that inhibit autonomy and freedom. These suggestions offer documentation as a legitimate stage in development. Among the suggestions is the creation of a new church with its ritualized practices, which would legitimize and concretize our faiths in human goodness and human growth. In this way we would not need external and unreachable authorities that supposedly set rules for human conduct for their own purposes. Another suggestion, already investigated by social science, comes from the successful use of the mediation process to be used for settling disputes between institutions and between nations. Further suggestions focus on the specialized uses of rational thinking in the use of solving human problems and disputes. It may become mandatory to identify and place special concentration on rational processes. At the same time we need to improve in recognizing irrational components, accept them as human, and allow them to function according to some plan or schedule. These suggestions are tied up with the existential questions raised in Adam's fictionalized soliloquy in Chapter I, and are presented here as possible solutions.

Bibliography 327

Synopsis

The thesis of this book is that autonomous behavior in the human being has now been securely anchored as a stage in the development of human personality. It has been recognized and described as a valid form of adult human behavior from the evidence supplied by a number of prominent clinicians and experimenters in the area of personality psychology. Furthermore, self-actualizing behavior has been shown to emerge as the more dominant form of expression in people after they have tried to get help with personal problems from the advocates of some of the newer psychotherapies. Autonomy has also been independently established as a necessary expression of life forces on the psychological level by General Systems Theory. Hence Autonomy is an important characteristic of the living organisms in their tendency to achieve a condition of minimal disorganization or "negentropy".

We can furthermore understand the lack of awareness in history of this human process for the following reasons: 1. Technological and scientific development did not allow men to develop long enough for it to emerge except for a few; 2. Pre-industrial technology further prevented Man from developing the physical security or the leisure that is needed for its exercise; 3. Religion and other ideologies forced Man to put his faith and trust in an all-powerful and warmly concerned deity rather than in himself; 4. Confusions about the real working of the human mind embroiled the philosophers over the ages to debate on the so-called faculties of Man and their interrelationships which effectively hid autonomous functioning under a number of other categories; 5.

Men so organized their society that they preferred dependency on a King or on an aristocracy. It took the development of machines to do Man's work, knowledge of medicine to keep him alive long enough, an acceptance of a democratic ideology and government, and the scientific investigations of mental processes and personality to see autonomy as a legitimate human form of expression.

The exercise of human autonomy has also led to some serious problems for mankind. We can attribute a sense of irresponsibility and lack of consideration, alienation, apathy, and even forms of anarchy to this. These difficulties have pushed whole societies to experimental solutions in which autonomy is subjugated either to irrational leaders or to a pseudo-scientific dictatorship called communism. If we recognize that autonomy is a stage in adult life, after the person has learned and accepted conformity and a sense of responsibility, we can distinguish between true exercise of autonomy and pseudo autonomy. Recent psychological observations about the development of morality also equate the development of the highest stage, namely consideration of the common good, with the exercise of autonomy. It therefore becomes possible for Man to take another look at the possible application of autonomous functioning to the solution of problems in our society, rather than magnify the latter with the slogan: "Let each person do his or her own thing."

We can begin here by carefully separating the use of rational thinking available in the autonomy stage from the irrational behavior found in all of us, including moments in the lives of self-actualizing people. Armed with this dichotomy we could then heavily lean on the rational thinking processes for solving problems. For instance, we could increase the utilization of mediation practices on all levels of society to settle the inevitable disputes that arise when the self-expressions of people clash with those of others. We could also organize and legitimate various institutions and practices which would allow people to freely express their irrational impulses. In this way these expressions would be isolated from the mainstream and would not hurt others except the participants who are willing to take the risk.

We are, therefore, at the choice point in history where we can accept autonomous functioning as a social goal in addition to our support in our democratic society and political institutions. We can reorganize our society to accept the facts of human development and personality organization and create the institutions that will help us solve some of our most pressing contemporary problems. The alternative possibility is that our problems may become so large that they may destroy our environment and life itself, or that we lose faith in our future and muddle on in conditions that penalize autonomous behavior as too dangerous.

Chapter I

ADAM'S SOLILOQUY: HUMANITY'S DILEMMA WITH AUTONOMY

One fine summer day long after he had been locked out of the Garden of Eden, Adam sat down on a rock overlooking the little pond close to where Eve and their two boys were preparing the evening meal. He had recently discovered how he could duplicate the fire of lightning by striking sparks from a rock into dry pieces of wood bark. He had then taught his family to heat the meat and make it taste differently. Now he could look forward to a meal of cooked, warm venison tonight in the hut which they all had built after Abel discovered how one could cut slabs of clay from a dry riverbed, place them on top of each other and cover them with hay. It now provided shelter for them from wind, rain or too much sun. A few days ago he had successfully experimented with sharpening the edge of a stone by striking other rocks against it. This tool now enlarged his world in several ways. For instance, he found that he could cut down reeds and bushes and had been intrigued with the idea that this tool could make his life easier. After he had gone off this morning he killed a wild goat with his homemade spear and then he tried to use the knife-like rock to skin the animal and cut it into large pieces. To his surprise this task took him half the time it usually consumed when he had used his hands and sticks. Now he suddenly found himself with an hour or more of sunlight to spare before his family ate their customary meal at sundown.

As he sat on the rock to listen to the sound of leaves whispering in the breeze and the frogs piping below, he saw his bearded face peering back at him in the still water, surrounded by puffy white clouds reflected from a brilliant dark-blue sky. It was not often that he had found the time to sit in leisure and think about his life and to contemplate his self-reflection. He savored the peace and leisure, but also knew that he would experience difficult moments, if he gave in to his solitude.

Here he was, placed on this bountiful earth as the pinnacle of creation and as the image of the most perfect being, and yet he had made mistakes and had suffered much -- along with moments of glory and triumph. How often had he marveled at the idea that he could think -- think about all kinds of objective matters and objects, about ideas, and even introspect about himself and his feelings without the need to touch anything or move from the spot. He did not even have to fix his gaze on the object contemplated. He remembered how he had been able to accept that he existed as an entity, because he could think with the aid of the symbols and words, which he and Eve had evolved between them. He remembered the moments of triumph as well as the pangs of fear when his awareness of an identity within him also made him feel alone and disconnected.

He reflected how this seeming disconnectedness had helped him define himself more clearly as an entity, even though he was part of creation and one of several human creatures who were destined to become the guardians of creation. After all, they were the closest copies of the exalted essence of God. He knew he was a man, and he had assumed certain duties in his home, such as hunting for food and materials, and doing much of the work of building and maintaining his shelter. He knew he was also a father who took an active part in training and teaching Cain and Abel. He knew he experienced moments of love and tenderness from his family and even from some of the animals around him. He acknowledged experiences of respect and even exultation when he communicated with God. He could identify pangs of anger when his plans went wrong or when someone else prevented him from following his notions. He remembered the minutes of fear when one of the raw forces was unleashed in God's nature and struck near him or puzzled him. And he wished he could forget the anxious moments when he contemplated the dilemmas of his independent existence and the uncertainties of a future, that also depended a good deal on his awareness of himself and of the direction he wanted to give it.

Yet, knowing his various qualities, both his powers and his weaknesses, was good for him. It provided him with an anchor of experiences and ideas which he could accept as belonging uniquely to him, and which became familiar landmarks to which he could also turn in moments of trouble or confusion. He learned to rely on them as his trademarks, because he could define his outer physical as well as his human essences by them, just as he could define the certainty of the sun rising and setting every day, and the existence of so many animals and plants to which he had given names after he had learned their attributes. He had realized that his own attributes as accepted by him and recognized by others were also similar to those of Eve and the children. And yet he knew that there were important differences between all of them and he sensed that some of his experiences were unique to him. That fact seemed all right and even reassuring at times. He only wished he could figure out why there had been such violent discrepancies in the self-definition of Cain, so that the differences between Cain and Abel were more remarkable than their similarities, even though both had seemed to share equally in the wisdom of Eve and himself during their early growth.

He was truly grateful that he could think in these terms. He also exulted in his ability to use his judgmental powers as a method of solving problems, both the problems inherent in harnessing his physical environment to his needs and the problems that arose out of the interactions with members of his family with their thoughts and ideas. The great potency of reflexive thought was unfortunately a double-edged sword. He reflected ruefully on the many occasions where he desperately needed an explanation and recalled the fear that took him when no answer seemed to come forth. What made lightning strike and hurt creatures of the creation, when they came too close? Why did the sun come up near the same mountain every day and set on the opposite side and where did it go when the sky was full of clouds? Why did Abel get sick the other night after he ate a strange blueberry, even though one of his rabbits had eaten some without mishap? And why was Cain so jealous of Abel and so full of anger towards him?

Adam shifted his position on the rock and lifted his gaze up from his own self-reflection in the pool. He drank in the golden rays of the setting sun and marveled at the puffy edges of the few clouds bathed in a rosy tinge. Yes, his thinking powers had led him into a lot of inner turmoil, as he had tried to formulate questions for which there seemed to be no answers. Why had God created him and his tribe? Was he supposed to continue the creation or merely guard over it as it appeared now, or was he to be a mere plaything for God? If God was so powerful as Adam had seen in the demonstrations of his creation, how could He dare to entrust all of it to a creature as imperfect and uncertain as he and other humanoids seemed to be? Did God make a mistake?.., but that was unthinkable and illogical! Why was he allowed to live only such a short time and why was he not permitted to watch over the changes that must no doubt come over the universe in the future? Why did he often not know what would happen next? And how could one plan or think clearly if one did not know what would happen in the next hour or in the next year? What would happen to Eve and to the children? Why did he have to worry whether and when he would die, and what would happen to Eve and the children if they died before he did? The uncertainties around such questions often tortured him, and now clouded his gaze, so that he barely saw the deepening red hues touching up the horizon.

He suddenly remembered that he had often used his power to answer many questions that also come up and had been as puzzling to the ones he had just left behind. It was fun and a source of a feeling of power to figure out answers, especially if you used your rational powers as a tool and in a logical sequence. He smiled at the delight they all shared after they had understood and used the healing qualities of the bubbling spring near the big window-rock. He had felt such relief when he figured out that some stars are always in the same place in the sky, so that they could tell him how to return to his home if his forays had

The Promise Of Human Autonomy

taken him further away than the fading of daylight. He chuckled with tender delight as he reminisced over the moments of experimentation and puzzlement when Eve and he had learned to give each other pleasure during moments of physical proximity and close sharing. Therefore knowledge could represent power as well as a trapdoor into blind and destructive forces that could suck out your peace of mind <u>and substitute blinding anxiety</u>. In addition there were other forces from within, besides the uncertainties over the big questions, which could spoil a good mood. Irrational ideas and feelings might suddenly emerge, even without warning. He remembered with awe how he had started to worry about Eve and her safety after a quarrel during which they had not made up, and had left him a little angry at her. Afterwards he was so consumed with fears of Eve getting hurt that he almost could not tear himself away from home for two days, until they made up. What about the nights when he woke up with a dream of monsters chasing him shortly after he had almost been engulfed by the fiery stream that came down from the flaming and smoking mountain? Such thoughts can certainly seem to take control over your thinking rather than being used as tools to solve your most pressing problems.

Adam reflected with some embarrassment on the time in their youth when both he and Eve had eaten the forbidden apple and tasted the first secrets of knowledge. Even though God had banished them from eternal protection and had forced them to become self-sufficient, they had also acquired the gift of thought in order to insure their new self-sufficiency. Even though thought can make you reflective and even anxious, as Adam was now, he took heart in the realization that thinking could be used creatively. He and his family certainly had not been lax in this exercise, and had encouraged each other to sharpen the creative edges of their thinking. This quality above all had enabled them to depend on themselves and gain a sense of self-confidence. He reflected with pride on their increasing independence. Even though he was far removed from the social security of Eden and from the abject dependence on its ever-present nurturance, he exulted in the knowledge of his autonomy. Its strength gave him far more triumphs than a mere existence based on immediate gratification. God was right when he placed the angel at the gate of Eden to prevent his return in the first few anxious weeks, but now the flaming sword seemed superfluous; He did not want to go back. Reliance on your own powers gave you a sense of knowing yourself better, a sense of being your own driving force. It enabled you to take some responsibility for being a free creature who had some knowledge of his strengths and liabilities.

Adam let his mind wander over the past and his many experiences, both in Eden and later in the wilderness. He realized that he had come a long way. Before he and Eve ate part of the apple they were very dependent and also very naive. No wonder the snake had such an easy time to coax them into disobedience. Since their exile they had become wise in the many ways of nature and about themselves. They had learned to use their thinking to fashion a language to communicate more elaborately than by mere grunts and groans. It enabled them to further their thinking into far-reaching ways, so that thinking became a tool to manipulate their environment alongside the tools they had fashioned out of rocks and sticks. Perhaps his present state of achievement was where he should be, since he was able to carry on their existence and take some responsibility as a governing force over the creation as he had been told. Perhaps his slow development and his gropings from dependence to independence, from confusion to the ability to make some predictions, and from moments of terror to a better sense of inner constancy all followed natural laws. Perhaps it would be true for other humans to develop along similar lines, as he was already beginning to observe in the concerns of his two sons. Perhaps his present reflection was even a stage in his own development and constituted a platform from which he could move on to find new questions and solutions and reach another plateau of progress.

It suddenly occurred to him that he could use this faith in new masteries and in a further expansion of his development. It would give him a weapon in the future to combat the uncertainties about future problems which his thinking also piled up around his shoulders. Perhaps he could use his faith in the continued use of thinking as a way of giving him back some control in the face of all the dilemmas he had brought up earlier. If he could accept that he could solve problems and be creative in the face of vexing questions, he would not have to fear the future with its sometimes overwhelming doubts.

Yet he had to admit that excessive confidence might only lessen the pervading feeling of great loneliness in the vast scene of the creation. He was master of only one tiny corner in it. And even in his tiny corner he was not always master of everything, and he had to see events happen from time to time where he lost complete control. He had to worry, for instance, about the frequent thunderstorms and lightning coming too close, or about the creek overflowing after a heavy rain and flooding him out of his abode. He had to guard his family from the ever-hungry saber tooth tiger and from the anger of the wild mastodon. He had to be skillful enough to find meat and food for his family and was aware that powerful forces beyond his control sometimes drove his animal herds away, perhaps to better feeding grounds. Or illness befell the animals so that his family might have to go hungry for a few days. He dimly realized how he minimized these real worries by remembering his self-built storehouse of expertise. His thinking ability had supplied him with solutions in the past. On that basis he had developed an inner security so that he would be able to draw on this reservoir of knowledge again when things got too tough.

However, he realized that this faith alone was not enough to sustain him at all times. His long-standing history of dependency on God in the Garden of Eden also had produced much inner pain as he had progressed towards greater self-sufficiency. The periods of inner certainty were counterbalanced by the much more potent uncertainties of nature. Everything seemed so capricious, and sometimes it seemed that forces were even working against him. In the supposedly orderly domain of God's creation, it was sometimes hard to accept the presence of a master plan when you could also observe randomness and uncertainty. At least there often did not seem to be a plan or a reason, as he could perceive with his own powers of observation and judgment. He knew he could fall back and often had to fall back on a blind faith in the laws and rules that were given to him in his own beginning. He would then have to remember them and exercise his beliefs in them. Otherwise he might sink into a panic for fear of having lost control. With some reassurance he thought of the few simple rules God had given to them at the beginning. He knew his own limitations and trusted the wisdom of God. He also consulted with Eve to learn new ways of coping from her own storehouse of experimentation.

Yes, it was good to have a baseline of fundamental laws which you could trust and accept without question. And they seemed to work almost all of the time. And yet, he even questioned these laws at times as he had done a few minutes ago when he had impatiently tried to analyze the secrets of creation. Questioning also was fun and gave you a sense of courage, but it could frighten you as well. You would then have to fear the sense of freedom when you had cast yourself off from the trusted base of old laws. It brought you into the land of ambiguity and doubts and could land you in strange seas with hidden dangers. Sometimes it seemed better to run away from the exercise of questions. He smiled when he remembered how often he had preferred to find something to do after starting with one of his doubts, like whittling on a stick to make a lance or just drawing on a rock wall with a piece of charcoal. He was aware that he had lost himself into such activities more quickly when he had been fretting about worldly concerns. It was also better sometimes to forget and to run away, although the power of thought would never allow one to run away forever. Often he had not been able to run away from powerful thoughts and questions, even when he had wanted to. Then he began to doubt his own strength and judgment. He usually wound up feeling guilty that he could not do better and solve these questions. Then he felt badly as though he had let himself and his family down.

Yes, the fear of the unknown -- out there and inside -- was a powerful force that could even still the knowledge inside momentarily. It was during those moments that he realized how much he needed the care and solace of others like him in order to nourish his own autonomy. God had not by accident supplied him with a companion to be by his side both during his youth and now. He could see even more clearly how Cain and Abel were able to draw support from him and Eve, and even from each other until a short time ago, just as he had drawn solace from the ever present order and from the instant gratification of his needs in the Garden of Eden. Hence he knew that he needed others for both support and company, and that others needed him. It seemed to be a law that the human required a community for strength and succor, especially when the marvelous thinking powers got him into states of almost unbearable loneliness or confusion.

This dependency on other creatures like him and on the community of humans also made him realize that he had some responsibilities towards others who in turn depended on him. Therefore, he shouldered a sense of leadership and of concern, because he had to reciprocate for the dependency he fostered on others. Eve and the children often depended on him for help, for care and for answers. Right now he could afford to indulge in all these reflections, because he had "earned" an hour of leisure by exercising his cognitive skills to create a time-saving device to skin his kill for the day. He was not needed at home for other tasks and he could therefore afford to be "selfish" and indulge in these moments of peace and introspection. Even though a sense of self and of creativity gave him the right to direct his energy into some channels of his own choice, he could not ignore the needs and rights of others, because they all needed each other. If he took time out to admire the forces of nature or think about his own concerns, he knew that others had the same right too. This awareness gave him an added responsibility: He also had to make sure that Eve and his sons had the freedom and opportunity to indulge in periods of self-contemplation or in the exercise of their thinking into creative channels. Similarly his sons had to inherit this sense of responsibility, so that their children and members of the future tribe could enjoy the luxury of sifting through ideas and arrive at a fairly constant and reliable sense of their own selfhood.

When he shifted the gaze from the deepening shadows of the surrounding hills to the pond below, he noticed that his mirror-image had become darker too. Perhaps his present preoccupation with his responsibilities had been influenced by the darker and more somber image of his face in the still water. He shrugged his shoulders because the linkage of cause and effect was another one of the frequently imponderable secrets of nature. However, he had to agree that the whole question of duty was an important one for the human being who had been freed from the fixed circuitry of animal inheritance. What really was the right mix of his rights versus his duties? Here was another one of the knotty issues about human existence that had been created by the ability to think. He knew he deserved this hour of leisure, but was Abel allowed to contemplate the clouds and sketch them on a piece of smooth wood while his herd of sheep was drifting further away and might become prey to a pack of hungry wolves?

Again he realized that the human animal moves perhaps quite lawfully through a series of stages in the formulation of answers about what is right and what is wrong in the human community. He realized that he obeyed God's laws at one time simply because he was afraid of God's wrath and punishment. When he recognized that his punishment of exile also opened up new vistas and sharpened his sense of freedom and his power to deal with problems, he also began to rely more on his own sense of right and of justice. Now he sensed that he governed his behavior much more often by what provided the greatest sense of good for his family and for his tribe, which included him. He realized that he had left behind an earlier standard by which he had obeyed laws and shouldered his responsibilities primarily because he wanted to be a "nice guy" and earn the approval of others. Now he realized that the laws he had inherited from God were formulated to support a state of existence in which each member could enjoy the most satisfaction by providing opportunities to satisfy needs both for himself and for others. Nowadays a feeling of respect for the needs and integrity of others was a predominant guide for him, because it rested on a sense of reciprocity as a central principle.

When he contemplated his own development, his present sense of justice seemed like such an easy principle to formulate. However, it was sometimes so difficult to apply it to a given example. For instance, did little Cain have the right to bang with sticks on a hollow log in order to satisfy his needs to expend excess energy and to enjoy the various rhythms he was creating? Did he, Adam, in turn have the right to stop Cain, because he wanted to go to sleep early after a particularly exhausting day? Was Eve right to suggest to Cain that he move further away from the hearth with his log, and that she go with Cain for the boy's protection, which also took her temporarily away from himself? When these dilemmas emerge it seems so hard to use the God-given power to think, and to rely on one's storehouse of possible solutions. It becomes much easier to rely then on God and his relatively simple laws. Did not God say to honor thy father and mother? Since I am Cain's father and want him to be quiet, I must prevail and Cain has to obey me. Then we both conform to a simple and well-formulated principle. It is when I get doubts about this simple minded solution of conformity that I also get guilty feelings about biting into the apple. Before that time, matters were so simple, because none of these questions had to arise.

I guess I have no choice but to also depend on myself, as well as lean on God. I escaped complete dependency and compliance, but my children won't -- at least in the beginning of their lives. They were so small and helpless and had so little experience that Eve and I had to be like God for them and preserve them from harm. It was certainly easier for them to obey our rules and our wisdom. If they had relied purely on themselves, they might have stumbled into the mouth of a crocodile or eaten a poisonous berry. Now they have to learn to think for themselves, just as I had to do it. And they will discover that it can be frightening to rely on one's own judgment and thought rather than blindly follow our advice. It is often much easier to obey the duties and the routine imposed by others. However, mere compliance also sabotages our God-given power to think, and our ability to develop into an independent person who can tackle and often even solve new problems; but that brings me back to my problem of where my responsibilities lie. Am I primarily responsible to God to be the shepherd over his creation, or only responsible to Eve and the children to give them a perfect and smooth future; or am I also responsible for myself and my own thoughts and needs? Should I not also respect my own ideas and should I want to encourage and expand them for my own happiness?

Since God has left us pretty much alone after our expulsion from Eden, I would want to trust my own thinking, and foster further self-development as I had to trust it in the past for solving the many problems we had to contend with in the wilderness. I know I get scared of what my thinking produces at times, and I am afraid of the unknown. However, I also trust my thinking power and I feel optimistic that it will guide me further and fertilize ideas in other human beings.

Adam felt happy that his leisurely thinking had provided him with new faith which could weather him over the loneliness and the absence of sure answers. This his thinking had also revealed for him. He got up, picked up the goat and the freshly skinned fur and ran the remaining distance to join his family.

These thoughts which we have anthropomorphically projected into Adam have also occupied human beings through the ages since that time. Of course, we do not expect that Adam enumerated all of these issues we have raised, or that he elaborated them so clearly in such a short time! Also he may not often have felt them so forcefully. It is much more likely that he -- like most of us -- may have been overwhelmed at times by doubts and by the mistakes of our own thinking. The diligent search by scores of theologians, philosophers, and social scientists over the ages is proof of that. Nevertheless thoughts such as these may very well have kept Adam on a more or less even course in his life, and carved for him a niche in the edifice into which countless human beings after him have also deposited ideas. This edifice now forms a trustworthy foundation for our understanding of the autonomous human mind and how it functions.

Chapter II

Early Technology and Economic Development as Deterrents to the Concept of Autonomy

Before we can understand the autonomously functioning human being and derive some of the scientific bias for this understanding, we need to examine why it has taken so long since Adam for stating that autonomy may be a stage and a normal function in the human organism, and for providing a political base for it. The very examination of this long history, which went along with the loneliness of human existential doubt and even self-torture, provides a better foundation for the principles we want to reaffirm from contemporary psychological and philosophical sources. The long gestation period of the concept of autonomy in the history of mankind is also reflected in the obstacles that often prevent people from developing to a more autonomous stage of functioning, according to modern social scientists. These same obstacles in history translated to present-day events can also cause regression in an autonomously functioning person to various forms of dependency, as again mirrored in history.

Now I want to take the reader on a psychological journey of what life must have been like before the contemporary life styles existed -- that is, before it was changed by the explosions in science and technology of the past 150 years. If we can strip away the consequences of the

Industrial Revolutions we can perhaps develop some empathy with our ancestors as they struggled with the concept of free will while they were buffeted about by the mostly unbridled forces of fate. Let us, therefore, just peel away some of the most important inventions of the last 170 years, so that we can appreciate how the lifestyle of today presents us with untold treasures of leisure and contemplation. These have influenced our thinking and our knowledge about the nature of Man and his interaction with others while they have, of course, also presented mankind with many new social and existential problems.

Television as a common medium of communication is only about 25 years old. It brings ideas, news, imagination and various forms of stimulation right into every home at the flick of a switch. It extends man's width and breadth of immediate experience way beyond the tangible world of his life experiences. Cognitive and emotional horizons are widened to include the whole world, so that the ideas as well as the disasters that originate in a distant and almost unreal corner of the globe are instantaneously available in your living room. Television and its somewhat older sister, Radio, brought the peoples of the world closer together, and allowed comparisons and often critical examination of the customs and values of other countries and other religions. Thereby these inventions have brought us all closer together on earth and have reduced isolation and eroded ethnocentrism. It has also made us more aware of the needs and problems of others and how they impinge on our own needs. It has sometimes quite forcefully expanded the life space of many people and thereby shrunk the world for them.

The airplane as a commercially feasible form of transportation is less than 70 years old. It has also revolutionized our lives, because it makes a reasonable method of visiting and conducting business across the whole globe available to many people. In addition, the plane allows materials, machines, and services to be rushed to places where they are needed in a hurry to maintain operations, to manage emergencies, and to supply risky explorations and experiments. Perhaps an even more important function has been a narrowing of the gulf between exporter and importer, or between the sources of excess and the areas of deficiencies. It is the airplane, backed up by the ship and by express surface transportation that has enabled an exchange of commodities in the world which were previously only available through exploitation and conquest. In this fashion the gold of South Africa can be fitted into the teeth or into the ornaments of Americans; or oils from beneath the sands of Arabia can move the automobile in Australia. In reverse, the technical know-how cultivated in a highly developed country and stored there in books and brains abundantly available can be rushed either permanently or temporarily to some remote jungle area to help develop a new resource or process.

The industry that developed and manufactured effective synthetic fertilizers in great quantities dates back to World War II. Together with successful scientific experimentation to develop hybrid food plants with greater yield and with greater resistance to adverse conditions, the fertilizer industry has revolutionized our style of life. Thanks to the choice of proper seeds for human food and for animal feeds, we can now grow and fertilize crops with maximal efficiency and then harvest them in record time with the aid of specialized and efficient machinery. It almost staggers the imagination when we learn that in some of the developed countries only 3.3% of the work force is required to grow and harvest the food which the total population requires for eating and for living well; and that includes children and older people. In other words this revolution has made it possible for almost 97% of the people available for work to engage their time and interests in other areas besides the production and procurement of food. All that is required from them is the minimal time for a trip to the grocery store to buy provisions or a trip to a restaurant to order them.

While we concentrate on the supply of food, we must not forget the revolution brought about by modern refrigeration. Pre-modern Man in the temperate and colder climates of the continent did not eat any fruit or vegetables, and very little butter or eggs during the cold months of the year. Since cattle were also dependent on plants being grown for feed, very little fresh meat was available during that time also. Absence of such foods during roughly one half of the year led to vitamin deficiencies and lack of proteins. Pellagra and nervous system disturbances were therefore much more frequent. The impairment of the nervous system and undernourishment led to further anxieties. It even may have increased the incidence of sensory disturbances and may have resulted in terrifying visions and other abnormal thought phenomena. Very often such events and the lowered efficiency of the body must have further contributed to feelings of victimization and to lack of control.

When we examine the revolution in living habits in recent history, we must not forget that the incandescent bulb and other wonders of electricity are not more than about 100 years old. Lights and other applications of electric power have contributed untold uses to our leisure time. We can now extend our lives past daylight into countless leisure activities and into manufacturing and services without limits. The electric motor and other electrical inventions have not only mechanized and speeded up our manufacturing and production endeavors but also have created untold devices that save time and human energy. Many of these can be used right in the individual homes in order to extend the leisure we already earn as interest from other inventions.

Perhaps the greatest transformation of traditional life styles was triggered by the invention and use of the steam engine around the turn of the 19th Century. It made it possible almost overnight to replace muscle power of Man and beast. The toil and sweat of the former on all frontiers of life was replaced by machines which ushered in an era we have aptly christened the Industrial Revolution. Not only could machines manufacture and process most of the tools, garments, building materials and raw materials we needed, but they could do it more quickly and more efficiently than the human being they replaced. Moreover, machines were applied or specially invented to pioneer in new areas of human endeavor which made possible manufacturing and exploration that had previously existed only in the fantasy of dreamers and writers. Machines were soon applied in the early 19th Century to surface transportation in the form of steam locomotives, and a few years later also to shipping so that the steamships replaced the clippers. These developments alone -- later abetted by the invention of the airplane -- made possible a rapid exchange of goods and services possible between far corners of the globe. Again, this technological advance enabled Man to meet his needs by relying for his needs on barter and trade rather than conquest and slavery.

Another great stimulus that antedated all these more spectacular developments was the invention and proliferation of the printing press in the latter half of the 15th Century. It provided a cheap and readily available source of ideas, plans and treatises for the common Man, so that he could form his own impression and reaction to the wisdom and to the new ideas available previously only to the elite or the clergy. Before the existence of the printed word such ideas were transmitted selectively only through proclamations, sermons, or through word of mouth, and they were closely controlled. The availability of the printed word also stimulated a wider need for literacy among the common folk, and sparked drives for universal education. Fertile soil was thus created for the understanding and use of the machines of the Industrial Revolution and provided a cadre of educated people who could be trained to build and service the machinery.

While we focus on the more spectacular milestones in the transformation from the harsh realities of our ancestors to "gracious living", we must not forget the quiet revolution in medicine that occurred in this century. Prior to the 20th Century a doctor could not do much more than hold the hand and soothe the brow of the great majority of his patients. He relied on a few herbal medicines, a number of crude procedures, and a whole host of placebo treatments such as leeches. In the overwhelming number of cases he had to wait until the patient "passed the crisis" and was therefore mending on his own resources if he got that far. The impact of modern antisepsis, biochemistry, cell physiology, radiation, and surgery have enabled the health profession to diagnose and treat a great number of diseases and almost eliminate such famous killers of antiquity as plague, undulant fever, infantile paralysis and pneumonia. As a result, infant mortality has been reduced astronomically and life expectancy has risen in developed countries to over 70 years. These developments have markedly reduced the capriciousness of life and provided a secure feeling that most anyone can achieve old age, that one's children are going to live and thrive, and that most illnesses and traumas along the way can be treated and ameliorated so that they will result at best in relatively brief disruptions.

If this enumeration of the solutions to life's problems conjures up a picture of too serene and predictable an existence for modern Man, we must quickly remember that we are still saddled with some important hazards. There are still some of the big disasters around that can spell death to some and widespread destruction to possessions and to the living fabric. Despite hurricane and tornado warnings and the provision of shelters and appropriate rules of behavior, these storms may still strike in unpredictable places. They are at least too destructive in their power to be always tamable by modern building material or by preventative measures. Tornadoes especially are so sudden and so incomprehensibly powerful that a person has no recourse but to tremble and pray, and then survey the vast desolation around him if he survives. Similarly, floods still cause widespread devastation in some places even though dams and levees have greatly reduced the regular catastrophes that have hounded the dwellers in the valleys of the Ganges and the Nile for centuries. Destructive earthquakes are more rare events, but they are as yet beyond any human understanding and control. They can therefore cause indescribable havoc and misery in a community. The scourges of antiquity like lightning, hail, and locust swarms have been leashed in most developed countries, so that they do not represent a major menace, but they can still strike and inflict minor damage in isolated instances.

While we have banished some of the major scourges of ancient time, we have inherited some new ones that arise from the malfunctioning of our complicated machines and involved technology. Air crashes and major explosions of factories, tanks or storage facilities provide mangled and charred bodies and twisted machinery beyond description. They not only strike terror in the hearts of those immediately involved or associated, but also may create some shock waves of anxiety in most of us, when we think of the occasional unpredictability of modern technology despite safeguards, inspections and feedback devices. The same sense of vulnerability comes from some of the lesser catastrophes, such as automobile crashes, fires, and the malfunctioning of equipment. However, there is also a sense of hope connected with these accidental malfunctions which pre-industrial people did not possess. Our technology and scientific sophistication and successes have also given us the faith that we can eliminate accidents and equipment failure, as well as even human error if we try harder. Further inventions, subsequent inspections and aggressive investigations, and the installation of checks and feedback devices can make modern machines even safer. They can warn us of their wear and tear, keep a check on the humans who process them, and even provide rules for the consumer on how to behave in the face of impending failure.

Nevertheless, the relatively tranquil modern life is still much truncated by some very traditional disasters stemming from the nature of Man. Not only can crime and, more recently, terrorism shake our sense of security to sometimes frightening proportions, but warfare is still a common enough occurrence to strike terror into some of our more highly developed regions. The people of Northern Ireland, of Beirut, and of Iran have been witnesses to that.

At this point, in order to give us a greater sense of empathy for our ancestors' lifestyles, we are reintroducing some of the uncertainties of modern life. Like our forebears, we are sometimes unable to find solutions to disasters or the reasons for their occurrences. We also experience similar anxieties when personal tragedy strikes us or those close to home. Do we not ask ourselves many questions when our good friend had to lose his job, our uncle had to die of a heart attack, or our neighbor had to be raped and robbed? Why do some of us have to cut down on all of the fun-filled activities of our lives because of the pain of arthritis?

We can easily rekindle these nagging doubts and reminisce in our inability to form explanations. We can even remember our sense of vulnerability and insecurity in the face of such contemporary tragedies beyond our control. Now let us magnify these doubts a thousand fold by projecting them into the lives of people living before the Industrial Revolution. Natural disasters struck repeatedly without warning or apparent reason, as there were no storm, flood, or weather forecasters and there were no precautions. Most people lived in precarious or relatively flimsy dwellings that did not protect them from the serious devastations of nature. Moreover, armies on the warpath or plundering hordes would frequently visit one's neighborhood without warning. Death or disease struck with frightening frequency and sometimes devastated whole communities and even whole countries, like the black plague of Europe. Besides the anguish of life's unpredictability the predictable part of life was very hard. Most everybody except the elite had to work hard and long hours to provide the daily necessities of life. Without machines and technological organization almost everyone had to pitch in to grow and produce his or her own food, make his own clothes and build his own dwelling. In addition he had to provide time for creating other necessities such as tools, or use skill to work for others to provide further necessities. Most men and women were spent by the time they were 40 and had used up their strength, health, and their motivation to provide further for themselves or for their families. It was therefore important to produce and train many children, imbuing them with the sense of duty, obligation and loyalty. They could then take up the slack and provide, when one's own productivity was curtailed either by excessive wear or by failing health. Not too many people lived into ripe old age. Again these conditions raised innumerable questions and produced nagging doubts.

Hence to our ancestors and even more so to primitive Man fate must have loomed as a terrifying and powerful force. There was so very little he could do to control natural forces or even human events and bend them to his will. He was, instead, very conscious of his lack of power and of the omnipotence of the forces around him. Even as late as the 15th Century Prince Machiavelli still had to conclude that fortune was tipping the scale in over half of our actions. In only slightly less than half the cases did we have the power to direct our affairs by our own will, and Machiavelli may have only been speaking for the more privileged classes. It was therefore realistic to leave more than half to chance. Machiavelli compares that minority control to the act of building a canal away from a river after a disastrous flood had inundated the plains and destroyed many houses and trees and denuded the soil. In this way the force of the next flood would not have to be such an unrestrained and disastrous affair, even if it could not be prevented.

In those times it was not wise to nurture one's own plans or to try to translate them persistently into action. The more humanity was able to swing the balance of control, understanding, and intervention over the halfway mark, the more its hopes and its faith into its own power could be raised. At such a point the expectations into the efficacy of one's own will become reality, they can become embedded into a basic recognition and into an official doctrine, giving up some of one's trust to fate, Providence and other forms of pre-determination.

I am conjuring up the frequent terrors of pre-modern Man and his questions about the meaning of his often arduous and problem-filled life for two important reasons: One purpose is to remind ourselves of Adam's plight when he questioned the riddles of nature and of life with the aid of his power of reason and consciousness. The other purpose is to help us explain why mankind could not readily reach a commonly recognized state of autonomy, or a state in which one had some power and the leisure to contemplate one's purposes and one's direction. I am sure that many individual men and women reached a sense of relative independence and self-reliance along the lines suggested by contemporary personality theory and described in Chapter X. I am equally sure that men and women received some inner sense of security from this private self-knowledge of relative autonomy which then also included a realistic acceptance of fate. Some prime examples in very ancient days are found in the thoughts of Socrates, Epictetus, and Marcus Aurelius. However, circumstances beyond their control made this perch a very precarious one and did not prevent many from toppling off and regressing to other ways of coping or not coping. This tenuous hold was further made more slippery by the absence of an official and openly shared recognition of autonomy as a stage in development and as a goal to be acquired by Man and integrated with other parts of the personality. In fact, official doctrine proclaimed the opposite as we shall see later. The repetition of disasters, the lack of control, and the capriciousness and hardships of existence did not allow the flowering and support of so subversive a doctrine.

There was one additional and very important economic consequence that arose from the scarcity in pre-industrial societies that inhibited any official recognition of human autonomy and contributed to its suppression. In almost all old-world cultures except in some very primitive societies the raw materials and their crafted derivatives were in scarce supply and were soon exhausted. The basic foods could be grown or caught by almost anyone, but even here the uncontrolled genetic mutations in seeds and cattle, and the vagaries of weather and pests made the growth and harvest a sometimes sparse or risky venture. However, spices and more exotic foods were scarce and frequently had to be imported from far away. Domestic wood and other materials for homes and for heating were often in short supply in nations that did not know the modern principles of selective cutting and reforestation. In arid countries devoid of large forests wood was soon exhausted and had to be found far away, cut, and then carried longer and longer distances to reach home. These conditions were, for instance, very true for the Roman Empire. Also, the abundant forests and fertile lands that covered the valleys of biblical Palestine were completely used up by the Turks and later by the crusaders who needed woods to build forts and fortifications. These lands became barren, and degenerated into deserts, wasteland, and swamps for centuries, until the new state of Israel came along with its ambitious reforestation and reclamation projects. They promised to transform the land and the landscape, so that it might once more become a land of "milk and honey". Any other woods more exotic than native varieties, and the marble and other more ornamental stones for the palaces and mansions of the elite had to be taken from far away. Quite apart from some of these more basic necessities, the gold and silver, the precious stones, ornamental feathers, special oils and perfumes were all very rare and had to be found and imported from faraway shores. If one remembers the relatively primitive state of pre-modern mining and metallurgy we can also easily imagine that metals for tools, weapons, and other implements were relatively scarce, and were not uniformly or reliably available.

All of these economic conditions mandated a social order in which certain people could command and amass the scarce resources. In order to guarantee a flow of these resources, the elite had to secure a social organization that allowed them the sole possession and use. They also had to command sufficient power to wrest these goods from places outside their own borders, and this power had to be seen as their duty and their right. It was therefore necessary for such an elitist group to build and command a large enough army to safeguard its own shores against other armies stealing its own resources and to conquer other lands or subdue them sufficiently to give up their minerals, spices, oils, skins, and even their manpower to them. Anthropologists have pointed out that the procurement of resources was the primary reason for the decline of the Roman Empire. Rome had to send its armies further and further afield in order to conquer an ever-increasing area of land and import the material and the slaves that were needed to fuel the appetite of the wealthy in and around Rome. Many of the famous wars and campaigns of European history were sparked by the search for more raw material, or were fought to insure the continued or increased flow of scarce resources needed primarily by the elite.

In such pre-industrial societies conflict was therefore almost inevitable. The only exceptions were some rather primitive societies who were relatively isolated from contact. Here resources were also scarce but available to all, especially if they cooperated in shared activity, so that some stable, pseudo-communistic societies could develop. Conflicts in the more developed societies required armies and with them further deprivations and dangers for the soldiers. But the first requirement was a doctrine that guaranteed the elite the wealth and the power as a right, and that normalized their needs to have that power and go to war to obtain more wealth and power. In addition, the lack of any doctrine about accountability of rulers and the absence of political checks and balances made whole nations frequently the capricious victims of power-hungry or mentally imbalanced rulers. The possibility of sudden wars and campaigns in order to satisfy the ambitions or fears of kings and princes contributed further to the terrors of pre-modern life and to the impossibility to plan one's fate.

It is obvious that the status discrepancies based on an economy of scarcity could not be a fertile soil for the concept of a universal human autonomy and freedom. Such ideas were dangerous, because they would have threatened to upset the status quo and would have menaced the privileged castes. It would have questioned their power to command everyone else to work for them, sometimes for mere subsistence or for social protection, and to go to war for them. Obedience to authority and not to one's own impulses and direction were therefore made the important values, and became the cornerstone of doctrines that governed an economy of scarcity before the dawn of machine manufacture and efficient transportation.

In any ordinary state of unpredictability and "normal" disaster, people experienced often a sense of bewilderment and confusion. Sometimes these were even punctuated by states of terror. We know from modern psychology and from our own experiences that even minor states of anxiety can inhibit action and judgment and efficient performance. Pre-modern Man also needed coping mechanisms to deal with nature-induced terror and with existential anxiety. He primarily needed to have some answers and gain some sense of order and direction in this sea of confusion. Hence in both ancient times and onward to the present mankind developed a theory about the universe that recaptured a sense of order and meaning. It further had to provide some coping devices, and many prescribed and often ritualized behaviors that could be used to combat panic and doubt.

As we shall see in later chapters that develop a more scientific basis for a development of personality which includes a stage of autonomy, we see Man as an organizing animal that must also organize on the cognitive level to conserve the energy and organization characteristic of life. We therefore need answers to the questions of "WHY", and we tend to look for causes and causal connections to make some meaning out of the buzzing confusion of stimuli impinging on us. Since animal and human life and human existence seemed both bewildering as well as organized and ordered in a miraculous fashion, various cultures developed ideologies that took both of these impressions into consideration and organized them into a coherent whole. The seeming order and functioning of nature was secured by the existence of a creator, God, who had made everything according to a master plan. In Western culture this idea was of course supported by the Bible and by stories handed down over generations about the revelations of God. If one walked about in a vast desert and suddenly found a solitary watch contentedly ticking away in the sand one would have to conclude that someone made that watch and placed it there -- probably for a purpose. It would be absurd to assume that all the gears and wheels just happened to fit together by accident. Similarly, the marvels of nature and Man himself had to have a creator. This same creator was such a superior power with such infinite wisdom and foresight that everything made sense in the creation and everything fitted together.

Hence the so-called disasters and sources of human terror were also a part of the master plan. They had a meaning and a place in it. Mankind was just too imperfect to understand and had to accept these superior signs of a greater intellect on faith. Hence the belief system and the faith created an adequate cognitive base with which one could field the existential questions from Adam on. The important point here is that the lack of control and the lack of understanding prevalent in our ancestors' world made it vitally important to secure a proper psychological footing. The capricious world was therefore partially tamed by cognitive and emotional devices. They were superimposed on nature as cognitive organizations and allowed people to regain some control. If one could, for instance, accept everything as proper and as given according to a master plan, then it was also possible to fit in terrible disasters, or injustices, or sudden change. As we shall develop later, existential anxiety that can paralyze and interfere with action can be laid to rest by a belief in a just and even perfect world. We need this belief to create some order into seemingly random events. Such beliefs helped people to accept events in nature and in their lives as being preordained and dictated by superior wisdom, and therefore made it unnecessary to wrestle with ways to change them. It is illuminating to contrast such a philosophy with more contemporary views that arose after we had learned to control our fate so much more effectively with some of the technology described above. After we had literally managed to "move mountains", eliminate some of the medical scourges of history, and travel to the moon, we literally began to believe that "the difficult we do today, the impossible we shall do tomorrow." If we cannot control cancer nowadays we fret and blame medical science or government officials, and we appropriate more money for research. We are working hard to understand and eventually predict -- and even control -- earthquakes and hurricanes. We are no longer like a cork buffeted about on the sea of unknowns. We are even beginning to see a possibility of understanding psychological problems such as mental illness, suicide and crime, or social problems such as poverty and alienation by marshaling our psychological and sociological insights. This new sense of power over nature and over our society provides a basis for the discovery and the understanding of human autonomy. It was totally missing in antiquity, where frequent chaos made beliefs in superior powers and dependency on authority figures a much safer bet. In fact, these crutches provided a mandatory safety net. We shall see in the next chapter how this belief system provided further security and rewards, even though it excused the physical, technological, and social organization of society and therefore inhibited any official recognition of autonomy.

We only need to say one more word about the elite and the leaders in the pre-modern era. The feudal upper classes enjoyed much more protection against the vagaries and terrors of life and were spared much of the backbreaking labor and illness-producing living habits. Instead they relied -- by law and by force -- on the toil and the procurement from others for both the necessities and for their many luxuries. Thereby, they also gained leisure time for contemplation and for creating a better base for trying to live meaningful lives even beyond the wane of their physical prowess. These members of the elite and of the clergy were of course also caught up in the very system of religious and social beliefs and in the ideological reactions to existential questions. They administered the machinery and the rituals associated with these beliefs. They were seldom allowed the luxury to stray from the ideology in their own thoughts, for fear of either punishment as a heretic, or self-torture stemming from the loneliness of unreciprocated dissent. They could not afford to entertain the doubt of being lonely and alienated misfits. Except for some notable exceptions further discussed in the next two chapters, they were not "free" to question their dependency on the system or assert the possibility of autonomy for them alone, even though they seemed to be freed from a goodly number of technological uncertainties. They had to subscribe to the same ideology regarding superhuman forces of control, who also gave them the right and the privileges to rule and enjoy extra luxuries. They were assigned a role in the system and they had to play it well and usually did with evident relish. We shall see in the next chapter how the system of beliefs integrated and explained away their relatively greater freedom to navigate, to think, and to secure their apparent autonomy.

Chapter III

Religious Doctrine as an Obstacle to Self-Fulfillment

We are now ready to examine the predominant belief systems which arose from the technology, social organization, and the reflections of our ancestors. Their ideology represented of course a bridge between the technological and human conditions they fashioned into large, complex societies, and the existential questions that emerged from their reactions to physical and social reality as they experienced it. It is my contention that the major values in the Middle Ages and beyond were one of three conditions which created a major obstacle to the unfolding of this idea, because only the more recent inventions and changes in our life styles enabled us to have the control and the leisure to allow the idea to become potentially available to everyone. We shall reserve for the next chapter a more detailed examination into the understanding of the human mind, which in the pre-scientific era was so encumbered with false assumptions and a misleading approach to its study that it also prevented further thoughts about self-actualization.

Many of the following assertions are taken from the Bible and the two predominant interpreters of the official Christian religion for many, many centuries: St. Augustine and St. Thomas Aquinas. These theologians had become the foremost interpreters of the Bible and of the official Church leaders. They became the theological authorities during the Middle Ages and their thoughts still hold some influence up to the present day. We shall further rely on some of the world's best known philosophers, if they concerned themselves with questions of human development along the lines laid down by religious ideology and with ethics. Hence we shall touch down with Kant, Hegel, Locke, Descartes, Hume, and Rousseau. We shall also take occasional excursions to the ancient Greek and Roman philosophers for comparisons, such as Socrates, Aristotle, Epictetus, and Aurelius.

A. Official Religious Doctrine as a Beacon of Light in the Midst of Chaos

If we can remind ourselves of the terrors of nature and the prevalence of death and disease in a life that was for most people full of hardships and unpredictability we can understand how the doctrines relating to God and the creation were like a miracle map. It suddenly illuminated all the confusion, brought order into uncertainty, and provided an officially recognized and accepted doctrine. This doctrine helped to preserve some happiness and kept hope alive. As it has already been observed: "If God did not exist, Man had to invent one." The religions therefore provided first of all a series of explanations. Since we are creatures that primarily rely on the cognitive manipulation of our environment, thanks to our cortical evolution, we require workable theories and concepts by which we can order the millions of impressions that impinge on our sense organs every second. Moreover, the Judeo-Christian religion had evolved as a master fabric of ideas, which pragmatically tackled and explained most of the existential and psychological reactions which people experienced in these days.

At its center stood a God who was infinitely wise and kind and powerful. He had created the entire universe according to a perfect master plan. His wisdom was beyond question and infallible, and he held the reins on all events on earth, including human fate. He further made His decisions in concordance with His pre-ordained master plan. He furthermore had provided a route to a better place than existence on earth, and had provided a plan and guidelines for behavior that would ensure the final, happy salvation. He was further seen as being primarily interested in men and women as those living creatures most resembling Him, and was therefore open to some dialogue. One could therefore ask Him directly -- or through His chosen intermediaries -- for favors on earth and for safe passage to the beyond, and expect some rewards, especially if one had followed all the rules He had laid down. This doctrine further explained the workings of the will and the existence of sin. It rationalized the obvious imperfections in both man and woman. It therefore provided a rationale for the existence and the power of the Church and its religious leaders. It gave them the power and the permission to provide ritualized means of the expression of ecstasy, of hope, and of restitution which the doctrine provided. The Church with the aid of the doctrine also made institutions available through which people could express their need for social and communal experiences. It provided measures and places at which important emotions could be safely siphoned off to provide relief, release, and even a measure of inner peace.

In this way men and women could exchange their individual contemplations on their short and difficult earthly existence as insignificant and powerless creatures for a master plan in which they and their tribulations fit meaningfully and even majestically. Suddenly they inherited meaning and a purpose. Everything made sense now and one could learn well-defined and institutionalized patterns of behavior and of feeling, which would banish reactions of terror, fear, and isolation. Marcus Aurelius expressed it more eloquently when he contemplated the loneliness that drove people into the arms of religion: "How small a part of the boundless and unfathomable time is assigned to every Man? For it is very soon swallowed up in the eternal, and how small a part of the universal substance? And how small a part of the universal soul? And on what a small clod of the whole earth thou creepiest? Reflecting on all this consider nothing to be great, except to act as thy nature leads thee, and to endure that which the common nature brings" (Meditations, Book 12, No. 37).

If pre-modern Man reflected on his accumulated knowledge and on the evidence from his senses, he was always struck by the existence of constant change and of uncertainties. Montagne reflected on the possibility that we can never have the answers to our questions when, according to Heraclitus, we can never enter twice into the same river. Or, according to Epicharmus, a person who comes to dinner after he was invited the night before nevertheless comes uninvited because he is no longer exactly the same person. Since change was ever-present and so unpredictable, the religious doctrine soothingly provided continuity and certainty. It was not dependent on one's own senses nor on one's own knowledge, but came as a perfect package well recommended.

If the doctrine of God provided explanation and a sense of identity and harmony, it also closed off further explorations into many self-initiated areas. Many such areas were either unavailable or forbidden. At best they produced shame and guilt feelings. They stimulated a fear of failing to gain access to rewards defined by the master plan, or a fear of official censure or even persecution. Hence the price our ancestors paid for peace of mind and a feeling of purpose and belongingness was the inability to search after one's own sense of identity and the pursuit of one's own ideas. These journeys were not recognized, nor were they officially sanctioned. One's identity was defined by the interpretations and inferences from the master plan, and was further reinforced by one's place in the society and one's parental plans. Rewards from these superimposed identities had to be sufficient at a time when terror and confusion over lack of control of life was always around the corner. The few courageous people who wrestled with new truths, like Galileo and Copernicus, experienced great personal hardships for their "heresy". Anywhere from 4000 to 30,000 less fortunate and lesser known people -- depending on different estimates -- were put to death in the 3 to 4 centuries during which the Inquisition went after so-called heretics. Many were found guilty of acts and ideas dangerous to the established religion. Many more were imprisoned or tried with the customary means of extracting evidence through torture.

We might say a word about the Greek and Roman philosophers and compare their pan-deistic religions with ours. Aristotle, Plato, Plotinus, and Aurelius, for instance, allowed men and women to go after pleasure, and to achieve both personal happiness and the exercise of reason for its own sake here on earth in contrast to the prescriptions set forth by

St. Augustine and Thomas Aquinas. The former lived in societies in which people had chosen to explain the problems of nature and the terrors lurking behind lack of control by the existence of many gods. This state of affairs is also found repeatedly in primitive societies with its beliefs in a multitude of spirits. Each Greek or Roman god was in charge of a particular force or process in the master plan. These gods were moreover much more closely patterned after the nature of human beings and were therefore not perfect. They mirrored the mixed emotions, the conflicts, and the doubts found in all of us. They were therefore "fallible", and were subject to intrigue of other gods and to prayer or bribes from human beings. They exerted their control primarily by their eternal existence and their greater power, but in their quasi-human form made more reasonable and approachable models for men and women. They could therefore in their own imperfections allow Man to be "imperfect" or to pursue his own needs and ideas with the hope of achieving some self-fulfillment. Of course, the Greek and Roman societies were strictly divided into tight hierarchical orders in which free men had the privilege to live like "human beings", while slaves were excluded from all the philosophical considerations about mankind. Slaves were therefore dehumanized and could then be treated like lower creatures that did not and could not feel or experience the lofty emotions and sentiments characteristic of mankind. It is sometimes amusing to see how the Greek philosophers used the strictly ordered and divided society to build further status ladders and then anoint themselves to stand at the pinnacle of achievement for Man. The God of St. Augustine and Thomas Aquinas by contrast was a perfect being who commanded the supreme good, and was gatekeeper to perfect and the only existing happiness -- after death. Hence a life of devotion, abstinence, and duty was required here, as we shall develop below. In such a doctrine, self-realization has no place.

It can perhaps be argued that a single and perfect God, who is elevated above the human being insofar as He does not share their "imperfect" thinking, was more successful in history. Such an idea perhaps crystallized society around what is acceptable and what is not. Perhaps the more permissive climate of the pantheistic societies may have produced more freedom of thought, but also may have fragmented human endeavor at a time when everyone needed to rally around a central idea and a central obedience to maintain control of resources and technology. The success of the Judeo-Christian ideology as a blueprint for human action and thought has certainly been demonstrated in history. It has caught the imagination of millions of people and has given rise to a refined and improved source of ethics, so that there is no question of its pragmatic value and humanistic basis regardless of its origin and its one-time support by a belief in a deity.

B. God as Master Builder and Supreme Authority.

The theologians in the Middle Ages have carefully interpreted and amplified the messages contained in the Bible. Even though men and women are universally recognized to be the most complex and able of all animals, and able to rule over the natural kingdom including all living creatures, they recognize God as a supreme being. He is far superior to men and women and by such a margin as to frustrate any comparisons. Man only retains his ethnocentric top position by making himself the preferred creature in God's universe, which was created in the image of God and made to carry on God's work and will as His warden and caretaker. God created the whole complicated universe, with all its processes and living creatures, out of nothing. He therefore stands revealed as an astoundingly wise and powerful inventor who knows immediately why and how He wants His universe to run. His rules and laws in it are similarly inspired by divine logic and are therefore innately given without questions. God furthermore transcends every object and process in the creation. As the donor of all laws and rules He expects obedience and compliance. He has, however, revealed Himself to Man at a few noteworthy occasions and as special privilege to the agent He has chosen in His universe to resemble Him and to carry out His purposes. He may reveal Himself again at any time when He so chooses.

How does the realization that man's intellectual powers and man's accumulated knowledge as potent forces in guiding us to some of our destiny fit in here? Thomas Aquinas argues that men and women are limited throughout eternity to a very narrow range of knowledge, since only God has the most perfect overview of everything. Since we are imbued by God with some of His qualities and therefore with some of His knowledge, the latter is a mere copy and usually imperfect. Also, our knowledge is necessarily divided, while in God it exists united as though it were accumulated in a supercomputer. God knows by one simple "act" of knowledge, while we are forced to specialize and delve into details. All we can do is try to get closer to the wisdom of God without even quite making it there, due to the immutable facts of the creation, which relegates us into an inferior position with regard to God.

God is therefore seen as the cause of everything insofar as God wills everything, and every creature on earth is subject to the providence of God. Nothing is therefore left to chance or to our wishes in this interpretation from the theologians of antiquity, in contrast to the writings of some ancient Greek writers like Democritus and the Epicureans. Thomas Aquinas argues that nothing was created without some idea of how it fits into divine goodness, since the aim of God's master plan was divine goodness. Hence individual items and all human affairs, especially those in the "corruptible lower world", are all subject to divine will. Nothing is due to chance. Events that seem subject to chance are still contained in a plan. Nothing can happen unintentionally in nature and in the whole creation. According to Aquinas, rational creatures such as men and women may govern themselves by their intellect and their will, both of which, however, require to be governed and perfected by the divine intellect and will. If this idea does not already inhibit all autonomy, the final blow to any hope of autonomous thinking is dealt by Aquinas when he states that the will is destined to move towards universal good. Therefore it is up to God to move the will, because God as the "first mover" originates the inclination towards universal good.

Thomas Aquinas solves the dilemma of being able to decide many behavioral choices in ourselves without the perception of an external compulsion as follows: He agrees that we are not "forced" in our will by God. He compares our wills to a heavy object that falls by virtue of the law of gravity without being "forced" to move downwards. Therefore

God does not force the will while he is moving it, because He gives the will its own inclination to move, but in the preordained direction only. Hence the will moves towards the universal good like the stone moves towards the center of gravity. We can act in accordance with an internal principle or motive entirely indigenous to the actor. Yet this internal principle is always caused by an external principle, namely by God's purposes. Therefore, to feel one is acting from one's own inclination is not contrary to being moved in reality by another outside force, namely by God.

This is a rather ingenious extrapolation from our often-experienced realization of our own autonomy. If that autonomy is purely illusory, it must caution you to question it at every step. If God's underlying influence as the master mover is always present in hidden ways, you are not really conscious of it until the wise spokesmen for God point this out to you. You can profit greatly by becoming aware of the divine purpose and your invisible ties to it. The process is very similar to undergoing orthodox psychoanalysis, wherein you go to an expert specially schooled in the inner recesses of the mind. He or she will make your mental processes clear to you, so that you can consciously accept them. This knowledge can then help you in guiding your future thinking and acting. Similarly, if you accept the divine connections with your thinking and accept the divine purposes, you can shape your thinking and then will in the "right" direction and go along in the pre-cast grooves. This new consciousness will make it a lot easier to follow in the pre-ordained paths of God's will. It will also help you to secure the rewards that are available at the end of that path.

It is clear that such interpretations of motivation leave very little to any human autonomy. You are first of all never your own agent or left to your own devices to determine your fate. God's purpose is inexorably tied up with yours, and He is ever-present in you in His role of the master builder as well as contractor. It also becomes necessary to question yourself at every moment to make sure that you have not violated the divine principle of universal goodness as interpreted by the contemporary theologians and priests.

In fact, if your will is pre-programmed and you are only experiencing autonomous thinking as another precast thought, it is blasphemy to assume that you can really think for yourself. If you do, you are denying God's will and the reality of God's creation, and you are subject to His wrath. You are certainly spreading your feeble, little wings too widely, and falsely taking on powers that are only reserved to God. False pride and a false, illusory faith in one's own powers are therefore dangerous feelings and merit punishment rather than either praise or a feeling of self-satisfaction and accomplishment.

Violations furthermore may cost you the final reward which God as the master builder has provided at the end. The emphasis here is so obviously on the need to learn the truth as stated in the Bible and interpreted by the authorities of the Church. We are really so weak that we can at best stop and listen and become more knowledgeable. The emphasis finally is on acquiescence and on the suppression of autonomous thinking.

C. The Predestination of Fate.

It is instructive here to take a look at the prevalent beliefs of the ancient Greeks and even of the Roman Empire before going to the early interpreters of our own Judeo-Christian heritage. If one reads the Greek philosophers, historians, and playwrights one is struck by their faith that the gods pretty uniformly determined the actions of men and women. The gods could perhaps be swayed by their own ambivalence or in inter-heavenly rivalries, or they could change their minds either quite capriciously, or by listening to human prayer and sacrifice. Nevertheless, it was their wishes -- no matter how often they changed them -- which determined the fate of men and women. Rulers and the organizers of military and trade expeditions routinely asked the oracles or the wise men for omens from the gods that might give them some advance inkling of the outcome. Similarly they looked towards their gods for advice, by asking their intermediaries or their priests for the best course of action. Free will was not even considered much of a possibility. Socrates felt that nobody moved without the knowledge of the gods. To attach oneself to a particular god, especially if he or she was in ascendance in the heavenly rivalries at that time, was like a valid passport or safe-conduct pass for a successful journey. Therefore the wise man always went along with "his" god. His best bet for a good outcome of a venture was to examine the world of the gods and see what was left for him to do on his own.

Montaigne describes military commanders through the ages who cajoled their men into battle by reminding them of the fatal necessity that our time and our lives were pre-ordained by God and were not therefore influenced either by our own boldness, or by flight from the battlefield, or even by the enemy's missiles. Preordination was thus used to force people into dangerous and fatal actions against their better judgment, in this way God or the gods have been used since the beginning of history to justify wars and battles. The composer Kurt Weill has captured this monstrous fraud in a devastating duet between two clergymen in the opera "Johnny Johnson", which revolves around World War I. In the duet -- or rather the juxtaposition of two voices -- a German minister and an American minister chillingly intone the identical prayer in their respective languages, so that the identical phrases follow each other. They both invoke the blessings of God for their respective sides and the justness of their causes; and they exhort the congregation to fight the war as a just one in the name of the deity and his blessing. Montaigne cites, for instance, the beliefs of some Bedouin tribes in the Holy Land that the number of days in the life of every person was prefixed by eternity. This faith was so unshakeable that the men rode naked into battle except for a white linen cloth, and only carried a Turkish sword for their protection.

Tacitus, the Roman historian, wondered at one point in his account whether man's destiny was always determined by fate when he remembered the story of Tiberius who always asked one of his astrologers to predict his own future after he had revealed the secrets in the future of the emperor. He then used to throw the astrologer into the sea from the cliffs of his castle. This murder constituted a test of their veracity as fortune-tellers for him, and was routinely failed by the seers! Finally Tiberius consulted one astrologer who began to tremble at his own impending misfortune when he was asked to predict his own fate following his forecast for Tiberius. Thereupon Tiberius embraced him, congratulated him on his validity and spared him from drowning. Tacitus uses this example as a possible argument against pre-ordination and adds further evidence that both good and wicked men have been observed to reap opposite rewards. He offers the possibility that natural causes may at times be responsible for our fate, and that heaven is not concerned with the beginning or end of the lives of men and women. The possibility therefore occurs to him that we do have the capacity to choose our own lives, even though he concedes that most people in his time believe that each person's future is fixed from birth. These contemplations again illustrate how the uncertainties in nature and in man's interrelationships created doubts and a variety of concrete solutions.

This uncertainty was taken out of life by the interpretations of St. Augustine and Thomas Aquinas. They added the insurance that our eventual fate could be influenced by our awareness of the divine purpose, and we could help it along by making our actions conform to God's laws and purpose. Thomas Aquinas agreed categorically with St. Augustine that men are predestined by God because every created thing is sent on course towards its predetermined end. If something cannot attain this end by the power of its own nature, it must be conveyed then by another force, very much like the arrow is sent towards its mark by an archer. Therefore a rational creature that is capable of attaining eternal life is led towards it by God. They acknowledge that this journey may be unconscious, because it can only be observed in the process of a person's life but cannot be actively seen by the person involved. St. Augustine further preached that God influenced the fate of kings and kingdoms, depending on their good or bad actions. He claimed that this principle explained the horrible fate of the Romans, because they worshipped false gods, and made sacrifices to them forbidden by Christians. God is therefore the real cause of our fate, rather than that of a more impersonal fate from the stars.

It is easy to see how mankind has always needed an external cause to explain the seemingly unlawful and capricious turmoil in his life and in the world around him. As we have shown in the last chapter, our ancestors had even more reason to run for explanations in order to regain some control and reduce the many uncertainties. We shall show in a later chapter how the quest for cause and effect and the search for explanations is a very real need, vital to the success of life, and is based on the principles by which the living system and particularly the cognitive system function. However, the followers behind the idea of predestination give up a great deal of valuable self-confidence. They may blind themselves to their own potentials and coping devices to make some of their decisions more autonomously. If God has predestined everything for us, we need not engage in much planning for the future, nor do we need to organize our thinking about the purpose and the meaning of our lives. We need only follow the rules of the interpreters of the divine fate to stay on the path that God has drawn for us, and we shall coast along with some serenity, even if we are buffeted about by rude shocks that may hit us without adequate explanation. We thereby exchange the existential fears about the meaning of our life for a canned explanation and a dependency on an unknowable master whose power and benevolence is assured for us from a long history of dogma and its contemporary guides and interpreters.

D. The Debt Owed to God for the Creation and its Supervision

It is implied in the writings of our early theologians that we are forever indebted to God for having created the world and us in His own image. This sentiment is not openly expressed, because such an expectation on the part of God would make Him look more like an "imperfect" human being, and would also impute to Him a need to get back some form of payment for His labor and His concern. Since He is perfect, He could not harbor such motivations, because they would be "selfish" and therefore almost sinful. Nevertheless the first Commandment: "Thou shalt have no other gods before me" expresses the spirit of such an expectation.

We find the feeling more nakedly expressed in a beautiful and poetic passage from the Greek philosopher Epictetus, who was -- true to his time - more "expressive" and not yet caught up in the notion that God had to be perfect: "Then after receiving everything from another and even yourself, are you angry and do you blame the Giver if He takes anything from you? Who are you and for what purpose did you come into the world? Did not He introduce you here, did He not show you the light, and did He not give you fellow-workers, and perception, and reason? Did He not introduce you as subject to death, and as one to live on the earth with a little flesh, and to observe His administration and to join with Him in the spectacle and the festival for a short time?... Go away like a grateful and modest man, make room for others: others also must be born, as you were; and being born, they must have a place." Such a spirit of gratitude for the gift of being created for a short look diminishes one's need to question oneself, and weigh alternatives including doubts that can eventually resolve one's own unique questions.

E. The Weakness of Man as a Prerequisite of his Dependency on the Power and Grace of God.

Nowhere is the status of an obedient and reverent child vis-a-vis a powerful authority figure more clearly expressed than in the comparison between man's and God's power. The Bible gives us many examples in which God determines the fate of men and women (among them being Adam, Moses, Noah, the Pharaoh of Egypt, etc.). There are numerous incidents in which God threatens absence of support and even death, if His commandments are not obeyed (e.g. Genesis 3; Deuteronomy 30, 15-26; etc.). In many other places God has "hardened the hearts" of incalcitrant personages. In other places we find clear expression of the abject dependence of Man on God. Thus in Isaiah, 64:8 it is written: "oh Lord, thou art our Father; we are the clay, and thou art our potter; we are all the work of thy hand."

We need only remember the Lord's Prayer: "Thy will be done on earth as it is in Heaven." Jesus reiterates the absolute power of God over Man. For instance, in the story of the vineyard keeper, Jesus tells how he pays all the laborers equal wages regardless of how long they worked, because the vineyard and the money was his (Matthew 6: 22-71). Further examples from the New Testament come from Romans 9, in which God is reported to have told Moses that He bestows mercy on whom he chooses: "So it depends not upon man's will or exertion, but upon God's mercy". It is similarly up to God to "harden the heart of whomever He wills". Recently I saw a bumper sticker that still nowadays expresses a similar sentiment: "God said it, I believe it, and that settles it". If you read further (such as Psalms 89: 6-8, Isaiah 40: 12-26, and the writings of St. Augustine and Thomas Aquinas), the theme of abject dependence on and reverence for God and His power and glory is repeated again and again. There is almost a direct denial that one can have any autonomy for oneself. Every good and worthwhile idea is not one's own, because it was placed there or sparked by God. One is asked to fall on one's knee to thank God for this great gift. One must further disavow all faith in independent ideas or else stand accused of false pride and idolatry. We are also reminded that God is everywhere and in everything. Nothing happens without either His presence or His knowledge.

The constant confrontation of the theologian and the philosopher with the imperfections of Man and the fallibility of Man's wishes is of course perfectly correlated with actual events in Man's life and with confrontations in nature as we saw it in the previous chapter. We are further asked to compare ourselves to this perfect, infinite, and powerful essence of God, and then try to aspire to get at least halfway --- or else! It becomes easy to see how the reawakened fears and doubts readily invited the proffered dependency on God, so that mankind fell back on compliance and stilled autonomous thoughts within them as unworthy and even as examples of our own imperfection. The result was that one felt very small and weak and was contrite for any contrary thought and apologized and did penance. Of course, one gained buckets of security, acceptance, and praise from the authorities and from one's fellow men. And of course one had been given ready-made answers to the questions which Adam and many people since have asked themselves. This emotion is beautifully described by Descartes (in Meditations III). He starts the thought by stating his own lack of awareness of any power within himself that "conserves" him from moment to moment. Hence he is the "same" person -- in terms of his thoughts and his intellect - from one period to the next without the need for "re-creation". This miraculous continuity proves to him that he is dependent on some other being than himself, which obviously created him in the first place. We shall see in the next chapter how our lack of knowledge about living processes both in the brain and in the mental realm created puzzles which men like Descartes answered by postulating God as the cause of these processes and from which he concluded our dependency on Him.

Freud has pointed out that mankind frequently needed to create gods in their own image and find a surrogate for the father, so that we can perpetuate the dependency relationship experienced for such a lengthy time in infancy, Hence our long history as dependent children; and the problems we must face cognitively and emotionally at many periods of our adult lives almost force us to project infantile dependency on God and even call Him "father". The father was and had to be overrated in childhood because the long maturation period of the human animal necessitated a long dependency period. The memory of this exaggerated father figure is often exalted into a deity and brought into present reality. The emotional bond created by this memory-image and connected with present reality offers protection from the real world, especially if it proves harsh and frightening. However, the reconstruction of a dependency relationship on a powerful and over-idealized father figure in the deity -- and, by extension, onto His interpreters -- robs us of the chance to explore our independence and our self-generated forays into our emotions and into our environment.

F. Man's Imperfections Preclude Full Comprehension and Require God's Help.

The theists, represented by such thinkers as Thomas Aquinas and St. Augustine, represented God as an ever unknowable and unreachable force -- at least as long as Man was alive during his brief span on earth. In contrast to the deists, who emerged during the 17th and 18th centuries, the theists denied that one could explain God and His nature with the use of reason. God is therefore solely available and knowable by means of (emotional) faith. A further implication was that nobody could ever comprehend the plan of providence. Reason could not fathom it out, and so it remained hidden, except that occasional glimpses were available to very devout and pious persons in great need. It can and does of course occur in occasional miracles and oracles. This doctrine was clearly an appeal to and a reliance on emotion in a controlled sense, and represents a devaluation of rational thinking. Nowadays we would say that the Church encouraged the controlled use of right-brain processes, while indicting left-brain processing as suspect in this area of man's functioning. In the previous two chapters we showed that reason was not very useful either to figure out the most burning existential questions of man's consciousness or to understand the secrets and especially the terrors of nature. It is probably a stroke of genius that the first church leaders of the early Christians interpreted the life of Jesus as a direct revelation of God to mankind. Thereby they helped to support the emotional components of mankind's faith, and therefore lent strength to the doctrine. The birth and death of Jesus was additionally full of miracles that could be accepted only by an active use of faith. Faith is, of course, one of the most vital forces in our existence and in each life, and we shall look much more closely and favorable on it as a legitimate and useful expression of the cognitive forces in the living system. We shall also take up alternative content areas for this "faith" force, which do not threaten to inhibit other legitimate stages of functioning in men and women, such as self-actualization. We need to acknowledge here that the deists' acceptance of a more aloof God, who has left the universe alone after the act of creation, encouraged a much more personalistic interpretation of religious doctrine and practice. Deism is also based more on reason and on experience rather than on blind faith solely left to the interpretations of a religious institution. This more individualized interpretation of God and the creation exists nowadays side by side with strong remnants of theist thinking.

Religious faith, of course, gave direction to men and women as they faced the chaos and insecurity of their world, especially when it clashed with their own plans and wishes. Among such massive doses of frustration the religious faith kept alive an inner flame of hope, which then rechanneled energy. As we shall see later, the Christian faith further nourished a hope for the future which lay beyond the misfortunes of life. It is precisely the faith with the support of important emotions that is feared so much by modern communist nations. Their reliance on a purely rational, so-called scientific theory of social organization has not brought forth any promises and hopes for a better world. They find that the "depraved" needs or a variety of other inclinations defined as "selfishness" was routinely branded as "sinful". People engaging in these actions or thoughts were threatened by rejection, blame, banishment, eternal hell, and even torture and death. Autonomous thinking did not fit in here. In fact, it is quite possible that the men and women who wrote and administered the doctrine occasionally experienced strong autonomy needs and were aware of what inevitably stirred in their breasts, because such manifestations accompanied a lawful stage in human life as elucidated later. These people were, after all, able to command a much better amount of leisure and their basic needs were more easily met as members of the privileged class. They must have been partly intrigued and partly alarmed by these internal stirrings. They may have even sensed that their own feelings were echoes of a more widespread human tendency. Therefore they had to guard themselves against further temptation, but had to make doubly sure that others, less "strong and fortified", would stifle any such "suspicious" stirrings and label them as evil and moving away from God. This reaction formation is noticeable in the often quoted statement of St. Augustine that "man's pride is the greatest stumbling block to our clinging to God".

Besides their function as interpreters, the Church also provided important gratifications for the need to belong and to be accepted in a community. It enabled people to feel more directly identified with their nation and town and with an immediate social group that could supply companionship and security. In addition the Church supplied rituals full of visual and auditory feasts. The great art and great music of the middle Ages was primarily concentrated in religious themes and institutions, and was literally woven into its services and other religious functions. Also, we must not overlook the awe-inspiring architectural marvels, the Cathedrals that illustrated the power and the glory of the Church. In addition there were the splendid uniforms, signs of office, and the gold and jewels on display with its priests and officers. Not only did these attributes and the rituals satisfy many auxiliary human needs; they also supplied the power to marshal and gratify powerful emotions. In this way the experiences of commitment, of solidarity, of existential meaning, of power, and of sheer ecstasy were released in a controlled fashion. They could be channeled into actions that conformed to the order and rules of the day rather than be left to smolder without supervision and perhaps erupt into an uncontrollable chain-reaction.

The bad feature of these important and necessary gratifications was its impact on crushing human faculties and capacities. Mill in 1859 accused many religions of using the slogan: "Man needs no capacity but that of surrendering himself to the will of God" as an indictment of self-will. Obedience and compliance were instead considered to be the only human good, and there was no redemption for anyone, until one's life was finally ended by death. Mill reminded us that different religions interpret the will of God differently and can label any act as sinful if it is not considered to be a duty to God. We can only gratify those inclinations that are permitted by the "god" of our religion. In addition, we cannot do so by our own preferences but have to proceed by the ways prescribed by the authorities.

G. Real Happiness only after Death: Happiness on Earth is Suspect.

For the Theologians of more ancient times happiness was defined as an ultimate "summum bonum", or "final blessedness", or "ultimate consumption", which supplied eternal peace in the contemplation of the "Divine Essence". This experience is only possible after life ends, when the soul of (some) people passes into Heaven. According to Thomas Aquinas, true happiness is not attainable in life, because happiness is a perfect good, excludes all evil and satisfies every desire. This is only possible in the City of God. Moreover, happiness also consists of a vision of the Divine Essence, and therefore just is not available on earth.

Furthermore, this final happiness cannot be obtained by Man himself and needs the helping hand of God.

Only the earthly life which molds itself to God can have a little measure of happiness in it. According to Thomas Aquinas we might be blessed with some peace on earth, "but such blessedness is mere misery compared to that final felicity". This view has tremendous implications. Any happiness on earth is merely "the solace of our misery". Thomas Aquinas even points out that the man who has everything is not really happy, because he only has satisfied his natural appetite. The "natural desire" of man is only satisfied by the perfect good of God-given happiness. So the "happy man" is really unhappy because the illusion that he is happy turns him away from what he desires "naturally". Thomas Aquinas therefore amends St. Augustine's statement: "Happy is he who has all he desires" by adding the phrase: "provided he desires nothing amiss"!

Also, only the earthly life which molds itself entirely after God's law can contain a small measure of happiness. Earthly life is at best imperfect because of its temporal aspects and because of the imperfections of the body. Hence, earthly happiness with all its deficiencies consists solely of a life devoted to God. Again we recognize a rallying cry for conformity. To experience real happiness one must participate on the lower stages in the appropriate and approved manner, and thereby insure a form of continuity. Kant tackled the more recent preoccupation with the pursuit of happiness as a possible human right in his time by showing how it only represents private happiness. It clashes with morality if it means the satisfaction of all desires. He therefore sets up a moral law as a "categorical imperative" (that is, something that imposes a given and absolute obligation on us), that one must be worthy of happiness, and not simply try to be happy. This ethical law dictates how we ought to act to deserve happiness rather than looking only after our needs. Happiness as a goal is dangerous, because it does not provide any standards for conduct. Therefore, it cannot be a condition of moral action, or a "moral principle" or goal. Instead, it can represent a consequence to the moral law which in effect commands us to perform our duty unconditionally. Hence the question of illusory happiness on earth points to the core solution of the issue for Kant: Duty comes before happiness. Adam Smith observed that in European education duties were demanded as forerunners and signposts to future happiness. The perfection of virtue was therefore required to secure happiness later. Heaven could be earned only by penance and mortification, more akin to the life of a monk rather than the "life of the liberal and generous spirit of Man".

Beneath this banishment of happiness until after death lives the very pessimistic conception which theologians had of life on earth. This was of course shared by the very real experiences of everyone else in the face of the many difficulties and in the face of a general lack of comprehension about mental processes. People not only viewed the body as very corruptible to evil desires, but despaired at any "perfect control" over vice. Each person tried to struggle against vice in view of the fact that one was only an imperfect copy of the perfect God, who had of course perfect control. Just as one seemed to be on top of the conflict or the temptation, "There steals in some evil thing", which may slip out in words if it does not find expression in behavior. Or it may merely insinuate itself into one's thoughts. Peace was therefore never achieved for long, because the war with one's vices continued unabated. Therefore, Man could not ever hope for the perfection of virtue. All he could hope for was the remission of sin. No wonder the idea of perfection was reserved for the creator, and his divine essence was promised as a compensation. However, this perfect standard was unfulfillable in the imperfection residing in Man, who was merely a copy of God.

One of the problems with such a conception of happiness as unattainable in the somewhat tarnished state of Man rests with the early definitions of happiness. They were of course handicapped by the inadequate and even faulty knowledge of human psychology. While all ancient philosophers and theologians agree that Man strives for happiness, it is never defined as an expression of self-fulfillment. It is instead defined as freedom from want, from misery, or as a sort of quiescent, needless feeling of peace experienced in a region of plenty. Such a state is really impossible in a living organism with its ongoing living processes, and is therefore more characteristic of the perfect stable equilibrium found in death or in non-living systems, except the consciousness to experience it is missing. Self-actualization, as we for instance understand it now, may involve tensions, excitement, and even deprivation of some lower inner wants. Human beings are also capable of ecstatic experiences and mystical experiences, which are however accompanied by pleasant tensions and intense feeling states. But, of course, we must not forget that the definition of happiness then functioned to justify devotion to duty and conformity to dogma.

In addition, the early philosophers such as Aristotle defined happiness as the secure enjoyment of maximum pleasure or as a good condition of one's property or body. Before the advent of Christianity with its intimate ties to God's plans, Aristotle and other Greek philosophers enumerated the building blocks to happiness as good birth, many friends, wealth, plenty of good children, an excellent body in fine condition possibly including beauty in addition to health, a happy old age, and topped by such ornaments as fame, honor, good luck, and virtues. Most of these were external criteria, and marked the upper status person. Inner criteria were added during the Middle Ages and then considered unreachable because of the nature of Man in relation to the Deity. Another problem with this kind of approach to happiness was that it tried to define it in such a way that everybody could agree on a general definition removed from more individualistic experiences. If the philosophers failed in this attempt then some people could not search for such a state. In other words there was no attempt to see happiness in terms of individual stabs at fulfillment which might then look very different to different people.

Hence early philosophers insisted that a science of ethics must depend on a first principle which becomes obvious to everyone. If happiness is to signify what each person thinks it to be for him or herself alone, it cannot supply this principle. The implication for education and social action is obvious. Both Aquinas and Aristotle realized that people seek different ends under the banner of happiness. However, they felt compelled to seek a definition of happiness that was appropriate to a human essence common to all. It could not be something that was determined by individual needs and temperaments. If people went by their own opinions or preferences, a "scientific" approach to ethics would be impossible.

It is only recently that a personalized happiness became first a right and then a goal for itself. Some of the Greek philosophers already saw glimpses of it in their contemplations. Thomas Aquinas, however, argued that happiness was impossible in life because his definition of it excluded any encroachment of evil and he saw it as the fulfillment of every desire. In their haste to define a general principle, some philosophers also pictured happiness as a permanent end state with such exalted properties that it seemed out of reach for anyone. It was also falsely seen as a life category rather than as a stage in a living process. When we examine in the next chapter the confusions that existed among these scholars about the working of human mental life, we can understand the faulty conception of human emotions. They were therefore unable to see happiness as a peak in a process. They were not able to employ process language, because they did not understand living systems in these terms. Under such handicaps in even the most basic terms of the definitions it is indeed impossible for the human being to be happy. The belief in a powerful God, who was greatly concerned with the fate of his most perfect creation, unfortunately became the icing that firmly covered this definition of happiness with a sense of duty and conformity.

H. The Power of God to Punish Transgressions.

Evidently it was not sufficient to stifle autonomous thinking in pre-modern Man by promising him a blissful state of eternal happiness unlike anything experienced on earth. Men and women had to be further motivated by the possibility that he would not get there automatically after death, but that he or she had to deserve passage by regulating both life and thinking. According to Thomas Aquinas God judges everybody as either good or evil, because He saw man's action to derive inevitably from God's creation. God judges us because He is man's last way station. It is therefore our duty to refer our actions to such an end. First of all our actions acquire merits or demerits in our own eyes. Next they are judged by the community because it cares for the common good. It is therefore logical for the governor of a community to judge our actions because he cares for the common good, first of all. (Obviously a corrupt or selfish governor was inconceivable!) Similarly God at the very end of this chain has the business to award retribution for things done well or badly in the community. Since He is governor of the universe and especially of rational creatures, it is His business to judge our actions with reference to His goals. Hence He gives out merits and demerits also. God, however, is an even sterner master than the community, which may overlook many actions of individuals. God on the contrary judges every action!

Locke points out that the awards and the punishments of another life are very weighty and have great power to determine choices in a person's life. Who would not want exquisite and endless happiness as a consequence of a "good life"? This reward system exerts a strong leverage to lead a "virtuous life" in view of the "dreadful state of misery" which eventually overtakes the guilty. These promises and threats are strong forces towards conformity. Since no one has come back from the "other life" and confirmed or disconfirmed the eternal rewards and punishments, and since they are described in rather vague terms and not subject to any further knowledge, a person has no choice but to accept the doctrine of the Church and its leaders. He better play it safe, if he subscribes to the central belief in a powerful and intimately concerned God. He must then, of course, give up his own inclinations and wishes.

I. Religion as an Explanation of Sin, Evil, and Deviant Behavior.

In the absence of a science of personality and of mental functioning, "evil thoughts" and antisocial action were very frightening to our forefathers and proved hard to explain. Here we find another of the salvaging functions of religion, because it jumped into this vacuum with ready-made answers. The explanations simplified this troublesome human aspect and brought order into some of the difficulties associated with living. At least one part of the hard and confusing world: the experience of inner Man, became intelligible. Thomas Aquinas starts with a comparison of pain with fault to derive definitions and a meaningful theory. Pain emerges from fault as a built-in consequence. Pain is an ingredient in God's creation and built into it as a logical reaction, signifying some form of punishment. Fault, on the other hand, is not part of the creation, but is a "disorder of the will" by which Man goes against the creation. St. Augustine also sees the will capable of going astray and doing evil deeds. It is then "lost" through its own fault and can only be restored by God, who gave will to Man in the first place. Here is one place where Man seems to have retained some autonomy to go his own way. However, such autonomy always leads one astray because it pushes the will away from the creation and from God!

The early theologians had a hard time with "sin" and with "evil". Since God represents the highest good, He would not and did not create evil. So how did it get there and how can it be explained? Evil is therefore defined as a "defect" in the will and represents an "accident". The will is not perfect, because it is only a replica of God's will and only God could possess a perfect and faultless will. Hence man's will can contain defects without faulting its creator with either negligence or malice! Of course by implication God still must take responsibility for creating something that can have cracks in it and become defective. Therefore we can understand why the logic of Thomas Aquinas etc. breaks down, when they try to explain the contingencies of evil. How is it conceivable that God can set up the earthly consequences (guilt) and the eternal consequences of evil (hell and damnation)? How can He punish something that He did not create? The explanation of the theologians is like a thin crust of ice that could break in easily under any exploratory step, but it goes like this: Sin is a defect coming from a created cause, namely "free choice". God gave this to men and women as a gift in order to make them resemble Him a little more. Hence they also have the "choice" to fall from God. However, once he or she has done so, he has no choice in avoiding God's punishment!

Again, the exposition of this doctrine about anti-social or even anti-self impulses gives some security at the expense of autonomy and responsibility for the self. One could, of course, pray to God, go to Church, and do penance. Avenues were available to reduce pain and to assure oneself the restoration of God's grace. Again with the advent of contemporary understanding of psychological processes we have different explanations and can find other avenues towards creating internal order in ourselves. We shall describe such avenues in greater detail when we take a closer look at the psychotherapies.

J. "Free Will" is either an Illusion or a Tiny Domain.

Let us again consult the religious authorities through Thomas Aquinas. He says in no uncertain terms that both the intellect and the will are moved by God who created the power of willing. The will might be stimulated by some good as the object of its choice, but it is moved "sufficiently and efficaciously" by God alone. He alone fills the capacity of the will and moves it. The will is predestined to be inclined towards its inevitable object, the universal good. "But to incline towards the universal good belongs to the first Mover". God is therefore the first cause of what men and women seem to choose to do freely, just as He is the first cause of every natural event. Moreover, the will as a "natural faculty" never moves itself into operation. It is always moved by reason, even in acts of choice. These acts are "also caused".

The so-called freedom of the will is therefore limited to a choice of means according to Thomas Aquinas. Another way of putting it is to assert that the will is by necessity driven to acts that lead to earthly happiness associated with the final aim of reaching the perfect good. As we saw previously, this perfect good is implicitly understood by reason to have this magnetic ability, because it was given by God. Therefore Man wills happiness by necessity. He has no choice to be unhappy. Therefore he has no choice of the end or goal, but only of the means or of sub goals to the perfect good. He can choose particular goods. For these reasons Thomas Aquinas does not see free will as an indispensable bridge to moral conduct. The will could move freely towards a variety of choices precisely because reason can entertain various perceptions of the good. But to the good the will moves and it has no choice but to follow along in its God-given track.

The Promise Of Human Autonomy

This explanation massively obstructs the range of choices and narrows human freedom to an almost tiny range of choices. Moreover, it does not attribute either autonomy or spontaneity to the will. This is further restricted by the additional limitations placed on reasoning power. While the will utilizes the rules of reason, the latter derives its rules and its goodness from Divine reason. Reason therefore acts like a beacon, because it can illuminate good ends and guide the will. Hence the goodness or any direction for the will depends again on "eternal law", much more than on purely human reason. When the latter fails we have no choice but to turn to Eternal reason. Since eternal law is not directly known to us, it percolates to us from our natural reason which it helped to spawn in the first place. However, the unclear pipeline again, necessitates a great dependence on the interpreting authorities, rather than relying on our own interpretations.

The clincher comes from Thomas Aquinas's assertion that there is really no distinction between what flows from so-called free choice and what comes from predestination, since God produces His effects through the operation of "secondary causes". Therefore what seems to flow from free choice basically comes from predestination. There is therefore no free will and its perception is largely an illusion. Again the loser in all these weighty arguments is Man who is thereby prevented from relying on his own decisions and his sense of self.

K. The Reliance on any Form of Autonomy is a Monstrous Defiance of God.

St. Augustine intimates in his own confession that a person is despicable if he strays from God's power by assuming either too much power or autonomy. He thereby "corruptly and pervertedly" imitates God and mimics a false liberty. He also thinks and acts in ways that "are not permitted to Man". He clearly states that any search for pleasure for the sake of pleasure alone is empty and even hideous. It is alright to pick up pleasure along the road to virtue, like the experience of sexual pleasure while one is fulfilling one's duty to beget children. It is blasphemy, however, to follow along the line of the Stoics, who claimed that one can find the supreme good in this life. Nobody can ever become happy by their own resources. Life is so capricious that one cannot exist without hope. The Christians provided that in huge amounts, so what else does one need to do?

Kant several centuries later produced "Proof" that any form of self-love is pure selfishness and conceit. It goes against the moral law as given by pure reason, and this conclusion therefore derived from the will of God. Only the certainty of a state of mind that coincides with the moral law is the first condition of personal worth. Therefore, one must suspect any form of self-worth that supposedly derives from this law. The law itself checks any such tendencies. Esteem rests solely on morality and is suspect if it does not. Our immediate feeling may be to see ourselves to be governed by our own choice and to accept that as an objective manifestation of the will. However, that feeling is really self-love, which is really a form of self-conceit if we accept these premises and their derivations as an unquestionable practical principle of operation. The moral law actually humbles Man and must therefore command the respect of mankind. If we accept the immediate feeling of self-worth instead, we are vain. We must therefore conclude that any exercises of autonomy and any search for personal pleasure or well-being is a monstrous sin, which exposes us to censure and consequent self-condemnation. The religious doctrine of our ancestors could not tolerate anything but a very narrow range of choices and a very rigid interpretation of man's feeling and thinking, befitting the official picture of God.

L. Faith as an Important Cementing Force Then and Now.

We have pointed out before that the problems inherent in pre-industrial technology and economic organization were responsible for a relatively short life span that was full of misery and unpleasant surprises. It is therefore not surprising that the prevalent uncertainties caused St. Augustine to observe that it required hope to live. The Church and its doctrine provided for the hope and also preached piety, so that one could look forward to some future salvation stemming from that hope. In this way mankind obtained some sense of inner harmony and a sense of order and even a feeling of control....even if it had to be achieved through some fairly simple, straightforward, but distorting rules. "We are made happy by hope" for something we cannot see. We may not see a present salvation, but we are promised and we hope for a future one at which time we are delivered from all disorder, evil and pain. St. Augustine and others preached that eternal life in heaven was the supreme good and that we could attain it by living right. Since we cannot see or know it, we must live by faith. Since we cannot live in the right way purely by ourselves, we can only do it with the aid of God, who is also the creator of the faith in us. Hence we have to believe in his assistance when we believe and when we pray to Him.

This is a neat package which has worked well for centuries. What is important to remember here is that Man as he is constituted by the forces of life and by his mental processes cannot live without hope or faith. We have tried to show how this particular kind of faith constricted the natural powers of Man to think and feel for himself. However, the person who rejects religious doctrine as too confining and as narrowing his creative potentials must substitute some faith in other vital forces connected with his goals and his values. It must constitute for him an important part of the map of his world by which he can navigate through the existential questions which Adam and millions of others have asked themselves since human consciousness first evolved. We shall later set out the scientific underpinnings of this principle about the functions of faith and hope in greater detail.

M. Changes in Religious Dogma to Personal Beliefs in the Service of Autonomy: The Shrinking of God's power.

If we have been a bit harsh with the Judeo-Christian doctrine about the nature of God, we need also remember that it has been refined over many centuries and has passed on through millions of people, including many of our contemporaries. It has stood a good deal of testing and feedback, and is consequently validated as "a good theory" by the yardstick of pragmatism: What works is good. It's power and conviction is evident in the tremendous effort and anguish which communist nations spend in their efforts to silence it and root it out. They do so because they claim that they have a truly scientific theory which also explains religion as "the opiate of the people"; that is as a drug that beclouds the recognition of the "truth, their truth". Unfortunately they have substituted a sometimes much harsher "cure" which acts like a guillotine for the human head and for human autonomy. We hopefully can convince the reader that there may be other, more scientifically-based principles which allow us to concentrate on the strengths of the human soul unencumbered by a claim to either an economic pseudo-theory like Marxism, or an abject dependence on a father-like God of great power and possessiveness.

N. A Recapitulation on the Power of Religious Doctrine over Man and its Waning in recent History.

We want to emphasize that the picture we have drawn of a monolithic religious doctrine belongs 2-300 years into the past. The first schism started more than 400 years ago with the beginning of Protestantism. This liberalization was followed by deist writers who disconnected Man's fate from God entirely and made Man rely on himself and work out his own relationship to a distant and disinterested God creator. This liberalization was of course fertilized by the new emphasis on liberty and the creation of new forms of social organization. After a succession of several revolutions in Europe, this trend finally culminated in political democracy in the U.S. and then eventually on the continent.

The doctrine of absolute faith in a strong and caring God figure belonged to a time period in our history where it was sorely needed in view of the conditions we have sketched out in the previous chapter. While mankind lacked the power to control its fate, men and women needed and kept alive a very powerful God to bestow meaning on living conditions and a sense of direction on their hopes. Therefore every man, woman and child allowed this God to determine every decision in their lives, guide their behavior and influence their thinking. He was used routinely to sanctify various forms of government and its rulers. Kings and princes in pre-modern days were hereditary and were sanctified by the Deity. Therefore an act of disobedience to the kings was most often also a violation of God's law.

Nevertheless we can also readily see how this religious doctrine has a powerful influence on thinking, quite apart from its comfortable fit with a technology and social organization that are not of its own making. As we have shown above, a doctrine that places so much responsibility, initiative, and power to shape behavior, into a central agent outside and above the human being, also has the power to inhibit independent thinking and the search for personal meaning and goals in life. In fact, these very acts are labeled as blasphemy and are punishable as heresy, if they get beyond the person's own guilt to the outside. Hence the doctrine created its own steam to inhibit free thinking, quite apart from the fact that free thinking was difficult in times when people neither had the time for it, nor did they experience a harmonious relationship with nature as a solid base for it. The doctrine succeeded here because it commanded powerful institutions which exhibited wealth and splendor. It was headed by powerful and highly intelligent men and some women who maintained intimate and often very explicit connections with secular government. Hence the danger was present and still is present in some corners of the globe that the institutionalized doctrine may retard the kinds of insights and speculations which we shall elaborate in later chapters and which gave rise to this book in the first place.

It is therefore interesting to study the changes in our religions over the last 200-300 years. When we began to invent machinery that gave us greater control over our environment, we did not need God as much as an all-powerful and autonomous regulator. We were learning to do some of this ourselves, especially as we also gained some ascendancy over the most crippling diseases and body conditions, and as we learned to change our lifestyles to fit in with the many new inventions. This development was necessarily hastened in the 18th and 19th centuries by the major revolutions. They gradually gave rise to governments that were no longer dominated by hereditary princes of dubious and even dangerous qualifications, and finally culminated in the democratic form of government supported by a rationally based constitution (see chapter IX for a fuller discussion). When religion was finally separated completely from government and the state, it became much more a private matter. This development also regulated God into a less compelling force to which each person could develop a more personal relationship. In this way ideas about God and one's religious inclination could also become integrated into one's autonomously organized ideas about the self and one's views of the world.

We have, or course, observed some persistent pockets where autocratic control is still vested in religious ideology and where strong religious leaders persist. This is true even in the so-called developed nations and has been found even in our own most recent past. There is still the danger that a soul-enslaving doctrine rooted in a strong and controlling God can flourish in a shaded corner, if it provides the fertile mix of a demoralized and powerless mass of people and sprouts a power-hungry, magnetic leader. The example of Rev. Jim Jones comes to mind here, in which the resultant conformity can even lead to mass suicide. We have some evidence that some other contemporary religious cults, such as the Moonies, contain elements of this conformity producing mixture. Also the parade of recent history has produced some religious leaders who have used their base in one of the churches to try to influence the thinking and acting of people in other than religious areas. Father Coughlin comes to mind as an example here. Despite such dangers that ministers and priests can be seen as powerful and semi-autonomous intermediaries for God, especially if they have strong power needs, the democratic and individualistic emphasis of our age has shrunk both the might and influence of God, and reduced the churches to functions other than thought-control.

Even the Catholic Church, which originated and housed the great developers of the principles for the religious climate, has changed greatly. While the Church is still faithfully built on the old cornerstones enumerated above, it has greatly liberalized its hold on its parishioners. It has done so in the most salutary way by giving up more and more control over vast domains of man's thinking and emotions, and has relinquished most of the supervision over his actions. It is nowadays confining its authoritative statements primarily to so-called ethical questions that deal with the relationship of man to man, with perhaps special emphasis on the relationship of man to women! There is no doubt in my mind that the Church will radically modify its stand on some of the remaining "heresies" regarding sexuality and the consequences of sexuality (such as the "life and death" issue) in the future, because I cannot see how such a proud and long standing institution would want to commit suicide in the face of ever-increasing percentages of dissident opinions and behavior emerging in recent polls of its parishioners.

Many contemporary religions, including Unitarianism, liberal Judaism, the Society of Friends and others have carried the principles of deism much further, and have permitted men and women to be truly autonomous in their life choices and have encouraged their followers to organize their belief systems privately. This appeal to individual freedom has even included the beliefs of their followers about a Godlike power, and their relationship to their church, so that sometimes no official dogma or prescriptions are even available for these content areas. Instead, such religious movements have primarily concentrated on the ethical principles of living in a modern world, and have provided many new social and emotional functions that are satisfying to some people. We shall take up again later the needs and feelings that beg to be answered by modern men and women and by their institutions in terms of the psychological principles we understand today. However, we also ought to remind ourselves from time to time that most of the above-mentioned religious principles still float around us as remnants of the past, and that they may at times inhibit the forces towards the development of adult autonomy.

Chapter IV

Experiences of Autonomy as Illusions Prior to the Science of Psychology

It may be hard for us to imagine what it was like for our ancestors only 300 years ago to navigate in a world where "miracles" were occurring daily, because the "simple" reasons and causes of common events were completely unknown and unknowable. Nobody knew about the electrical and acoustical properties of lightning and thunder before Benjamin Franklin; the circulation of the blood was not known or understood before the surgeon Harvey discovered it; the many chemical transformations that occur in combustion and the very nature of matter were completely misunderstood before the experiments of Priestley and Lavoisier; and the very origin of Man was shrouded in speculation and controversy before Darwin and others. Before the invention of the microscope by Leeuwenhoek in the latter part of the 17th Century mankind had no way of discovering the secrets of life and of living processes that were locked away in the cell. It was therefore not possible to understand how a human being was conceived. Many theories about this most important question existed. In those days of male supremacy there was even doubt that the woman contributed any seed or any part of the newborn human being except to provide "heat" and the womb as a depository.

If little was known about our bodies and how they functioned, even less was known about the workings of the mind. We therefore finally arrive at a third major reason why a focused concern and systematic study of autonomous processes in the human mind could not have been possible until the last 50 to 100 years. In the absence of experimentation on mental processes and without any knowledge of neurology, there was pure speculation which was painfully convoluted. Even if some thinkers "hit" on bright ideas and hunches that later blossomed into "truth", there was no chance to get agreement or to integrate these hunches fruitfully with other ideas about the nature of Man. We must, of course, remember that there was no scientific psychology before the 19th Century, and science as an acceptable enterprise and as a source of respectable knowledge was also a recent phenomenon.

The first major obstacle to any scientific investigation was the monolithic position of the Church during the Middle Ages. Religious dogma as partially described in the previous chapter discouraged any ideas or conclusions that might have questioned the state of the world and the nature of Man according to the "Gospel". We need only remember the difficulties and the hostility which greeted scientists like Galileo, Copernicus, and later people like Darwin, Freud, and Semmelweis when they suggested new, important theories from their empirical observations. One of the biggest obstacles which any science including psychology faced, was the criterion of truth or of "reality". It took much liberalization of social institutions and of political doctrine to allow mankind to trust other criteria than the accepted and traditional pronouncements of authorities about the word of God. Eventually we began to listen to scientists and to the philosophers of science when they substituted repeated and repeatable observations under maximally objective conditions to investigate alternative hypotheses to the accepted traditions. It took even more time to accept the probabilistic definition of truth instead of the idea of an absolute truth. This definition rests on the tradition developed in science that a predicted finding is "true" if it occurred less than five times or even less than once by chance out of 100 observations. It could then be accepted as a true state of affairs, even if chance could never be completely ruled out as a possible explanation. This definition of truth, of course, gave us a different orientation to our world. We could now accept truth as an approximation to an ideal which was subject to change, and which took into account error and the fact that we can never measure or observe the state of nature with perfect accuracy. The very approach to nature, even with the finest and most delicately calibrated instruments, has an unknowable effect on what we measure. This of course is the famous Heisenberg indeterminacy principle. Therefore we accept a statistical definition of truth by accepting the average of many repeated measurements or observations as the "true state" of the process we are observing. These very philosophic mutations in our definitions about certainty in nature - including Man and his thoughts - helped to create the fertile ground in which the hypotheses of human autonomy could grow and flourish. The acceptance of uncertainty as an approach to truth rather than search for the truth gave men the possibility and the faith to fall back on their own use of reason and on their resources rather than lean on an outside authority.

In psychology there were a number of special difficulties very much related to the subject matter of the young science and to the specialized nature of observations that was required here. First of all, all methods or observation had to be invented from scratch and tried out in repeated forms before we could trust the data to be reliable. Reliability in psychology involves a trust in our observation as being repeatable or capable of being shared with another observer. One of the biggest obstacles was and still is the question of maximizing objectivity. Psychologists have tried to develop ingenious methods to keep their own values and needs and their personalized perceptions out of the observations and measurements of personality processes. They have for instance used peer ratings, subject self-report measures, letting the subject behave under conditions where he can be objectively observed in carefully controlled situations, etc.. And still we are plagued by the possibility of the experimenter unwittingly influencing his subject to perform the behavior which supports his hypothesis, as the experiments of Rosenberg and his students at Harvard have shown without so far yielding definite clues about how this experimental bias is transmitted to the subject. Psychology also had to break away from an initial emphasis on general laws about human behavior toward a study and understanding of individual differences. Only in this way could it investigate the manifestations and processes of human personality. When this area became a legitimate place it was further necessary to set up crucial experiments that would bring some order among the proliferation of theories about the functioning and development of the personality. While we have not yet been able to declare one theory the winner over its rivals by virtue of some clear-cut experiments and objective evidence, we have been able to narrow the field considerably. At least we have been able to forge a metatheory that can incorporate the seeming disparities of several approaches. In Chapter VI we shall show that certain common principles about people functioning at different stages and levels of integration emerge from a number of personality theories. We shall try to show later (Chapter VII) how there is some general agreement on self-differentiation and self-productivity among different theories which emphasize different parts of the personality as important. Finally we have had to overcome the interwoven multiplicity of factors in the human personality which cannot be easily separated for the sake of study. We had to derive special methods and special techniques of manipulation to deal with the huge banks of data that come from our in vivo observations of the interrelationships. We have learned to study these interrelationships while keeping the person functioning in a relatively undisturbed way. Thus we keep both the process intact and open to scrutiny.

Let us go back once more before there was a science of psychology and see what happened to the study and the contemplation of Man's thinking and feeling. This was the era in our history when such study was exclusively undertaken by philosophers. Philosophy then had important functions and had its professionals and its supporters. Moreover it was an important faculty in all European universities. When psychology first started out as a young science its practitioners came from the discipline of philosophy, and psychology was taught in philosophy departments of psychology. They may be found paired with philosophy in one department or one division.

It is not hard to project ourselves into the reaction of both the philosophers and the general populace when they stopped to think about their own minds and consciousness before anything was known about either brain neurology or psychology. First of all it must have been another miracle that our minds can think -- sometimes rationally -- and that they can register emotion, command muscle and bones to work, and that they can store vast elements of information and knowledge as memory. A mind could do all this without visible things floating around in the form of levers or containers acting in the form of a reservoir. All such wizardry again provided a need for a creator, and pointed a path to God. If he had created us in his own image and bestowed us with some of these divine powers it was merely the manifestation of divine essence at work. This fact in itself was a proof of God which occupied some of the philosophers, notably Descartes. It also prompted Hume to declare after he had contemplated our complete ignorance about the process by which an idea pops into our mind, that it appears "like an act of creation" since it seemingly arose from nothing!

There was one additional handicap in earlier times which prevented even the thinkers from making any intelligent approach toward a better understanding of mental functioning. This approach characterized all investigations about living things. The approach was similar to what any of us would do if we found a strange box washed up upon a beach that contained a multitude of levers and wheels all carefully machined and interlocked with each other in an orderly manner and seemingly functioning together to produce some meaningful but unknown end result. We would carefully examine this machine, observe and wiggle the various parts. Eventually we would carefully take it apart and study each part and the function it plays in the whole until we had some idea of its nature and its relationship to the whole machine. By this analytic process we would also eventually figure out the purpose of the machine itself. In other words our understanding would proceed by an analysis and an understanding of its parts.

This approach is known as structuralism and is of course a most useful and logical way of entering into a nonliving system. It is also a royal road to the understanding and repairing of the defects and breakdowns that occur in most man-made machines and inventions. The approach fails in the understanding of living processes precisely because the parts and their so-called independent functions are not the important clues to the functioning of the whole. In the living organism, whether single cell or Man, an analysis of its contents does not yield the secrets of the life within it. Instead, we unlock its gates if we concentrate on the processes or on the interaction of the parts and understand the nature and the laws of these interactions. Among the most important characteristics of living systems is movement and change. Any understanding of these eludes us completely if we try to freeze the action and concentrate on the artificially isolated and still components which are then distorted in their interaction by their death. We shall take up this discussion in more detail in Chapter VIII where we shall try to show that General Systems Theory, as a general approach to living systems, allows us to do just that, and understand it's working. Let us here only indicate that the discovery of the importance of the process in life occurred slowly in intellectual history. Hegel's postulates on the dialectic process is one of the first attempts. The statement that "the whole is more than the sum of its parts" is perhaps the best slogan from those who concentrated on the pattern and organization of particles rather than on the particles themselves in exploring living processes. This slogan was also first sounded in scientific psychology in the movement called Gestalt psychology which is associated with such people as Kafka, Kohler, Wertheimer, and Lewin in Germany around the turn of the 20th Century.

Structuralism in philosophic contemplation of the human mind, of course, also preceded by a painstaking analysis of the so-called mind into its "visible" components. Hence in pre-scientific days mental processes were sharply delineated into separate faculties which acted like unrelated capacities and almost took on the character of watertight compartments with doors and valves that could be opened or shut. The list of separate faculties included for instance the will, reason or intellect, desire or inclination, passion, sensation, and of course, the soul. All of these were separate from the body and its parts. The difficulties that were created with such an artificial separation is for instance seen when Thomas Aquinas tried to explain human happiness and argued that it is not alone due to will but also due to intellect, because the act of willing to achieve something is not enough. Otherwise the man who wanted money would be happy just by daydreaming about having the money. It requires the knowledge that one has something one wanted as well as wanting to be joyful about having it. Such a contemplation of happiness as an end process and as a separate state sounds strange to us now when we regard "happiness" a. as an emotional feeling that accompanies many interactions within the person; b. as an experience with many different meanings depending on the organization of physiological and psychological components; and c. a stage in the processes of motivation and perception which marks off certain peak periods.

This early division of mental phenomena into arbitrary categories and the inability to figure out body-mind connections created some of the confusions in philosophy which led to the more famous controversies during and after the Renaissance. These controversies are merely part of our history. Hume was one of the first to break the stranglehold of the medieval Thomists on the mind as a slave to processes entirely due to God's creation and control as outlined in the previous chapter. His skepticism saw the mind as a compository of impressions from the senses, from internal feelings and from memories. For Hume mind was not an entity but more of a process which owed its sole existence to the input that came through our interactions with the environment. Since these impressions traveled through questionable channels he even questioned the reality of the outer world and the reality of reason, as well as the ideas we have formed about the world, ourselves and a creator. An attack of a similar nature was launched by Locke through his concept of tabula rasa through which he saw mind as a more passive receptacle that collected ideas and impressions like a soft wax can pick up stones and sticks. These ideas were of course direct challenges to the religious doctrine which insisted that we see the mind as an encyclopedia of fixed ideas of right and wrong etc. created by God and endowed with capacities to govern over His creation and supplied with mirrors that can reflect more or less accurately the reality outside. Kant resurrected the sacred reality of reason but did it in such a way as to fling down another challenge to the church. He tried to show that "reason" or rational ideas like, for instance, mathematics, exist in us as innate knowledge, and did not come from learning or maturation. This reason can order experience and sensation without prior learning. Therefore he put back a governor or an organizing principle over the interaction of internal and external events which Hume had approached more as a process than anyone else heretofore. However Kant was also a compulsive structuralist and again created watertight faculties in his "mind". He placed faith, religion, soul, and God beyond the pale of his reason. They could not be proved by reason because they did not come under the principle by which reason brings order to experience and sensation with the help of the a priori principles available to it. These contemplations reside in another absolute and given "faculty", namely in an absolute moral sense. This faculty is also independent of sensory experience and exists in the inner self as a given principle of morals. It is just as certain and as absolute as mathematics. This moral "categorical imperative" is also innate and is required as a source for our religion, our faith, and our moral action. It is easy to see why the Church tried to suppress Kant's views because it was strenuously opposed to the placement of the religious belief outside the pale of reason, even though Kant resurrected it as a "separate but equal" mental power.

These "quarrels" were most noteworthy for our purposes in the contemplation of the contemplation of the "will" as we shall see below. We only need to remind ourselves at this point that the approach through structural analysis created static faculties like will, reason, and faith. They stagnated in their dissected isolation, even if their relative passivity was gilded over by much high-level intellectual concern. And it did not help matters if this concern was motivated of course by the highest motives, namely by the intense intellectual curiosity of mankind. This type of concern therefore completely ignored processes like motivation, and stages in the development of skills, needs, etc.. It was only the understanding of the processes of change that later led scientists to a better grasp of the emergence and functioning of self-directed behavior. As we shall see later, this functional blindness to these processes by early philosophers was primarily removed by the development of a freer political climate. It was unnecessarily prolonged by the need to be a structuralist in the absence of any guidelines or previous knowledge. When Man could search for answers because he was given autonomy as a political right he was also able to free his mind from old dogmas and thereby develop new methods of investigation and new approaches to study. The new political climate was ushered in not so much by the philosophers and the scientists but by popular movements such as democracy which of course arose on the cornerstones of technological changes and on the speculation of some thinkers about the nature of Man.

One of the problems for the earliest thinkers from Adam up was the understanding of Man's mind vis-a-vis the motivation of the animal. In the more dogmatic categorizations set down by Aquinas, animals act merely from natural instinct and cannot use judgment. They have only a choice of picking a direction into which to run if they are programmed to see danger by one of their instincts. Man on the other hand has "free choice" in what to do to get to a goal. He is master of his actions through his reason and his will. Nevertheless in his choices each man was limited by God, because he could only choose the means for his actions -- as what to pick up. He could not choose goals because the will was so constructed by God as to have the built-in objective to strive for the good. Hence all human action was inevitably oriented toward an end state or goal which had been previously ordained by God. Our reason made it possible for us to know the end and the universal truth of the divine will, again defining a difference from the animal mind. Therefore we can "freely" will a choice of action but only because we know the end. This rather fragmented and pessimistic view of Man left him with his knowledge of the end as the only reason for his choice of action; we could move toward the end voluntarily rather than be pushed toward it by "naturalistic causes", as was true for animals and inanimate objects.

Subsequent philosophers tried to liberalize and expand the choice points for the human being in contrast to the animal but again fell over the obstacles created by the structuralist approach of separating the mind into compartments. Both Rousseau and Locke saw the animal as an ingenious machine to which Nature had given senses so that it could wind itself up and guard against forces of destruction or disorganization.

Man was the same machine with the important difference that he had some share in the operation of Nature and in his own impact on Nature. Man was therefore able to deviate. Therefore a hungry pigeon would starve next to a piece of meat and the hungry cat would do likewise next to a bowl of fruit, even if they could derive some nourishment by picking the unfamiliar food. Man deviated here because he had the ability to deviate from nature. He knew when to acquiesce to his natural impulses and when to resist. This consciousness of his liberty gave him a certain sense of power in his willing. However, this formulation was still a pretty limited definition of human mental abilities.

The arbitrary distinction between desire or wishing and will caused many philosophers to attribute the former only to animals and the latter to humans, and further added reason to the choice made by humans while irrational brute choice was solely available to animals. Thomas Aquinas realized that human choice may be affected by brute choice but is not determined by it because only "elevated reason" can really determine human choices. Hence the interplay of forces from the unconscious and the processes of motivation, as well as the complex interaction between cognitive and motivational processes, were not understood. This is why both Kant and Hegel were able to argue for a pure will which for them meant a free will. It was independent of any sensory impulses or stimuli and could not be determined by them. When Hegel saw freedom as the essence of will we can recognize the absolutistic and arbitrary division in components at work. Stages of development and the dynamic interplay of forces were not considered. This form of thinking created a model of the human mind that contained switches which can be turned on and off like those activating an electric bulb. Hegel also gave Man a "will" which could turn off the switch of the animalistic impulse or channel them to be "his own".

A similar problem was encountered when we look at attempts to define reason or the utilization of rational thinking. As we shall see later the latter is such an important ingredient in the furtherance of autonomous self-regulation. Kant, resurrected "freedom" from the minor role it had during the Middle Ages, yet spent many pages of his famous treatise to argue that the concept of freedom came from "pure reason" which he had defined as a separate and very airtight category in the mind. It was isolated from "natural law" which was not free. His invention of pure reason was done in order to say that it does not follow natural law, because he did not see it as playing a very helpful function for Man. He saw Man much more frequently governed by the (false) choices from the will, the instinct, and other faculties which obeyed natural law. According to Kant, reasoning things out usually brought about more unhappiness than when one relied on instinct. We need only remember that science had not helped people in Kant's time. Kant called them the luxuries of understanding. In the midst of this confusion he was making a heroic attempt to contribute some sense without adequate data. Despite his compulsive efforts and his mental convolution, his arbitrary separation of functions did not give him a better understanding and took him further away from the idea of "freedom" as an ingredient in very "natural" and empirical processes in human experience.

Once the hold of clerical dogma about the dependency of the mind on God's wisdom was broken, the long-standing controversies about the question of a free will versus a strict determinism became a favorite battleground for philosophers. This concern is of course very relevant to our search for a better understanding of human autonomy. The scholars of the medieval church had not great problems in this area. St. Augustine for instance took the pre-Christian thinkers, such as Cicero, to task for doubting the possibility that God had foreknowledge of everything on earth, including our own actions. He called this doubting sacrilegious and then went into long deliberations to prove that there is a "free will" despite divine preordination. God allowed us to use our wills to order and understand the causes embraced by his foreknowledge. He therefore allowed us to play around with our "free wills" and gave us a narrow tether. Since God's will, however, resided in all creatures including men, all wills were therefore subject to God's will. Thomas Aquinas defined the narrow limits of choice given by God more exactly. First of all Man cannot be the first cause and the first mover. He is also the creator of our so-called voluntary judgment which operates according to the laws that He has set. Any choice we make presupposes the help of God. He has set the limits insofar as he has created a finite set of ends and goals which cannot be questioned.

For one thing, the will cannot choose to move either toward good or toward evil because -- according to the "First Principle" -- it is clearly programmed to move toward the former as its proper object. However, Thomas Aquinas claimed that the will was "free because one had the option to move one's hand or to keep it still. He went into a number of convoluted demonstrations to show that there was no contradiction between labeling this a voluntary act and yet seeing it as proceeding from God as the mover of the will and as the originator of every natural law. Since this action is not connected with good or evil, it lies outside the predestination and allows Man the power to choose. This narrow "free choice" is possible because of the existence of reason. First of all reason was given to us by God so that we could discover the divine "pleasure principle": namely, that Man was destined to want and to move toward the perfect goal of happiness. God gave us reason for the purpose of giving us the power to understand this "First Principle", a privilege of understanding that animals did not have. However, Man could not will to be unhappy. Therefore it was not possible to choose ends, only means. Reason could help here, because we can reason about the conclusions of the First Principle and we can choose how to acquire the rewards inherent in the First Principle. However, Thomas Aquinas admitted that it was not always too helpful to figure out the paths toward the end goal of happiness. Therefore reason often could not make a judgment without further inquiry. We see again how the very limited range of independent action is made so doubtful that Man had no choice but to consult authority. Since Thomas Aquinas also stated that Man could not really know the truth without divine help it became obvious that other authorities like the Church became the proper "movers" of the will.

Hobbes restated the ideas of Aquinas in even less ambiguous terms by tying up Man's so-called liberty in a necessary chain of causes that start and end with God. Since, for instance, water must flow down a channel it can be said to have the "liberty" to do so. The chain of causes in nature proceeds inevitably up to God as the only one who can have a clear overview. He makes sure that the liberty of Man conforms to the necessity of His will. The actual range of Man's so-called liberty is neither further defined nor explained by Hobbes, nor is it seen as a contradiction. The reasons are obvious. Thomists and others were not able to go further because of the limited knowledge of mental processes available to them.

Montaigne goes even further than that by accusing anyone of presumptuous vanity to claim to be above nature just because he supposedly could use a will and imagination. This was false pride because this very imagination was the source of sin, sickness, irresolution, and despair; that is, for all the evils that befell men. The reason it was hard for us to believe that we are governed by the laws of nature was that we did not experience this causality in ourselves. He therefore claimed that it was more honorable to accept control from the laws of nature and therefore from the hand of God than to "act regularly by a licentious and fortuitous liberty." It was therefore also safer to entrust ourselves into the hands of nature than to adorn ourselves foolishly with acquired goods from education. Here we go full circle in-so-far as Montaigne quite nakedly spelled out the Thomistic need for faith and dependency and to return to a safe harbor where any independent sorties outside are fraught with dangers. This was especially true for Man at the stage of his understanding where he did not yet have the chart or the navigational aids by which he could understand both the shoals and the reefs of the new horizons of the mind.

During the Renaissance the problems with free will were taken up more vigorously but again ended up with unresolved controversies. Locke opened up the small range of "free action" just a little further. He decided that we had the power to suspend the execution and satisfaction of any one of our desires. We then have the privilege of judging and weighing the consequences of the various choices by which we could satisfy the desire before we go into action again. He considered this very limited function of free will a great gift of God. When we therefore stop and think, we have already done our duty, because that is all we have within our power. God moreover is such a merciful father that he will readily forgive us if we have acted too hastily or made mistakes in our deliberations and choices.

Kant, as we have indicated above, liberated will a little further. He postulated that we have ideas beyond our sensory experiences that present themselves intuitively and cannot be proven to exist or to be possible. These ideas came from pure reason and were therefore not based on any law of nature. One of these was freedom which unconditionally commanded as well as inhibited certain actions as was typical of other "categorical imperatives". These laws were imposed on us a priori by our reason and proceeded from the Divine Law-giver who created us in this fashion. Freedom and the other two ideas -- God, and the immortality of the soul -- were therefore matters of faith like the belief in the highest good from God which was realized in the world through freedom. Man's will with the aid of pure reason arrived at the same laws that had already been set up by God, and he became therefore "free". If the will did not have this built-in compass of pure reason it could not function in this marvelous uniformity and could not arrive at the same universal end. Only in the kingdom of God did all rational beings devote themselves completely to the moral law. In our lives, however, progress was possible. Here freedom was built more securely into the mental faculty called the will and given a built-in set of guiding principles which one could trust. However, the trust was based on the assumption that they and the mind were created by the all-powerful and infinitely good-hearted God. Through this form of reasoning we are again detracted from a more dispassionate examination of mental processes per se. The debt owed to prior religious thinking is seen more cogently in one of the major conclusions reached by Kant and later elaborated by Hegel: the essence of will was duty. Doing one's duty was the pursuit of the inborn good. Therefore the cornerstone of their moral philosophy was "in doing my duty I am by myself and free".

Descartes similarly concluded that Man's will cannot add anything to the nature of goodness and truth because he arrives to find both already determined by God. Therefore, as Man accepted these more willingly and therefore "more freely", the more clearly he saw the good and the true. Spinoza was against the free will because he could not conceive the human mind to be the cause of his own actions. Since each volition had a cause and since the infinite will came from God, He alone was a "Free cause". Hence freedom for Spinoza did not lie in the will and did not enter into choice, but merely entered in when we did not feel compelled to choose ideas that were superimposed on our own nature.

Hence different conceptions about the will seem to lead to different conclusions about the location of it in Man or in God. In those days determinism always won out and cause was centered in God. Determinism was, however, continually challenged by the persistent emergence of freedom in human consciousness and also because it arose again and again as an immediately felt idea. Prior to our more scientific understanding of experience based on stages of personality development and stages of personality integration, it was "explained away", or considered illusionary, or was anchored in set ideas like other faculties, in reason, or in divine will.

Even James still had to accept the possibility that our consciousness of freedom may be a delusion. For him the question was insoluble on psychological grounds because he could not draw on a science or body of knowledge called psychology. We did not yet possess experiments and observations about dependency or independency, conformity versus creativity, degree of congruence between attitude and behavior, self-knowledge and self-delusion, etc.. James resolved the dilemma extra-scientifically. For him a doctrine of determinism was incompatible with moral responsibility or with a distinction between virtue and vice. Since he felt that a free will was therefore indispensable to the moral life he chose to believe in the alternative view that freedom is possible. His own ethical position caused him to "solve" the free will controversy by saying that freedom is possible. His own ethical position caused him to "solve" the free will controversy by saying that the first act of free will should be to believe in free will! Here we see how skepticism itself can be a voluntary choice! We must also remind ourselves that the controversy about free will is far from over. We shall see below where it has been picked up again by modern psychological thinkers who have substituted fixed mental or body-mind relationships for God's will as the predetermined causes for all thoughts and ideation.

Another famous attempt to split off compartments in the mental sphere is the long-standing dichotomy between body and soul. We need not recount the many words that have been said and written about the independent existence of the soul and its ability to survive the body and exist eternally. Suffice it to say that this approach to map the structure of the mind obfuscated any clear understanding of thinking and behavior. Thomas Aquinas who has written extensively on the properties of the soul also split intellect off from the body. The former did not need a body for its operation for the following reason. The perfect end-state of happiness for Man was defined as the vision of the Divine Essence. For this experience a body was not needed. We are nowadays aware of the important interactions between somatic and psychological processes, and we know that we need their secrets to explain the organization of processes at various levels of human functioning, including the level of relatively autonomous functioning. Hence we substitute a "psychosomatic approach" for the division and analysis of separate components.

Another smoke screen that obscured a better understanding of some of the more fundamental psychological processes like perception, sensation, and cognition was the long debate on what is real "out there" and what is illusionary or a figment of our own imposition on the world. Initially medieval religious dogma froze any controversy by asserting the existence of a reality created and ordered by God. This view allowed no doubting, because it forced the acceptance of the authority. Later these views were assailed by the skepticism of Hume, who questioned the existence of any reality outside our sense impressions, and by the phenomenology of Husserl. These thinkers were willing to accept a very personal and simplified definition of "reality". There were no controlled psychological experiments on sensory illusions or on the effect of attitudes, needs, and group forces on perception. We did not yet know the sensory stimulus, and configurational conditions under which people could agree that they saw and experienced the same thing. Nowadays we don't worry so much any more about whether there is a "reality" beyond our eyes and ears and skins. We have become "practical" with the pragmatists by accepting an unseen radiation from a nuclear bomb as "real" if it shows up on our Geiger counter. So we have relegated the "reality controversy" to the scrap heap of unanswerable and meaningless questions with the help of the positivists and operators. We still cannot answer the question whether you and I see the "same thing" when we both look at a traffic light and stop our cars. However, we don't care as long as we both learn to call the "it" a "red light" and behave "appropriately" to it. Hence we have accepted consensual validation as an approximation to "reality", just as we have accepted a relativistic and statistical criterion of truth for an absolute, either-or benchmark. We have also accepted that "reality" differs for people of different cultural backgrounds, learning, needs, and personalities. These differences are important determinants of behavior in some situations, but become relatively less important and even meaningless in many other situations as, for instance, a reaction to a traffic light or the reaction to the "color red". We don't really have to give up the task of defining a human "reality" because we might eventually want to perform the "crucial experiment" suggested as a joke by Reichenbach. This "experiment" will involve the surgical hook-up of the sensory nerves of one person with the brain of another. The first person would then look at the color red while the second closes his eyes and reports what he "sees" through the eyes of the other, and then compare the statement with the experiences of the first person. We only need to make the obvious conclusion here that our present understanding of perceptual processes and stimulus qualities, and of the interaction of motivation, learning, needs, and body states with perception, help us over the roadblock of "what is reality". In this way we can move on to a better understanding of how all mental processes develop before a new level of integration called self-actualization can occur.

As we shall see later, various levels of functioning in Man are usually attained by a different integration of hereditary, bodily, and learned components and imply the achievement of a new level and sometimes a higher level of functioning. This is also based on the satisfaction of inner needs or the resolution of important problem areas. At such a moment we are also speaking of the familiar human correlated experience of "happiness". In the pre-Christian civilizations some philosophers like

The Promise Of Human Autonomy   IV

Plato defined happiness as a spiritual well-being or as an inner peace which was synonymous with the soul. During the thousand or so years in the Thomistic straight jacket, happiness was yanked out of the grasp of the earthbound human being. Thomas Aquinas decreed happiness to be synonymous with the perfect good. This was wanted by Man "by necessity" because it was built into him by the way God created Man. Therefore Man could not will "not to be happy", because that end was determined by God and was not opened to choice. Only the means of getting there was somewhat open to choice. However real happiness was then also removed from the functioning human being entirely by defining it as an inevitable reaction in the presence of the "highest good". One could only meet this state after death in heaven. Hence basic happiness -- wanted and built into us as a fixed need -- was completely unattainable on earth or through any of our choices. We had to wait patiently, and in the days of bad technology and impotent medicine one did not have to wait too long! One would of course have to insure this blissful if delayed state by choosing one's life wisely in conformity with God and his church-based interpreters -- because wrong decisions might land one in Hell or Purgatory where one was deprived of this state, sometimes forever.

Kant accepted the proposition that Man fashions happiness and his final purpose. Since Kant had built freedom as one principle into the faculty of desire he agreed that Man could develop a sense of self-worth from what he received and enjoyed from the use of this freedom. But even Kant could not base this process on anything but divine influence. He correctly saw this development of self-worth as part of the process by which Man, through contemplation, imposed meaning on nature which would be a wilderness without Man. For Kant this imposition of meaning and order proved that Man was the final end of creation because now the world had a purpose. This phenomenological fact of superimposed order and meaning was explained by Kant as proof of the existence of a higher intelligence which produced the world and Man in it. Unfortunately Kant's exposition of a God-created and built-in moral sense also turned him away from the acceptance of happy feelings as legitimate reactions in themselves. For Kant an action was good because it was done to obey inner duty or because it emerged from the inner and given moral law, not because it may have good results or was accepted as wise. This moral law which legislates all our behavior did not come from experience for Kant. Since the only worthwhile accomplishment was a will that followed this moral law, happiness became unimportant. Instead the most important thing was to do one's duty. So it was again duty above beauty or happiness. Morality became the doctrine of how we made ourselves "worthy of happiness" rather than how we could strive to be happy.

What literally jumps out at us in all these discourses is the acceptance of "happiness" as an end-state or as a final place in which a person would have no more wants or needs. Here we see again the structuralist fallacy at work. If happiness is split up from other processes and defined as a separate entity or state with certain finite and rigid properties it becomes indeed an impossible experience. It becomes an illusion or has to be resurrected as "real" by raising it to a superhuman status not possible in life as we know it. We still see remnants of this confusion among the people who search in vain for this kind of happiness because they equate it with an almost perfect inner harmony or lack of tension. When we equate happiness with utter satisfaction or bliss and couple it with complete cessation of frustration and the absence of any further motivation or excitement, it becomes "unhuman" and unattainable. This kind of long standing equilibrium is not characteristic of processes in the human organism and is indeed only possible at death when there is a complete cessation and therefore a "perfect equilibrium".

Motivation was therefore another area in which the structuralist biases of the pre-scientific era created artificially cloudy conditions. We were then again prevented from illuminating the mainsprings in the human being that pushed him toward a better definition and enhancement of himself or his ego. Motives were split up into arbitrary categories and studied separately. Moreover, any dispassionate study was made impossible by assigning value labels to most motives. If a desire was good, it had a different destiny and required different principles to explain both its origin and function. If it was bad it was looked at very differently. Naturally these labels were superimposed by necessity from a dogma about human origin, functioning, and destiny that came from the highest and unquestionable authority of God as revealed in the scriptures and interpreted by the church.

Nowhere is this confusion and lack of understanding more evident than in the discussion and explanation of sinful and crazy behavior. Already in antiquity there was a lot of discussion about "evil", "passion", "emotion", "envy", and "wrong judgment". These "bad sides" of Man were all lumped together and seen as deviations from an ideal of pure reason or from a faculty of "free will", which had been given to us by God. These deviations were therefore "mistakes and imperfections." They had to be "explained away" and guarded against. They were certainly not understood as "normal" parts of a living process, nor were they seen as integral reactions within the total personality as we understand now. This view and the correlated compartmentalization of mind was well expressed by Marcus Aurelius: "The movement toward injustice and intemperance and to anger and grief and fear is nothing else than the act of one who deviates from nature. And also when the ruling faculty of the will is disconnected with anything that happens, then it too deserts its post. For it is constituted for piety and reverence towards the gods no less than justice".

Saint Augustine defines virtue as something that can only be obtained by learning and is not given by nature. It emerges only from a continual war with vices that are also inside of us. Only the virtues, like temperance, prudence, justice, and fortitude can bridle the carnal lusts and prevent them from winning. The vices are in us continually until the next life when they miraculously dissolve. Note here in passing that the virtues -- as well as the vices or the "seven deadly sins" -- are isolated entities that are acting separately and in qualitatively different ways. Saint Augustine and other theists had a hard time explaining sin and evil as constituting legitimate causes. If Man was created in the image of God and if God was eternally wise and good, how could He create evil? It was inconceivable that He either made a mistake or overlooked a defect, or was too weak to insure His creation against such disturbing factors. Saint Augustine spent a lot of torturous thinking and writing to explain away one after another of such hypotheses. He finally arrived at the conclusion that there was really no cause for evil and that it might defy explanation. Since no one could understand the defect there was no need to explain sin and vice since they were after all defects! If therefore these reactions were beyond explanation and could not be integrated into a coherent picture of created Man they could not be understood.

In addition to sin the whole realm of psychotic and neurotic behavior was beyond the tale of understanding. It was therefore often attributed to the work of the evil or malignant spirits and treated accordingly. Saint Augustine described how this demonic possession could happen to any wise Man and bury his intelligence. It was, of course, not possible to accept transient, alternative mental states such as mystical experiences or temporary neurotic reactions as legitimate or normal complements in human experience. In addition the absence of fresh fruit and meat in the long winters of Europe prior to the invention of refrigeration created deficiencies in vitamins and other essential foods. These often brought about weakened nervous systems and might have resulted in brief hallucinatory experiences or anxiety reactions. Such terrifying experiences were not understood and were also attributed to the devil or to a punishing God. Too often these deviations were feared and were hastily labeled as demonic in origin. Again, the arbitrary division of the world into black and white categories prevented an understanding of process and development.

Hume took another look at the dilemma regarding evil and crime. If we called such acts sinful we were also assuming that they were ultimately caused by God. Such an assumption questioned God's attribute of perfection. Hume therefore concluded that the question remained a mystery which pure and unassisted reason had not been able to handle. This was one of the reasons that propelled him to his skeptical conclusion about a world that we would never be able to interpret.

A final obstacle to the discovery of a developmental sequence which includes autonomous functioning was the emphasis on setting up general laws about both inanimate forces and living creatures. It was perhaps understandable that our ancestors had to simplify the task when they had to approach and comprehend the profusion of natural phenomena. Since stars were all similar and again different from wind, rain, lightning, and these again were different from animals and again from Man it seemed logical to explain "stars" and "animals" and hence "Man" as general entities. A law that explained one specimen of the species then had to do for all. Individual differences had to be pushed into the Procrustean bed of generalized knowledge. It did not occur to our ancestors at that time that this exclusion of observations created the very blind spots that kept a fuller explanation at bay. In personality psychology, for instance, it was the study of individual differences which gave our scientific thinkers beginning with Freud the insight on which they could build a system about personality organization and development. Therefore Mills was able to observe in the middle of the 19th Century that individual spontaneity was not recognized as deserving study or experimentation, or having any intrinsic worth. In view of the general acceptance of conformity, spontaneity did not become an ideal for either scientists or reformers. It was, on the contrary, viewed with jealousy and characterized as a troublesome and perhaps rebellious obstruction to what reformers wanted mankind to accept for their salvation.

The first scientific attempt to understand consciousness and the "reality" of thought was made by Freud. As we saw earlier, philosophers and theologians with some notable exceptions like Hume and Husserl had assumed that the contents of our thinking was either trustworthy as immediately given in consciousness or was influenced by God's will. Freud was able to show that such incidents as slips of the tongue, selective forgetting, repression, and the work of dreams all put thought and thinking on a very different basis. Using an anti-religious, naturalistic approach, he was able to discover another dimension of the mind in the form of unconscious forces. He then set up an intricate pattern of concepts to explain the relationship and the development of the two realms of "thinking" and of "willing".

Freud thereby completely converted the controversy about a "free will" by substituting strict determinism. Conscious thinking had suddenly become a minor part in a total organization in which every idea and thought was necessarily anchored to additional forces in an unconscious substratum, and lawfully derived from it. Furthermore these underlying causes were universal forces fixed in our nervous system both by our neurological inheritance and by the uniform pattern of our early development.

While Freud did much to propel our understanding of the complex functions in personality, he has been accused of imprisoning the mind into yet another straight jacket consisting of the unconscious id. His diagram of the forces acting in the adult human being has been compared to an iceberg because four fifths of the personality is submerged into unconsciousness and is not available to awareness. The large id or storehouse of basic urges and wishes is totally unconscious, the medium-sized superego or suppository of ideals and conscience is primarily unconscious, and the somewhat dwarfed ego has its roots below the consciousness barrier. We are therefore seen as creatures that are largely dominated by powerful unconscious forces. The little ego has the herculean task of monitoring between these forces and effecting a compromise between them, external demands, and the stimuli impinging on us from our senses. It can do little more than compromise and adjust the raw forces of the unconscious to the realities of civilization. It can at best convert the powerful wishes from the inner side so that they become "civilized" in the channels of their expression. In this way it can allow them some satisfaction and therefore some tension release without getting the person into trouble either with his environment or with his own unresolved impulses. The primary focus in this model of personality is on tensions and tension release, and elevates adjustment to the highest form of development. In Chapter VI we shall trace neo-Freudian and the more contemporary models of personality that have added insights and enlarged the sphere of conscious functioning so that we can put spontaneous and even autonomous thinking on a more legitimate basis and see them as criteria of adult stages of functioning.

At this point we want to end the discussion by attempting some resolution of the question of free will which so hampered our forefathers in their contemplation of thought. As we already saw, they could not move beyond an all-or-none position and therefore could not adequately tackle the understanding of the process characteristics of human thinking. Many contemporary thinkers and scientists solve the dilemma in the following way: In the first place we are now aware of the tremendous multiplicity of ingredients that go into every act of human thought and feeling, thanks to modern psychology and neurology. Hence there are almost an infinite possibility of choices available to each of us at every moment of the day. Our knowledge of the effects of body processes and heredity and of the past, -- including maturation, learning, and the availability of choices in the present situation -- allows us to narrow down these infinite possibilities to a much smaller range of choices. Thus we know that an anxious and undernourished violinist with a mouse phobia is not going to continue playing nonchalantly while a mouse is running across the stage in front of him. Thanks to modern contributions to the study of human consciousness we can lawfully endow the human mind with more choices than was allowed either by Freud's ego, superego, id model or by Skinner's behavioristic model of learned and reinforced associations. We also know that sudden transformation of components can occur even on the mental sphere so that new patterns and reorganizations can form. In different sciences this system change and the hierarchical reorganization may be variously called mutation, fission, or an act of creative thinking. These phenomena occur, first of all, when certain elements, under special conditions, are present. If and when such a phenomenon forms and begins to function it may have new properties which were not contained in any previous system nor caused directly by any of the separate elements in the new system. Nevertheless the new system is "caused" or predetermined in the sense that the new relationships operate by virtue of certain guidelines which explain the system's novel behavior. Therefore it obeys "laws" which eventually "explain" its original formation and its functions. If these laws had been known and a computer had existed that would instantaneously record the properties of the ingredients at the moment of the formation of the system, the new creation could have been explained or known at the moment of its occurrence or perhaps a fraction of a second beforehand. At this point predetermination becomes a meaningless issue. A separate issue is the fact that we are also dealing with the world as it is experienced by the human being. This world is just as "real" as the examination of the human choice from the more "objective" view of the outside observer. In our experience of our world our thought in many contexts appears very free and "uncoerced". It therefore has a property of being a proper product of our will. In addition we tend to preserve energy and prevent disorganization as living systems, which we shall show later. We maintain a form of organization on the cognitive level by trying to find causes and explanations for our experiences. Hence we have a built-in tendency to superimpose organization and order on nature and to try to arrange it in a cause-effect sequence. This is true for both perception and thinking. Searching for causes pushes us to overindulge at times, especially if we are obsessively trying to gain security in a seemingly fluid and ambiguous area. Finally we must remember that we can never know the true state of nature, including human nature, because we have learned from Reisenberg that our attempts to intrude into nature for its secrets produces slight but unknowable change in the very state we wish to observe. Hence we are forced to arrive at a probabilistic picture of nature and of reality including human volition.

In view of all these considerations the question of free will versus determinism becomes a meaningless dichotomy. This ancient dilemma dissolves into a more realistic issue. We can instead tackle the following questions: 1. How much was act A. of person X predetermined by what we know of him, his past, his present, and his own subjective estimation of his choices? 2. How many new laws do we need to set up to handle the unique product that emerges in act A? 3. Are we sure that we have determined the ingredients validly? 4. How much uncertainty can we afford to retain in ourselves and in person X before feeling that we can give up looking for sufficient causes for the act?

It is almost reassuring to create "order" into seemingly capricious "human" nature by resolving an ancient source of great insecurity like free will. We can do this with the aid of systems and probabilistic approaches. We realize that we foreclose understanding by pushing hastily constructed boundaries over the events and then categorizing them along these boundaries. In the face of inadequate knowledge of important factors and processes we may superimpose wrong boundaries or enclose events together that belong apart or vice versa. We now understand that events in nature never repeat themselves nor are "the same" when they are repeated. This realization caused Bertrand Russell to remark that a "miracle" has occurred when I cross the street in front of my house for the thousandth time the moment the sun is at a certain angle, three other people are passing nearby, a yellow car is coming from the left and a red car from the right corner, and my thoughts turn to the lecture I have to give. According to our definition of a miracle, juxtaposition of all the events at that moment of time will not coincide again in a million or more moments. Yet we are not compelled to "explain" it and if we do we can approximate it by pinning causes to most of the components of this moment. When we can explain a class of events like a lunar eclipse or the fertilization of an ovum in terms of repeated basic and required processes, we do not need to worry about a particular instance even if that has some idiosyncrasies not shared by other such instances. Similarly we are more confident if we can explain the general social forays, social interactions, hobbies, and interests of a shy, introspective, obsessive young man primarily reared by an overprotective mother. We may be disturbed when we could not predict that he took a rifle one day and wounded a few passers-by from his apartment. Yet we may find new connections when looking at his behavior and that of similar young men so that we can eventually spot the system before the potential outbreak occurs. Similarly we cannot predict what various people will do or think when they have reached a sense of personal identity as young adults and begin to reach out for more self-actualizing moments. But we can capture their individual behavior along a track that can be understood as a lawful process which occurs only after certain antecedents and which obeys certain behavioral characteristics and not others. Suppose we can in addition use our knowledge of living systems to explain different levels of thinking and feeling as the reorganization of components so that they reach levels of greater complexity. Suppose further that we can observe the products of complex functioning and fit them into wide categories without being disturbed that many diverse behavior patterns still seem to "fit" in. At that point we are beyond some of the existential doubts of our forefathers. We do not have to foreclose the anxiety by inventing narrow and arbitrary categories or by leaning on authorities that either forbid further search or promise a superior guidance if we give up our search. Instead we will be in a position to tolerate existential anxieties and become satisfied with less than perfect understanding, especially if we have theories that explain our very existential anxieties and our fear of uncertainty as natural parts of the human process. These theories were not available prior to the science of mental functioning and could not serve as a beacon to light up important areas of Man's functioning, including the experience of autonomy, of choice, and of self-enhancement

Chapter V

DEFINITIONS OF AUTONOMY AND ITS BEGINNINGS IN HISTORY AND PHILOSOPHY

Before we delve into the more recent scientific observations of the development and properties of autonomous behavior in the next chapter, we might stop and define it more vigorously. In the last three chapters we have been assuming a general dictionary definition of autonomous behavior that is immediately accepted by most people including presumably the reader. In its more general use autonomy is seen as a state of being self-determining in which the person experiences and acts out a self-directing freedom which includes moral independence. The quality of liberty within this definition includes the state of being free which means one has the power to make choices and is free from physical or arbitrary constraint. At this point we are not examining whether this state is good or bad or contributing to the common good nor to the welfare of the person. We are also not examining the restraints that may have to be placed on this state of freedom so that it does not lead to anarchy and to harmful results for others.

While there is this element of self-determination in both autonomous behavior and self-actualizing behavior, there is also an important difference between these two modes. Autonomous behavior may be a brief sequence of actions and feelings in which the self experiences primarily a sense of initiative and direction for these. Self-actualizing behavior also involves such behavior sequences, but represents a more complicated and inclusive sequence. Here the autonomously directed behavior is intertwined with a general direction or goal beyond mere self-expression or the expression of personal initiative. Here the goal is to bring about a project of some importance and involves some time duration in the individual's life. This goal is tied up with important goals with the self or with attributes of the self, the enhancement or enlargement of which produce a feeling of growth, satisfaction, and even ecstasy. For instance, the person may want to widen his horizon by contacting and experiencing more people in order to learn about them and about himself and to experience his reactions to friendship and to involvement. Autonomous behavior may involve joining groups in which he shares interest or may involve increased travel or a greater amount of self-disclosure and attempts to engage the attention of others to himself. Self-actualizing behavior would include all of these plus the mulling over and evaluation of these experiences, plus the resultant feeling of success, failure, change, and possible ego expansion or personal growth. As we shall see later in Chapter VI, self-actualizing behavior requires longer preparation in personality development and requires important prerequisites. It is more exacting and involving of energy than the shorter sequence of autonomous behavior. Self-actualizing behavior therefore characterizes a process in the individual or a definite sequence with a definite beginning, middle and end. It occupies a larger stage in the attention span or the preoccupation of the person, although it may be interspersed with many pauses and even by confusing behavior, frequent withdrawal and even conflict.

It is therefore possible to show autonomous behavior without being engaged in a self-actualizing process. Children, for instance, can engage in autonomous behavior but are rarely engaged in sustained self-actualizing experiences. Whatever self-actualizing behavior they show may be fleeting and rudimentary, because their selves are so fluid, experimental and poorly organized around a definite identity. On the other hand, all self-actualizing activities always have to involve autonomous behavior, by their very definition. We shall be talking primarily of self-actualizing behavior in Chapters VI to VIII in which we try to define its important role as a legitimate stage in the development of all human beings. Autonomy as we address it in this volume should therefore be seen as synonymous with self-actualization only when we discuss autonomy in its vagaries in history prior to the development of scientific psychology and when we try to see what previous theologians and thinkers have said about human characteristics and development. Only then do we revert to the more narrow definition of autonomous behavior as a tendency to make choices. Very often in Chapters III and IV and at the end of this chapter we have no choice but to equate autonomous behavior with self-actualizing behavior because the various problems outlined in the last three chapters have put blinders on those philosophers so that they could not even contemplate the valid existence of self-actualizing behavior.

I would therefore define self-actualization more in terms of behavior that we can recognize both in ourselves and in our neighbors. We shall then have a clearer bridge to the observations of psychology and to the experts on personality development. If we look at self-determining behavior as a narrow variety of actions and feelings we are better able to distinguish it from behavior that is not self-actualizing. It then also becomes possible to reexamine the philosophers and writers of the past to find glimpses of their recognition of this behavior in their own attempts to understand and prescribe human progress.

In general terms independent actions have a positive and a negative connotation. On the positive side they imply self-sufficiency and adequate power. On the negative side they imply freedom from limitation and freedom from being subjected to the will of others. Marie Jahoda includes the criterion of autonomy as one of six headings with which positive mental health has been defined and studied by various psychologists (<u>Current Conceptions of Positive Mental Health</u>). Within this context autonomy is defined as the regulation of behavior from within and as a trend toward independence from the pressures of the immediate environment. It includes a connotation of self-protection from the bad influences of the surrounding world. Here and for our later arguments it is very important to mention that many psychologists quoted by Marie Jahoda include a balancing capacity for conformity within their definition of the capacity for autonomy as a criterion of mental health.

Perhaps we can clarify the ingredient of self-actualization in self-generated behavior by giving a number of diverse examples. A carpenter is remodeling the kitchen of his home after he and his spouse have agreed on the general contents and on their approximate location. However, he shops and bargains for all the components and puts them in place including the electricity, plumbing and decorations. A craftsman, or someone knowledgeable with tools and materials, slowly builds his own house by subcontracting and by inviting friends to come on weekends over the month to help out. A person is writing a poem to express a feeling of adventure about having flown an airplane for the first time. A person is baking a complicated and decorative cake from recipes of various ingredients, while adding some individual touches, and enjoys the successful outcome and the appreciation of the people consuming the cake. Another person is opening himself up to the sounds of the waves and of the wind at the beach and quietly appreciates the sensation and the emotions as he experiences his reactions. Another person aims a certain amount of satisfaction and even exultation from moving his muscles in rhythmic coordinated fashion in some sport such as skiing, sailing, or even jogging. Even going on a walk either alone or with a friend, enjoying the trees, the plants and other sights, as well as the exercise itself, fits in here. Another person puts a good deal of energy and time in bringing up a child and marvels at the child's individuality and his capacities under the person's tolerant guidance. The obvious examples also fit in here, such as writing a book or play, painting a picture, or exploring a new idea or area.

In all of these examples some of the initiative must have come from the person rather than his engaging in the act because it was ordered, wanted, or supervised by someone else. Also the person so engaged should not primarily want to prove something to himself or to others. Nor should he want to best somebody or win out over others. He should not primarily want to act for the sake of compensating for something "bad" or "weak". He should not want to escape from something or somebody. He should not primarily act for the sake of gaining praise or attention, or love, or to raise his self-esteem from a low position. All of these reasons and motives may be involved in a truly self-actualizing activity to some extent, but they should be functioning in a subsidiary way rather than constituting the primary motivation.

The Conflict between Glimpses of Autonomy and official Doctrines in History

In the remainder of this chapter we shall take a quick journey through history, in order to take a look at how mankind and its philosophers tried to deal with this kind of autonomous behavior. Naturally, long before the more scientific or systematic investigations of mental processes began people got glimpses of their own autonomy and of other people who managed to function at a self-actualizing level. Hence before we set out the principles in the next chapter with which the contemporary science of psychology has legitimized autonomous behavior as a developmental stage, we want to take the reader on a quick journey over these observations in history. For many of our ancestors who stopped momentarily to contemplate the discovery of their own or other's self-initiated thoughts and actions, it was an illicit pause, sometimes even fraught with danger. The early philosophers tried to wedge their discovery into the existing doctrine of the strict determinism of the will and of the intellect. Especially in the Christian world that dominated Europe after the disappearance of the Greek and Roman civilizations, the official dogma told Man that nobody could and would deviate from God's will. Anything contrary arising autonomously in Man was impossible or a form of blasphemy, probably put there by the devil, as we saw in Chapter III. It is therefore amusing for us, as unconcerned spectators, to see the early philosophers sometimes frantic efforts to nail down more boards over the loopholes of their own breakthrough of autonomous thinking, to prevent further leakage. Despite all the anguish and refutation of arguments against determinism the very self-evident breakthrough of self-realization bubbled out of the broth of ideas. Autonomous thought was ever a willing star in the wings to jump on the stage and share the spotlight. Perhaps that is why it was considered so important in the Middle Ages to foster a religious feeling. The latter was defined as a somber and cool contemplation and helped to prevent these breakthroughs from happening too often.

The Greek and Roman Philosophers

Aristotle did not have too much trouble in accepting that men had moments of depending on themselves and to tolerate that as a valid characteristic of life. Even though life was created by the gods, and the dependency of the gods on themselves was the best and most eternal part of life, this trait also had to rub off on Man, because Man represented life. Aristotle therefore did not have any guilt feelings when he borrowed freely from the life characteristics typical of the gods. They had invented them for themselves and therefore also for us. As a matter of fact he had no pangs of false modesty when he proclaimed the philosopher to have reached the pinnacle of potential achievement of human happiness. After all, the philosopher contemplated truth for its own sake and used reason to do so while all other people may have used such thinking merely in the service of achieving other ends. In addition the philosopher contemplated while at leisure. The use of reason in this condition was superior because it provided pleasure in itself, and the positive attributes of self-sufficiency were associated with this activity. We see these ideas as the beginning of autonomy even though it was primarily connected with the use of reason and with the role of the philosopher who wanted to pat his own back. For Aristotle it was most like being a god who already spent most of his time in contemplation. Contrary to Christian philosophers he felt proud that Man could try to bring out the best in himself, without once connecting it to a blasphemous competition with a god. In fact, he concluded that the gods must value the philosophers most since they were most like the gods when the former had chosen this life by their own will.

Even more astounding were the ideas of Epictetus as written down by his many eager students. Epictetus, living around 60 to 138 A.D., started out as a Roman slave and was later freed. After being expelled from Rome for his radical views he finished out his years in his native

Greece in self-chosen Poverty and expounded the views of the Stoics. Epictetus talked about the dignity of Man before this became a fashion in the social commentaries and psychologies of the 20th Century. The dignity of Man was up to each person alone. Anyone could sell his mind and his compliance for a price, and many people did so, which Epictetus likened to "holding a chamber pot". In contrast, he cited famous examples of people in history who had chosen death or exile rather than submit to their captors' demeaning orders.

To become free to follow one's own integrity, one first had to learn the rules (of God) because one could not undo the order of the universe and one had to maintain one's mind in harmony with it. Here he anticipated our present recognition that some conformity and a sense of moral order is a prerequisite and a foundation for the expression of self-actualizing behavior, as further discussed in Chapters VI and XI. Freely accepting the harmony of the world and its rules assures the person a sense of tranquility. A further requirement was that people grew out of their inevitable dependency on others. Eventually one could lift up one's own head as if released from slavery. One could recognize then that one is endowed with the same wonderful mind as a god. One could then cast away sadness, fear, envy, malevolence, avarice, and even desire and intemperance. God's inspiration was of course seen as an essential ingredient. The other alternative to this maturation was searching for something that was stronger than oneself amidst sighs and groans and a hunger for tranquility that was forever elusive. Here one was looking for it in the wrong place.

The identification with God's rational powers also lifted us above acclaiming citizenship of a particular town or country according to Epictetus. Such an allegiance did not necessarily grant us power and safety nor the absence of fear. As a citizen of the world one derived a sense of power and a peace of mind from one's own power of reason, after one had recognized it as a gift of God. Here we see the beginning of autonomy, because Epictetus recognized a self, even though it was derived from no one but God. This recognition allowed Man to release himself from all bonds to others. Tyrants and thieves may have power over our bodies and bodily wants but they do not have power over our reason. To think merely of bodily needs is to shrink one's self-image to that of stomach, intestines, genitalia, etc.. Epictetus described a person who merely begs for favors, money and status as dead, and labeled him a "carcass". The use of one's reason could also banish a feeling of loneliness. When a person could enjoy the stars and his own existence, he was no longer solitary, nor was he helpless. When we take up Maslow later on (Chapter VI) it will become apparent how Epictetus expressed the same polarity in his two contrasting modes of existence.

It is therefore very evident that Epictetus, like some others in antiquity, had some pretty clear ideas about the inner sense of autonomy and the liberating effect of free choice. Epictetus used it as a bulwark against tyrants and against the vagaries of chance. It helped him build his own stoic way of life on it as a foundation. He was able to use his own rational integration to look differently on a life that was full of surprises and often beyond one's control. Notice how he still had to claim this power as a gift from God rather than as something he could fully claim as having originated within himself. In those days all knowledge about men and the self had to be indebted to God. One had to give thanks to God for having stumbled on this knowledge, and one had to know God first before deriving laws about one's own nature.

The Roman Emperor Marcus Aurelius (121 to 180 A.D.) was another remarkable thinker for which he is known much better than for his very just administration of the Roman Empire. He asserted that the most worthy endeavor of Man was to initiate for oneself and to restrain oneself in conformity with one's own constitution. These conclusions will then bring a feeling of freedom and happiness which will not be gained by thirsting after fame or praise. The mind was for Aurelius a citadel in which a person could place trust and could turn to in case of trouble. Plotinus, who lived in 205 to 270 A.D. as a teacher in Rome sided with both Aurelius and Aristotle by proclaiming that everyone has the potential of achieving happiness if he relies on his reason rather than living exclusively the life of sensation. Here, too, Man can approach the life of a god and could experience moments of a "perfect life" which characterize gods' lives all the time.

The Bible

When we turn to the Judean and Christian religions we find in the old Testament a very different kind of god from those of the early Greeks and Romans: one who placed a heavy curb on autonomous behavior as we saw in Chapter III. In the books of Moses God is very paternal and high-handed. He asked Abraham to sacrifice His son as a test of Abraham's allegiance. He commands Noah to build an ark and escape the flood while "consecrating" the sinners around Noah to a watery grave. He visits ten horrible plagues on the Egyptians for keeping the Israelites bondage and even resorts to the murder of innocent children to achieve these ends. His impatience with the deviants and His unwillingness to try rehabilitation is illustrated in His scorched-earth policy in Sodom and Gomorrah. He is severely punitive when anyone disobeys him, as when He turns Sarah into a pillar of salt when she looks back on Sodom against His injunctions. Moses is punished for invoking God's name to enhance His own status and will not allow Him to go into the promised land with the tribes He has lead from Egypt. He thunders at the impatience of the Israelis for turning away from Him and for adulating a golden calf. In the Book of Kings the breakdown in the Jewish nation is severely punished by misfortune and even by conquest. It was therefore not a good idea to deviate from God's law and wishes.

In the New Testament, this God was considerably softened by Jesus who pushed God more into the distance when His son appeared as God's real-life intermediary. Jesus placed emphasis upon one's own conscience and judgment. By taking on suffering upon himself, he also appealed to Man's sense of control to monitor his own behavior and let his own conscience be more of a guide. Retribution and reward was removed to the time after death rather than threatening at any moment from a wrathful and harshly judging God. This process freed Man somewhat from his ever-present fear of this God as an external source of control. It placed control more within, especially since internal control became a royal road to Heaven or Hell. New rules for "walking in Jesus' ways" were available as blueprints for this control.

Speaking of the Bible, the whole story of Adam and Eve in the Garden of Eden is a marvelous parable of the birth of human autonomy. God's punishment for breaking the bond of extreme dependency on Him was to set Man free to do his own thing in the wilderness. Even though it was banishment from the "Social Security" of the dependent child, it was also a sojourn into freedom where Man had to try and could also rely on his own ingenuities. Gaining knowledge now became synonymous with being conscious of oneself and of one's resources, until Man also became aware of his tendencies to mature toward self-actualization and toward the knowledge about himself that made this book possible.

The Philosophers of Medieval Europe

When we look critically, by contrast, at the early Christian theologians in Chapter III we discover a great deal of suppression of valid self-knowledge, partially to sweeten the adjustment to the intolerable conditions of health, and economic and political factors as described in Chapter II. St. Augustine, in the 4th Century A.D. insisted that God was the origin of all good ideas in Man while bad or sinful ideas represented a perversion of God's will. There is very little room for any autonomy when Man is defined in such a way that he must forever try to approximate God's will and to let that be the main yardstick and originator of all thoughts and values. Nevertheless a little glimmer was provided for autonomy by allotting to Man a combined sense of knowing and of willing. Even that was not genuinely motivated from within but was merely generated from the Holy Trinity.

Saint Thomas Aquinas in the 13th Century reiterated these ideas, asserting that any seemingly voluntary acts must be traced to some higher cause, because everything in nature is traceable to God as a first cause. God is therefore the ultimate cause of what Man freely chooses to do. Hence autonomy does not exist and is illusory. The intellect was a mere passive power to understand nature, because only the divine intellect has the power to act. We only have the choice to be obedient and to approximate the perfect state or take the consequences.

Autonomy was a denial of God and was blasphemous. Free will was just given a minor role in choosing between means to the goal. However, Aquinas promised a tremendous explosion of self-determination and a use of the free intellect once Man had made it to Heaven. Exposure to the essence of God opened up to Man a chance to be a carbon copy of God.

The Breakthrough of Freedom in the Renaissance

This monolithic theme of Man's dependency as more fully expanded in Chapter III, had a long stranglehold on the experience and discovery of autonomous thinking. Fortunately, for the people of the Renaissance and for us it did not last forever. Already in the 14th Century two religious leaders (John Wyclif, an English priest, and later John Hus, a popular preacher and director of the University of Prague) rose up to ask reforms of the Church, which was by then hopelessly corrupt and involved in many schisms. They advocated the idea that Man could get salvation from God without the need of the Church. Man could rely more on himself and let the Scriptures and not the Church be his main guide. This dangerous appeal to independence from indulgence, absolution and favors dispensed by the Church for money was successfully labeled as heretic, and suppressed. The Church's doctrine prevailed over another hundred years until Martin Luther nailed his thesis to the doors of the church of Wittenberg in 1517.

Luther repudiated the authority of the Church as being the intermediary between Man and God. He would, of course, not have succeeded if the invention of the printing press had not made the newly translated Bible available to many more people besides the aristocracy and the wealthy few. Luther preached that each individual has the right to get his own instruction from the Bible and could direct his own conscience accordingly. He therefore freed Man from tradition and from dogma. Instead he urged Man to rely more on himself. This was the beginning of the movement that launched autonomy as a legitimate source of judgment and revealed the possibility to Man that he was destined to be free. At first autonomy was limited to one's own experience of God. Darwin's theories of evolution expanded this application of autonomy because his theories provided the idea that Man might have evolved through the operation of chance and through such laws as the survival of the fittest rather than because of God's intelligence. If the possibility existed that Man was not the purposeful creation of a powerful ruler but the end product of cold, uncaring chance combined with the laws of nature, then Man was thrown back on the both frightening as well as exciting fact that one could control one's own destiny and manipulate future evolution. In other words, one would have to be one's own authority.

Matters began to move more swiftly toward our present era. Montaigue was a French moralist who lived from 1533 to 1592. In 1580 he began to get glimpses of what we are talking about nowadays. Grandeur of the soul for him derived from the knowledge of how to govern oneself rather than in pushing toward achievement. The worst calamity was to despise oneself, while self-acceptance to even a modest degree was a better choice than craving for eminence. He pointed to eminent men in history who still appeared serene after having lost everything because they still had themselves to fall back on. This inner self and certainty was secure from plunder and violence. It could be hidden and treasured, as Epictetus had pointed out hundreds of years earlier in a different context. This inner treasure became the true fountain for happiness because it was entirely "free". It represented our true liberty and constituted our private retreat. Even though we acquired happiness from wives, children and material goods we would be able to refresh ourselves from this private reserve. All of this was made possible by our possession of a mind that was flexible. "The greatest thing in the world is for a man to know that he is his own." Such lofty appeals to autonomy were later incorporated into descriptions of actual experiences in the developing personality by the contemporary psychologists inhabiting Chapter VI.

Descartes, the French philosopher and mathematician living from 1596 to 1650, elaborated further on these ideas. He started with the assumption that every person must make some choice that curbs desires and inhibits the notion that one can change the world. However this free choice could bring about contentment even though it might require long exercises and meditation. He cited ancient philosophers who were able to free themselves from the vagaries of chance and from poverty or illness by accepting the limitations of nature. They also were able to convince themselves that they had complete power over their thoughts. They gained self-esteem, a sense of power, and of freedom by ceasing to long for things. They often were more "enriched" and even more so than some people with lots of riches. The description of this solution in life sounded very much like Erik Erikson's ego state of integrity, which occurs as a central choice point in late maturity of the individual after he has secured an identity, learned to be intimate with others, and has involved his surplus energy in creating things or in creating a new generation, as we shall see later.

Descartes was discouraged to extend these excursions into self-actualization because he accepted a very limited power of human intelligence and understanding as contrasted to the nature of God. This enfeebled intelligence had to miss many of the fine points of the infinite understanding available only to God. For these reasons Descarte could only accept a very limited and imperfect free choice. It was a gift from God, and even he felt that you don't look a gift horse in the mouth. Rather than grieving at the realization that a much more extensive and infinite intelligence existed out of the reach of Man, Descartes consoled himself with the strength and further knowledge which this experience of divine grace bestowed on us.

It was apparently still hard for the philosophers of the Renaissance to reconcile their beginning recognition of true liberty and self-reliance with divine ordination. If one conceives the possibility to exist at times in some form of private isolation -- as Descartes tried in his famous soliloquy -- then to will something seems to be synonymous with appearing to be freely relying on one's own self. One can even experience sensations and thoughts in one's private self without any proof from rational thought. Descartes accepted the joy of that experience very much like the present-day phenomenological psychologists. He, like they, did not care to find proof that this experience was "real". The philosopher Hume later declared that it was an illusion or even a false sensation. He claimed that we suffered this illusion and even foisted it upon ourselves because we are driven by an almost frantic urge to believe in liberty. Descartes, however, foreshadowed our present evidence of self-actualization as a legitimate form of behavior by saying something like this: "I don't care. To think and to experience feels good and even real, so let it be part of us." He could not take the further step of accepting it as a "real" experiential phenomenon that is embedded in the mental sphere as a legitimate manifestation of life processes (see Chapter VIII). When he tried to question its "reality", he had to reduce his enthusiasm because he believed that our reality testing was circumscribed by the imperfect intellect which God had chosen to bestow on us in order to forestall any competition with His supreme power.

This conclusion was also shared with a Dutch philosopher, Spinoza, around 1670 (He lived from 1632 to 1677). Since for him only God as an infinite being could be free, the human mind could not be a free cause of its own actions. True self-determination and free choice was therefore not possible. Will was then reduced to steering the person clear of causes from the outside that might compel the human to be one way or another. It could also determine which of two foods one might eat or whether to lift the arm or to lower it. Free determination could not however extend into the moral or ethical sphere. At this point in the thoughts of our ancestors Man was still bound up in the straightjacket of the Augustinian view that pictured Man to be a weak puppet in a God-dominated universe.

Spinoza, however, left open a little spark of self-building which represented a forerunner of our contemporary observations about self-actualization. When Spinoza invited reasoning in as a proper power in Man he saw reason dictating to Man that he should try to love himself, and prove himself, and preserve his own being. Hence both virtue and happiness were rooted in the success by which many people could preserve their own being.

The Promise Of Human Autonomy

The Industrial and other Revolutions: Kant and Hegel

It took over another hundred years and perhaps the stimulation from both the American and the French Revolutions to get the philosophers into the mood to claim a greater degree of freedom for the mind. The most noted examples are the two German philosophers Kant and Hegel who published their penetrating examinations of the human mind in 1781 and 1816 respectively. Kant tried to "solve" the problem of a free will that was not anxiously checking itself out against God's direction and that had contributed significant choices in seizing political power and thereby greater self-determination. He gave the will greater freedom by hitching it to an inborn function called intellect or pure reason. This existed separately from other mental functions. The power of reasoning existed as a completely separate entity. Moreover it was built into us as a faculty with its own immutable laws of operation which followed the rules of logic and other abstract principles of reasoning. Some readers may perhaps recognize this faculty with its absolute, unexplainable and given characteristics as one of Kant's "categorical imperatives".

Anyway, rational thought existed as an end in itself which could not be further explained. Every person saw his own existence as an end in itself and as part of an objective principle that had the characteristics of a universal truth. It followed from logic that a perfectly given and ordained principle has intrinsic value or worth. Kant called this worth "human dignity". However, Man also conceived of the existence of others as ends in themselves. Again this generalization was accomplished by the same inborn powers of reasoning that got Man to see his own worth as an end in itself. Therefore it followed that Man saw the laws that he both creates and obeys as being synonymous with those given by everyone else around him, He respected these laws because he realized that such laws are inevitably created anew by every rational creature. Duty therefore becomes synonymous with dignity. After Kant had clearly isolated intellect from all naturalistic observations of human behavior and human experience he concluded as a logical proposition based on reason alone that autonomy was the basic human reaction to this dignity. Thanks to the faculty of this inborn reason we have a completely free will and could legislate to ourselves and therefore experience a state of autonomy and an ego. The only problem was that freedom did not follow the laws of nature and was a mere idea that could not be understood. It became "inevitable" because our reason makes us think consciously of a will unrelated to other "faculties", such as desire, feeling, emotion, etc. The explanation for the inevitable existence of such an idea is that it is defined as a "categorical imperative". It has characteristics similar to that of a gene that has been inserted miraculously into Man in perfect and unchanged form -- presumably by God. Existence of God and of a soul became matters of faith for Kant.

Autonomy of the will was therefore emancipated somewhat from the constant dependency on God's wishes and became a law unto itself. Freedom was no longer a matter of faith but rested on reason which could be proved to exist as an objective reality. The moral law, which was another built-in categorical imperative, proclaimed the autonomy of pure and practical reasoning. Reason regulated itself so that practical reasoning became identical with freedom. Hence freedom was at the foundation of all moral laws. We don't become directly conscious of freedom but only directly conscious of the moral law. Only after we became conscious of what we ought to do, did we recognize that we were free, or else we never would have discovered the moral law within ourselves. This circular reasoning elevated a sense of autonomy to a lawful place but never tied it in with the real experience of feeling and reaction. Autonomy was initially rooted in the properties of practical reasoning or with pure will which for Kant were identical. Autonomy of the will was a property which became a law unto itself. Self-regulation of pure reason became freedom for Kant. Freedom and a free will were inevitably subjugated to the moral law also existing as a given "categorical imperative". Therefore freedom was the foundation of all moral laws since everyone arrived at the same conclusions from their built-in identical imperatives. We became aware of our freedom by becoming conscious of the moral law existing within us. Whenever a person realized that he could make a choice from knowing that he ought to do so, he recognized his own freedom. However, without the existence of the moral law within us Man would have never known these connections.

The reason Kant had so much trouble to convince himself and others that autonomy was a legitimate experience and a goal was that he separated reason and its derivations completely from "nature". Nature for Kant meant the operation of the senses, of emotions, of passions, of wishes, or needs. The sum total of these faculties made us "natural" creatures that obeyed the natural laws that explain behavior from various psychological forces. According to Kant we could at one moment live in a world of senses and as such completely separate from reason. At the next moment we could function very separately in the world of pure intelligence in which Man was really his proper self. Kant did not see the dilemma he created for himself and for modern Man when he spoke of two separate reservoirs within Man, namely one of rational powers and one of moral ideas. Kant was aware that men are affected by both the forces of nature and by the inborn blueprints of ideas; but he was not interested nor scientifically equipped to work out the laws of their interrelationships and to solve the puzzle of how Man integrated his reactions and experiences into a total process. We meet again one of the many dilemmas about understanding psychological processes if these are approached as things that can be compartmentalized into several separate parts. It followed from Kant that freedom -- defined as one's independence from the compulsion of another person's will -- was the one and only original and inborn right of everyone who subscribed to possessing human characteristics. This freedom included the inborn operation of pure reason and a moral sense of duty. Hence one could not be bound to another person unless both shared this dutiful and reciprocal relationship when each had independently decided from his own intrinsic existence his reason to conform. This inborn right gave Man the right to be his own master so that Kant gave his blessings to a form of self-actualization. He diluted this by concluding that there is really an innate right of common action because similar conclusions are reached by identical intellects operating in each one of us. If each one thought about the laws and duties for oneself and for mankind independently, the laws would still come out exactly like those that are already existent. This rigid conclusion made it difficult to legitimate change and to understand changes in Man's personal development over his lifespan. We shall also see later -- in Chapter XI -- how contemporary psychologists have solved the ideas of a shared moral foundation underlying autonomy. As we saw above, this preoccupied Kant to the point where his solution raised new questions. The main contribution of Kant was to enliven the ability to make choices with a basic and supreme good stemming from its own intrinsic working principles. The goodness of the will did not have to be judged by what effects it produced or what ends it chose. Furthermore the will could become the ultimate cause of other good events in a person's life, including his desire for happiness.

Hegel also squarely accepted self-determination as a basic property of the human being. However, he derived it from his vision of the interrelationships of forces within the person rather than basing it on an arbitrary program of reason that was cemented into some corner of the mind. Hegel perceived the essential unity of a body and a mind working together. The body was the embodiment of one's freedom. Since one felt with one's body and since this influenced one's mind the resulting consciousness of these reactions within oneself created freedom for the person to become his own property and take possession of himself. At first the will was very subjective but as one moved from childhood to maturity the will freed itself and became a fully actualized and less subjective will. Eventually Man could develop an inner life that was somewhat emancipated from natural force or from external constraint. At that point it also became independent of the guidance from parents and others. A person at this stage could take full command of what he wanted to do.

Hegel's will therefore could and did reflect on a person's own individuality. He further set up an ego that reflected on its own attempts at self-determination. The ego defined the self and integrated the feelings of being restricted and determined with the feelings of being a separate person with an identity of one's own. The resultant will had freedom as an essential property just as the body had the essential property of weight. Self-determination was considered an important force because of our need to translate our wishes into action. It was therefore the absolute right of personal existence to find satisfaction in asserting one's personality and attaining one's goal. The will was further involved in both the organized moments of determination and in the moments of free-roaming and disorganized self-reflection. The will gained unity or organization as both of these tendencies were reflected in the self and then determined its individuality as a universal characteristic of mankind. The self-identity of the will filled the will with a sense of freedom. Freedom was therefore involved both in determinacy and indeterminacy. Hegel had described more of the kind of process characteristics that we shall meet again in the more sophisticated models of personality and self-actualization, as shown in Chapter VI. Again his conclusions set off self-determination as a lawful human function.

Hegel still defined reason as a gift from God but He allowed us the power of self-determination and allowed Man to exist for himself and not as a pawn of other forces including that of tyrants. Unfortunately Hegel partially invalidated the release of Man's mind as shown above by asserting that the State is the final union between the subjective (self-development) and the rational will. The State represented the form of reality within which the individual enjoyed his freedom. What this implied was that we have to accept that the State and its laws embodied our complete freedom. The State represented the universal and essential will of each member in Hegel's thinking. Its laws (of morality) were rationally based. Moreover the self-worth and spiritual reality one possesses was only gained through the State. The State represented the divine idea on earth, and all of its laws reflected universal and rational arrangements. Hegel concluded that only the will which obeys the laws was free because it obeyed essentially itself as reflected in the law. The end result of this unfortunate and circular reasoning was that conformity to the State was still required. Hegel recognized this contradiction in his reasoning but answered that the savage was not really free because his life was marked by brutal passions and by violence. Freedom was therefore not natural and original but had to be won with the aid of discipline and intellectual and moral powers. The State's limitation of the brute emotions and of the raw instincts was really a form of emancipation. Unfortunately Hegel's extreme sense of obligation and his need for an outer security limited his ideas of self-actualization to a relatively narrow sphere of Man's functioning.

John Locke and William James

We can quickly glance over another attempt to free the mind from having to obey God's direction and of disowning heretical self-determination in order to win salvation. The British philosopher John Locke in 1690 threw out all inlaid concepts and faculties. He saw the mind in the form of a blank wax tablet (tabula rasa) which acquired all of its structure through sensation and association. This process was carried out by a passive intellect similar to dough picking up the crisscross patterns of a cookie cutter. Everything in the intellect was therefore introduced by sensation, so that Locke presented a great antithesis to both Kant and Hegel. This idea also freed the mind of preformed principles but left it too passive to influence and determine much of its own destiny. In the beginning of scientific psychology the Kantian tradition of inlaid laws of the intellect fortunately prevailed so that the first laboratory investigations of attitudes and sets of responding produced important principles of organization of this mental functioning. We were then able to see that the mind selected and integrated perceptions, sensations, and ideas. As we shall see in Chapters VI and VIII we have been able to discover the laws of self-actualization by sticking to the fact that living processes are primarily characterized by organization rather than by mere addition and subtraction as Locke had in mind. These tendencies toward an organized process dictate the need for a governing center or an ego and then imbue it with a tendency to move autonomously toward self-involvement rather than merely reacting passively like a slot machine reacts only to proffered coins.

William James was one of the first psychologists who specialized in the observation and explanation of mental processes. He was struck by the need to deal with interrelationships of factors in the personality and with the complexity of the process. However, he did not have the advantage of later methods of observation of both normal individuals and of individuals with problems. He was aware of the controversies raging over the idea of "free will" in history, but could not honestly add more information from his own limited observations. Hence he made the conscious choice to believe in free will rather than in strict determinism of thoughts. He found the latter incompatible with moral responsibility and with his own inner experiences. He chose to reject it but on purely personal rather than scientific grounds. For his free will was indispensable to moral life on a purely personal basis. Therefore he chose the alternative of freedom rather than predetermination. This was perhaps a more honest and courageous position than that of Kant who equated freedom with a heavily "constructed" will which was an inborn characteristic in Man as a gift of God.

We might end this survey of prescientific identification of autonomy by adding the eloquent voice of one more observer, namely that of Leo Tolstoy. He also observed that one could develop autonomy over one's own fate. Hence in his novel <u>War and Peace</u> he placed these observations into the Russian officer Pierre as he contemplated his harsh and perilous living conditions when a prisoner of the French army under Napoleon. As the army retreated homeward from its disastrous occupation of Moscow, Pierre was marching with other prisoners in a column of their army in retreat and was subjected to many horrible experiences and deprivations. He reflected on these as follows (Book 14, Chapter 12): "While imprisoned in the shed Pierre had learned not with his intellect but with his whole being, by life itself, that Man is created for happiness, that happiness is within him in the satisfaction of simple human needs and that all unhappiness arises not from privation, but from superfluity. And now during these last three weeks of the march he had learned still another new, consolatory truth -- that nothing in this world is terrible. He had learned that there is no condition in which Man can be happy and entirely free, so there is no condition in which he needs to be unhappy and lack freedom. He learned that suffering and freedom are very near together; that the person in a bed of roses with one crumpled petal suffered as keenly as he now, sleeping on the bare damp earth with one side growing chilled while the other was warming; that when he had put on tight dancing shoes he had suffered just as he did now when he walked with bare feet that were covered with sores -- his foot gear having long since fallen to pieces.

Chapter VI

THE ANCHORAGE OF HUMAN AUTONOMY IN CONTEMPORARY PERSONALITY THEORY

The time has come to show that human autonomy is more than an occasional spark in a philosopher's eye and more real than the seeming delusions of idealistic and self-preoccupied dreamers. Let us make a visit to the laboratory of today's social scientists to find what they had to say about the development and functioning of personality and to ask them if they found any evidence of self-regulated behavior. I think we shall discover a solid body of both empirical observations and clinical investigations that have been incorporated in psychological theory. They all form an impressive base on which we can build further. Even though there are some differences between some of the theories on the exact nature and functioning of autonomous behavior, there is also a broad band of agreement weaving through them. As a respected researcher I am convinced and I hope I can convince the reader that autonomy or self-actualization is a recognizable behavior pattern, that it represents a lawful stage in the development of personality, and that it has identifiable antecedents and prerequisites.

Before we start on this journey, we need to remind ourselves that animals are already engaging in so-called autonomous or self-regulated behavior. Perhaps one of the most startling facts of nature is the complicated and unrehearsed sequence of behavior found in some insects. It is startling because the behavior is so complex and so "intelligent" in an animal so low in the ladder of evolution and brain development. Let us take for instance the case of the solitary wasp. When a larva of this species emerges from its egg it finds itself next to a fat, live caterpillar which is imprisoned inside a hole on the ground. The larva begins to eat its heart out from the juicy insides of the caterpillar, and it grows and grows until the caterpillar is dead and eaten up. Then the larva spins itself into a hard cocoon. All during this time it has never seen either of its parents and has never attended wasp school. Also mama wasp naturally did not leave any textbook in the hole. However, upon emergence from the cocoon a flying adult female wasp will find a mate, become impregnated, dig a hole in the ground, and then go on a hunt for a nice fat caterpillar nearby. Upon finding its "babysitting food larder" the wasp stings into its nerve center so the caterpillar is slightly drugged. The wasp then pushes and cajoles the half-stuporous animal toward the hole, pushes it inside and then seals the hole up. She does, of course, not forget the most important act in the sequence: just before sealing the entrance to the hole, the wasp deposits her tiny eggs on or near the caterpillar's body.

This sequence of events is complicated and unlearned and can be found repeated many times in the social insects and in amphibia such as frogs, turtles and fish. They emerge out of their eggs as fully functioning adults without ever having seen their parents. We recognize at once the work of so-called "instincts" which are the blueprints and triggers for action and that are laid down in the genes and transmitted from parent to offspring. Now that we can manufacture silicon chips for computers the size of a baby's fingernail which contain 50,000 bits of information we can appreciate how nature can manufacture complex molecules of DNA that contain long sequences for actions. All they need is the proper triggering device of enzymes and related chemicals to send the appropriate impulses to muscles, glands and nerve fibers. Then the fascinating hunt of the wasp for the caterpillar is played out as though switches are slowly triggering complex circuits into action in a preprogrammed sequence. The higher we go in the animal kingdom the more learning is required before the animal can assume adult behavior independently. We all know that birds need to be taught to find and pick up their food. Even seal babies have to be shown how to swim before they can master their native element. Though we admire their wasteful and complicated diving games in the water, they would drown if they were thrown into the water as babies without being shown and helped in the beginning.

And then comes Man, who has evolved with the most complicated brain structure so far found in the animal kingdom. He is the most helpless and immature of all animals once he is breathing and eating on his own outside the mother. One of the most convincing theories (Wilson) about the evolutionary sequence is that the first break away from the anthropoid apes was an animal that could walk on his hind legs rather than move on all fours. This fact enabled the animal to carry his head higher for a more complex overview of the environment. His forearms also became free to manipulate food sources and eventually tools. However, he had to have strong leg muscles and a relatively light frame to be able to outrun his enemies and thereby survive. Eventually the exercise of more complicated behavior patterns of which he was capable seemed to benefit also from increasing brain development and brain size. Eventually a mutation created the "big head" with a larger cortex and an enlarged cranium over the ridge of the eyes to contain that fabulous piece of machinery, the human brain. The alternative of enlarging the pelvic bone structure of the female to carry, nurture and then thrust out the big head came out only half finished and immature. Therefore the baby could not walk until he was about a year old, unlike the foal and calf and even the monkey baby. The reason for these inabilities was not primarily the weaknesses of the leg muscles, as anyone watching a kicking baby can see for himself. The main cause is the lack of development of the nerve centers and of the nerve fibers dealing with posterior locomotion. Also the nerve fibers reaching down to these regions are not yet maturely developed. Similarly the bones of the head are still soft and wiggling plates which will grow for a month until the adult size is reached and they fit together to form a protective shell. In the meantime the brain cells, underneath, mature and grow fibers to connect to each other and to other parts of the body. The compromise of an immature organism existing outside the womb included a special bonding between parents and child that necessitated protection of the infant and transmission of survival techniques from the parents via learning. The human child, as a result, is not mature until about 16 to 20 years of age and learns most of its behavior and thinking repertoire from others.

As mankind has "evolved" into more complex social organizations and more complex civilizations or cultures, the learning period has to be elongated beyond the point of physical and physiological maturation. We have accumulated more and more knowledge, and schooling now goes on through college and even into graduate school for many people -- sometimes into their late twenties. And now the abundance of material to be known and mastered is so vast that "adult education" has become a thriving industry. Some adults learn new skills all during their lives.

What these evolutionary and maturational facts tell us is that human autonomy is often not very visible. It takes much longer for a human being than any of his animal ancestors to become independent and even to act like adults before maturity and learning have laid down the guidelines. Much later men and women have to break away from the long period and the relative safety of their dependency. That process is quite a struggle for most of us and requires new integration and experimentation as well as a fertile soil and adequate reinforcement. However, the analogue of autonomous behavior is already present in the solitary wasp and the social bee, the bird, the seal, and the monkey. There it is triggered by instincts and mediated by some autonomy of choice even though the instincts also severely restrict the range of solutions. They can even sometimes produce ridiculous rigidities that are counterproductive, such as a duck's imprinting on a red ball or on a human being. In the human being the largest stage available for the enactment of autonomy is in our cognitive arena abetted by the skill of language. Finally it is firmly anchored in the self or ego, as we shall see in the following theories. We shall also meet a scientific explanation behind the need for a central self in the cognitive area of a living organism in Chapter VIII. We shall also take up in that chapter the possible evolution of a self-structure after its need arose in an inadequately functioning humanoid prior to the development of the self.

At any rate the nurturance, growth, and expansion of this self-structure is the basis of various explanations of autonomous behavior.

The very first men who pioneered in creating a working model of Man's personality and who recognized an important place for autonomous behavior were the famous disciples of Freud, namely, Carl Jung and Alfred Adler. And it is also interesting to note that their recognition of the central position of self-realization were among the most important reasons why they eventually broke away from Freud. We have already mentioned that Freud's first attempt to create a clinically based systematic model of Man's personality placed a heavy emphasis on unconscious forces and on early development. Freud developed a model of forces within the personality which obeyed certain instinctual urges that clamored for attention and release. These forces were then molded by an acquired superego or conscience and were allowed to have limited expression by an ego structure which also acquired rational judgment along the way. This ego converted the inherited "pleasure principle" -- or "everything is done for the pleasure of it" -- into a "reality principle" ("You better watch out that it is O.K. with everybody first before you do it?") through which the undifferentiated needs came out in a civilized form. They could then be expressed in a limited but adequate fashion without evoking too much counter pressure from a watchful conscience and from the social environment. Most of this conversion and adaptation process was acquired in the first six years of life and was largely enacted on a stage submerged below consciousness. Moreover all adult motives and wishes were secondarily derived from more primitive urges and represented compromises with them. Therefore sublimation -- or the conversion of a raw, uncivilized wish into a form of expression that was seen as the highest development to which human motivation could rise. It meant that all so-called adult strivings could be understood as primitive urges squeezed into socially acceptable and even valuable channels. This model assumed that there was a finite and predetermined quantity of energy which absolutely required investment or else it would dam up and blow the lid. It had to be channeled and squeezed to fit the narrower pipes required by civilization and its replica in the superego. The model therefore stressed the reduction of tension as the prime explanatory principle for all human activities. One had to let this energy out and give it passage. The model gave the ego the role of governor over this domain; however, it could do little more than compromise or adjust. Genuine autonomy or growth beyond the early formative years was therefore not possible, although the theory was and still is a very powerful explanatory tool to understand when something has gone wrong. Freud also was very aware of the long dependency on parent figures and the relative immaturity of the human organism. He used childhood memories of his patients to reconstruct the development of the personality as it was interacting with other powerful figures. It is for these reasons that he saw the pattern of early relationships with parents as the most important template for all relationships in the future. In this way his concept of transference, or the projection of early perceptions of parents on later authority figures, became such an important clue toward the understanding of a person's later attachments.

Carl Jung felt that the person's orientation to the future was as equally important a determinant of behavior as his attachment to the past. For Jung there was a continuous and often creative development, so that the search for unity became an important motivating force. For Jung self-actualization became the end goal of psychic development. Toward this end the various subsystems in the personality had to become fully differentiated and developed rather than carry out old and repetitive scripts to reduce inner tensions. Jung called this process individuation and used it to explain the development of unique aspects of the personality and the constant search for creative change even in the later years of life.

Alfred Adler, the other famous pupil and associate of Freud, became increasingly impressed with the existence of a more spontaneous energy that was directed toward self-realization. When he became convinced that this was the main driving force of the ego, he broke with Freud. He saw the ego as a more potent part in shaping the personality than the basic drives which energized Freud's model. Adler then coined the term "guiding fiction" to denote a potent goal or purpose in life which we all develop to achieve a sense of unity and coherence. All basic drives eventually become subordinated to this force. This force becomes identified by the age of four or five and increasingly guides life from then on. It determines the "style of life" which for Adler was synonymous with the self or the ego. It also determines both the unity of the personality and one's own individuality.

Before moving on to the more systematic attempts to include this driving force in individuation and self-realization as a vital part in the forces shaping personality, we should remember three other pioneers who were struck by its preeminence and forcefulness. Kurt Goldstein was a neuropsychiatrist who worked extensively with brain-injured soldiers of World War I. He became increasingly impressed that the disease or the injury itself was not solely related to the disturbances in perception and behavior which he found. The symptoms could be understood as an organized attempt of the person to deal with the lesion and with the deficit, because every person seemed to behave as a unified whole. Goldstein then tried to set up some principles which governed this unified organism and its behavior. To achieve unity and direction on this sphere the person operated with one single drive, namely self-realization or self-actualization. This drive soon incorporates diverse individual drives. Hence the most potent motive in Man was the constant attempt to realize his inherent potentialities. It is the creative trend of human nature.

Andras Angyal was a psychologist who, like Goldstein, was born in Europe and then emigrated to the United States. Like Goldstein he switched from research to private practice in his later years. He was also impressed that human beings strove so hard to assert themselves and to expand their area of self-determination. He therefore pictured the human being as an autonomous, self-governing entity who asserts himself actively rather than merely reacting when something provoked him. He therefore coined the operation of two major motivating forces by which the organism achieved unity even though these were seemingly opposed to each other. One was the drive to autonomy and self-determination, by which the person consolidates and increases his self-government. It manifests itself through Man's exercise of his freedom and is reflected in his spontaneity, his self-assertion, and his mastery over his world. His second tendency is the drive toward self-surrender or homonymy because Man realizes that he cannot use violence or force to increase his mastery over the environment and expand his autonomy. He must achieve it by practicing obedience, understanding and respect for the laws of the environment. Hence he also tries to become harmoniously integrated with super individual units which he considers to be greater than himself, such as the family, the group and the nation, or a cause and an ideology.

The fourth pioneer was the American-born psychologist Carl Rogers who created the first major rival theory to Freud's system of psychotherapy and hence to his theory of personality. Rogers rejected the operation of unconscious forces and felt that personality could be understood in terms of the on-going processes of the moment. These were all potentially available to the actor and to the observer. He therefore was not interested in knowing the person's past in order to explain present functioning. He was influenced by the phenomenological approach. Furthermore he relied heavily on the concept of self as the key to the understanding of the personality. This self gradually crystallizes all of the experiential world (called the phenomenal field) of the developing person and becomes differentiated and organized. The important point for us here is that Rogers endowed the self with a single, all-empowering drive: primarily to maintain, actualize, and enhance itself. While this proposition is borrowed from two other phenomenological psychologists, namely Snygg and Combs, its emphasis on self-realization is the cornerstone of Roger's theory and is therefore similar to the observations of both Goldstein and Angyal. It will be echoed again later when we consider Maslow's theories later on.

All of these pioneers built their observations on their clinical practice. They were not primarily interested in the study of various aspects of personality functioning. Even though they saw mainly people who asked for help because of their inability to function, they were nevertheless impressed by the forces toward autonomy and independence both in their patients and in people they observed outside their private practice. We now turn to three psychologists who arrived at a more systematic and differentiated conception of personality and of the place of autonomy in it. Even though only one was a practicing therapist, all three were trained in the scientific method and wrote their major work during the forties and fifties. They were therefore heavily influenced by the movement to study personality more objectively and experimentally. We shall at this point refer to Erich Fromm, Gordon Allport and Abraham Maslow in turn, showing what legacy they left for the contemporary builders of sophisticated maturational stages in the development of Man and his personality.

Erich Fromm was a German psychologist who first became a practicing psychoanalyst in America after finishing psychoanalytic training in Germany. In his writings he is very much concerned with changes in the Freudian model of character formation, because he felt that Freud did not transcend his own culture of origin and based his universal theory of Man on what he knew from his own origins. Freud therefore ignored the way of relating to other people as an important ingredient in personality formation. For Fromm, character is not determined by the organization of inner forces but by how Man relates himself to the world (<u>Man for Himself</u>). Specifically character is determined by how Man acquires and assimilates things and by how he relates to others and is reflected in them. These relationships become the core of a person's character and determine how energy in a person is channeled to future relationships with objects and with people. Man's character then becomes the reservoir of actions and decisions and takes over from the instincts. The important point for us is that the only constructive solution for character development and the highest form in Fromm's character types is the productive character. In this mode Man uses his own powers and realizes his potentials. He is more free and can face his doubts and his isolation. He is guided by his own reason and is not dependent on others. He experiences himself as the captain of his fate. This character is primarily associated with creativity, self-realization, and spontaneity, rather than with mere activity or the amount of energy invested (<u>Escape from Freedom</u>). Man is constantly struggling to free himself from his history of long dependency in order to express his individual self. He must free himself from a world that gave him security and reassurance. There is subsequently a driving force towards this individuation which can add inner strength, and integration to the personality and to new relationships with close ties. Nevertheless there is also in all of us this fear of freedom because we have to give up the security and identity with others. This fear of isolation can create anxiety, insecurity, and even desolation which then propels the individual to escape from freedom and productivity. The four other or nonproductive character types, which can develop out of the interaction of the growing person with his world, are foreshortened solutions of the productive type and are predominant in certain cultures. Fromm analyzes some contemporary cultures to show how each favors one type of human interrelationship and therefore produces a correlated type of non-productive character formation.

One of these, the marketing personality, has a recent appearance in the history of Man and is predominantly found in modern capitalism. Here a consumerism and marketing ideology determines the value of anything by the laws of demand and supply. In this system the self and its attributes assume exchange value. The question one must ask oneself in such a system is: "Is this role in fashion? Does this behavior sell? This development favors conformity, automatic existence, the constant change of roles, a loss of self, and an inner emptiness. Fromm therefore criticizes capitalism for its inhibition of true freedom and for normalizing one of the escape routes from productive character formation. In his later books Fromm is primarily concerned with the effects of various cultural and economic organizations on character formation and on the growth of Man to his highest potential. We only need to remember that Fromm sets up as the all-important force in Man the constant struggle for freedom and independence which is rooted in Man's long dependence as a child. This struggle is both evident in normal development and in neurosis but may be absent in the nonproductive character types once they have been fostered by the culture and become "normalized" by the majority. This majority then considers itself well-adjusted even though it has given up the struggle for true autonomy.

Fromm therefore -- together with Maslow, as we shall see later -- does not see neurosis as a dead end. He pictures it as a sign of active struggle to solve the basic conflicts between an old need for dependency and the search for freedom. Fromm also in his latest book (<u>To Have or to Be</u>) echoes a point made by Maslow that inner security means living in the "being mode" in which one feels "I am who I am". In this mode one is not afraid to lose what one has, including one's sense of security and identity. In such a state of autonomy one feels that one's center is within and that one can be sure of one's capacity for existing and for expressing one's powers in normal day-to-day living. This mode is contrasted to living in the "having mode" (according to Fromm, the predominant character structure in contemporary society) in which one is constantly afraid of losing what one has. One is therefore preoccupied with crime, economic change, sickness, or death, and loses sight of a love for freedom and gives up the chance for growth and to venture into the unknown.

Gordon Allport started as a social psychologist and conducted some of the best initial studies in such areas as social attitudes, rumor, racial prejudice and human values. Since many of his studies took him out of the laboratory of Harvard he became more and more interested in the nature of Man. Later he began to build a system of concepts to define the workings of personality and also to include his increasing conviction about the uniqueness and individuality of human behavior.

He also attacked some older theories for forging a model of human motivation in which Man merely reacts to inner and outer stimuli. In addition, he took to task Freud's tension-reduction model for its reducing all motives to primitive forces in the past and thereby putting an undue stress on early life. Allport, like Maslow and Goldstein, acknowledged the motivating effects of pressures, drives and conflicts. These indeed cause reactions that are sometimes glaringly noticeable. However, for Allport there was another and perhaps larger arena of human motivation, namely the arena of conflict-free growth and self-actualization. Hence Man cannot be fully understood as an organism that is only trying to seek an equilibrium and who is merely trying to adjust. Real growth only occurs through risk-taking and exposing oneself to new tensions. The striving and the synthesis of a self which Allport saw as an organizing center (and called the "proprium" to distinguish it as a composite self of selves from Freud's ego), is for goals that are not always easily attainable and not necessarily correlated with happiness. Happiness may become a glowing by-product in the attainment of a goal, but it is a momentary state rather than a goal in itself. Allport, like Maslow, therefore sees the "growth motives" as forces that may maintain tensions in the interest of distant and often difficult goals, quite in contrast to the action of "deficit motives". The latter indeed bring about a reduction in tension and achieve a new equilibrium. The growth or self enhancement striving is a qualitatively different type of motivation because it aims toward a unification of the personality and is oriented toward the future rather than toward the satisfaction of momentary needs.

In order to support this type of motivation more meaningfully, Allport added the concept of "functional autonomy" to the process of motivation. It recognizes the spontaneous, changing and future-oriented character of much of adult motivation. Therefore some adult motives can be seen as self-sustaining, contemporary systems that are not rooted in or explained by the past. They have of course the antecedents in the past, but are functionally independent of them. The concept implies that we can generate new energy rather than using up old forms of energy in new form. Motives can therefore be newly acquired so that they are not mere tensions from antecedents which were involved in a motive of the past. Instead they are now invested into growth. We shall see later in Chapter VIII how General Systems principles support this idea of energy generation and the investment of energy as characteristic of all life in lieu of a static conception of the living organism moving from one homeostatic level to another through a mere re-adaptation to inner and outer "disturbances".

We owe to Abraham Maslow a more differentiated model of human motivation which culminated in self-actualization as the highest stage of human development. Maslow started out as an experimental psychologist who worked with animals. He then switched to the study of sexuality before Kinsey made it fashionable. He finally settled on a study of motivation after establishing the major principles of his theory of motivation. He soon became such an enthusiastic advocate of the peak experience and of other advantages of growth motivation that he became an inspirational writer in his later years.

Maslow (<u>Motivation and Personality</u>) showed that human motivation moves from birth on up a ladder to more and more complex stages. At each step a new form of motivation emerges and becomes predominant. It can only be reached if the previous form of motivation has been satiated sufficiently. Hence the five need levels are arranged in a hierarchy, and a need level can only become potent if all lower need levels have been satisfied. Also, at any need level both fixation and regression is possible. The human being starts with a concern for physiological needs, moves on to a safety need level where he becomes primarily concerned with security, protection, and familiarity. Then he becomes preoccupied with love and affection or with the belongingness needs. Moving on to the fourth level he is primarily motivated by the esteem needs and wants to gain self-respect, mastery, reputation, and prestige. He may desire achievement and assume independence. It is only the fifth level that marks the highest achievement in Man, and guarantees positive mental health. This level creates the need for self-actualization or a desire for self-fulfillment. Even though any human being is genetically and potentially capable of achieving this level it is reserved for older people and can be fully attained only around the age of sixty (<u>Psychology of Being</u>). Younger people have not achieved either a full identity or a full sense of autonomy. They have not yet experienced loyal and enduring love relationships and they have not yet made peace with their impending death or laid to rest their ambivalent feelings about parents and other authority figures.

In his further attempts to define, describe, and study self-actualization Maslow gave us additional qualities to think about (<u>Toward the Psychology of Being</u>). First, people on this level try to actualize their potentialities, capacities, and talent. They may see this behavior as a fulfillment of their mission, or their call or fate. They search for a fuller understanding and acceptance of their own nature, and they are constantly building toward a unity or toward an integration of themselves. Maslow points to such terms as growth, individuation, autonomy, self-development, and self-realization as being synonymous with self-actualization. When he studied a sample of forty self-actualizing people in greater depth -- the majority were well-known historical and contemporary figures -- he listed fifteen qualities they seemed to share with each other: a. more efficient perception of reality; b. increased acceptance of self, others, and nature; c. spontaneity and simplicity; d. problem-centered rather than ego-centered; e. a quality of detachment and a need for privacy; f. autonomy or some independence from culture and the environment; g. continued freshness of appreciation; h. capacity for more numerous mystic or peak experiences; i. increased identification with the community and with the human species; j. interpersonal relations are deeper and more profound; k. democratic character structure; l. keen discrimination between means and ends, or between good and evil; m. philosophical, non-hostile sense of humor; n. creativity or originality; and o. ability to transcend their culture and resist enculturation.

Self-actualizing people further are operating in a "being mode", rather than in a "deficiency mode" (motivated to get things one feels one is missing) because they are not primarily motivated by the basic deficiency motives on the four lower levels (<u>Psychology of Being</u>). Therefore they can almost be said to be "unmotivated". This also aligns Maslow with the eastern philosophical views which see health as the state where one exists above having striving and desires. In addition such people are oriented to one or more of the "being-values" such as beauty, truth, goodness, order, oneness, justice, etc.,

Finally self-actualizing people are more frequently and more intensively experiencing so-called "peak" experiences, or experiences that fill one with awe, ecstasy, beauty, Mystic experiences, religious experiences, "Eureka" experiences, and even some sexual orgasms belong here. However, Maslow found that such experiences are also occurring in college students and other people at any time in life, even when they are not yet functioning primarily at the self-actualizing level. Hence a person in a peak experience may take on temporarily many of the characteristics found in self-actualizing people, and peak experiences form only a part of behavior characteristic of self-actualization. This finding made Maslow realize that self-actualizing (or any motivated) behavior is not a static, all-or-none state. It can be more accurately described as an episode in which the powers within the person come together in a particularly efficient and even very enjoyable way. He then becomes more open to experience, more individualized, and more spontaneous, and also more independent of his lower needs. Self-actualization is therefore a matter of degree because such people have more peak experiences, and they occur in waves alternating with valleys in which lower needs may also predominate very temporarily. Therefore happiness is also a transitory state and only temporarily accompanies gratification. For Maslow this is an important insight into the functioning of human motivation (as we shall see when we look at living systems in general in Chapter VIII). This contrasts with an old theory of happiness on which we have been raised, which describes it as a permanent and final stage typified by Heaven, the Garden of Eden, and the good life. It is embodied in the ending of any love story: "and they lived happily ever after..." Hence people who experience a generally high level of fulfillment still experience periods of mild discontent, usually about issues not relating to them personally or immediately. Maslow calls a discovery of a higher state of discontent in the midst of basic gratification his "grumble theory".

For us it is important to remember that the basic experience of and quest for autonomy is rooted in the self-actualization stage in which the needs that arise can be met more by the person himself. Lower needs below self-actualization can only be met by other people and the subject depends more on the environment than on themselves. Such a person is more dependent on others' approval, goodwill and affection. He must, like Fromm's marketing personality, adapt, be flexible, and be responsive to the environment because it may fail him and thus bring disaster. All this adds up to a lack of freedom. The self-actualizing person is less dependent and more self-directed.

Before passing on to some of the attempts to construct sophisticated and all-inclusive models of human personality functioning including autonomy as a stage, we need to say a word about Martin Buber and Rollo May. Martin Buber (<u>I and Thou</u>), the German-born philosopher, wrote a book in the middle Twenties -- before psychologists quoted above took a hard look at the dimensions of experience -- which has found many echoes in existential writers and among psychologists who, like Maslow and Fromm, have attempted to define higher and lower stages of functioning. Buber sees the I-thou mode of relating as a fuller and more complex way of experiencing both the self and others. This mode is contrasted to the person who relates on the I-it mode. In the I-thou mode one can lose oneself and ignore lower needs as we already found in Maslow's formulation. For Buber one can leave the world of causality and step into the world of being and relating. In this mode one can find the "freedom of one's being and of being" (p. 100). In this mode the ego can differentiate itself from other egos and can afford to "lose itself" and can and does experiment and experience. This formulation solves the "free will" controversy by postulating stages of greater involvement, more intense relating, and therefore greater autonomy.

Rollo May, the American psychologist and existentialist writer (Man's Search for Himself) also posits a final stage of consciousness -- his fourth -- which he calls "creative consciousness of the self". It occurs after a separate stage and consciousness of the self and is characterized by the ability to transcend oneself momentarily, to experience ecstasy, and to exercise both insight and creativity. May does not see it as a permanent or terminal stage but as a process occurring in waves, because one can live very little of one's life at such a rich level. Glimpses of it give us meaning, direction, and hope, so that we can "lose ourselves" in experiences of mysticism, alternate states of consciousness and religious feelings. May again reiterates the process characteristics of higher motivational stages concerned with autonomy that we have seen in others so far. They come much closer to the real characteristics of living processes than the erroneous assumption of a long-lasting state of "happy autonomy". We shall emphasize these points more authoritatively in Chapter VIII. At this point we also bring May into the discussion because, like Fromm and Maslow, he describes the experiential characteristics of autonomy (Love and Will). May talks about a sense of vitality which becomes the energy to reach out, and sharpens and refocuses the world by various creative forays. This state of vitality is also characterized by a more pronounced sense of intentionality. Man can lift himself above many situations, and he can be creative without any reference to himself and without losing his footing.

Another brief mention must be made of Marie Jahoda's attempt to define positive mental health (<u>Current Concepts of Positive Mental Health</u>). She lists autonomy as one of the six headings by which positive mental health has been defined and studied by social scientists. It is noteworthy in view of our later concerns about unbridled autonomy that she reminds us that some theories of mental health have included a balancing willingness to conform as part of a capacity for autonomy.

We are going into the end stretch of touching down on some of the most noteworthy authorities on human nature in our search for scientific evidence for the lawful place of human autonomy in the behavior repertoire of Man. We are reserving the best tidbits for the end because they are ambitious attempts to sketch out a very systematic sequence of reaction, feeling, and perspectives that go on in adult life alongside physiological changes, life experiences, and self-evaluation. They accomplish for the post-pubertal years what Freud accomplished with his brilliant observations of the developing forces inside the growing child. They belong here because all three of the following scientists include autonomy as an important stage or as a milestone in their exhaustive investigations into adult development. As we shall see, they are really not in basic disagreement and give credit to each other in their attempts to understand human nature. They merely differ in emphasizing some components differently or fleshing out some of the components more fully. They include the pioneer Erik Erikson and two relative newcomers to personality theory, namely Daniel Levinson and Jane Loevinger. The latter two published their major work in 1978 and 1976 respectively.

Before Erik Erikson's two books developing his theory about the stages of the ego from infancy to old age, the whole area of adult personality was like a vast desert about which little was known. We should qualify this sweeping statement by reminding ourselves that a great deal was known from the insightful writings of novelists, playwrights, poets and even philosophers. Shakespeare, Goethe, Dickens, and Tolstoy are some of the many gifted writers who immediately come to mind here. When I speak of a desert in our knowledge I am referring to the fact that after Freud's authoritative statements, no personality scientist or clinicians dared to investigate whether adults developed or changed in any systematic manner after puberty. Freud had shown that all the adult motivation and behavior patterns could be derived from childhood dynamics, and most of them were occurring before the age of six. His ingenious system of dynamic forces in the personality, all obeying certain laws, seemed sufficient to explain any adult "cathexis" (the attachment of an inner wish to an outside object), whether it was the twenty-year-old man ogling after a buxom blonde sauntering down the street; or a 65-year-old woman dreaming of the time she was able to saunter down the street in this way and wistfully wondering what meaning life would have for her after her nearby grandchild left for college and her husband retired to stay home all day.

It was perhaps not quite an accident that it was someone from Freud's inner circle who first set foot in that desert to risk the starvation and banishment which the master had predicted by stating that the desert was devoid of cases. Erik Erikson had been a teacher and a student with Freud in Vienna and then became a clinician later on and a practicing psychoanalyst as well as a professor at American universities. When Erikson set out on that journey through Freud's desert he came well-equipped with his work with children of various ages and his studies of various Indian tribes. These studies gave him many insights about child and adult development in addition to his intimate experiences and overview on at least two western cultures. Erikson developed a series of principles which explained the growth and differentiation of the ego from birth to death. Under his creative pen that ego changed markedly and very graphically at least in five more well-marked stages past the age of six all the way up to old age. With each stage the person was concerned with different issues, and directed his behavior into different and sometimes new directions.

Also, this ego which developed so systematically as a built-in force in the personality (regardless of whether the person was a Sioux Indian, a Eskimo, a German, or an American), was the ego of Freud! Erikson has perhaps done more to resurrect the potency of Freud's theory than anyone else, because he has added potent explanatory principles to Freud's exposition of early development and of psychopathology. Moreover, his theory has corrected some of the more glaring deficiencies of the Freudian model. For one, the little ego of Freud has become stronger and more commanding of the forces in the personality. It has literally been expanded above the threshold of consciousness. Also as the ego solves one major growth problem after another in Erikson's system, it invests new energy into new areas or questions. In this way it is no longer a component that merely reacts to old and rekindled energy from within, and the principle of mastery replaces the constancy of energy and the pleasure principle of Freud. Erikson also clothed the forces operating from the ego at each of its developmental choice points with concrete behavior that can be recognized in all of us. Freud's forces were sometimes so general and devoid of behavioral descriptions that any behavior could be explained by them, often to the anger and consternation of the "victim". Finally, the ego stages were well tied up with evidence from anthropologists about changes they had observed in diverse cultures, so that it suddenly appeared that each culture has had to take into account the inevitable growth that had occurred among its people in pre-ordained order. It did so by accepting and normalizing its institutions and practices to make allowances for these stages, such as setting up rituals and trials for the adolescent's effort to establish an identity. This is not the place to set forth the eight ego stages and the time and character of their occurrence. Suffice it to say that Erikson sees each stage as a new problem that needs to be tackled by the growing ego after it has mastered a previous "nuclear conflict", and that therefore becomes more differentiated and stronger through physiological maturation, further development of inner energy forces, and the addition of life experiences or learning. At that point the ego is at another choice point, and the choice of appropriate behavior determines the degree to which the ego solves the developmental task at the new stage. What concerns us here is that Erikson labels the second way station of the growing ego as the struggle between autonomy versus shame or doubt. After the ego of the infant has developed a basic sense of trust, the child begins to venture out at age two or three with a better development of muscles of legs and arms and with a better perceptual acuity. He then experiences either a sense of some autonomy or independence or freedom of self-expression, or he experiences a constant inhibition of such experimentation by parents or by the action of seemingly capricious occurrences or disasters in an unsupervised environment (like falling off a chair). The latter kind of disaster produces basic reactions of shame or doubt. Erikson sees this struggle -- like all the other ego conflicts -- to continue into later life on different levels of complexity than mere locomotion or "getting into things" which was characteristic at the toddler stage. After this ego stage has been dealt with in the growing child, the ego tackles the dichotomous task of either developing a sense of initiative or a feeling of guilt. Next comes a sense of industry or a sense of inferiority. The adolescent years are those of Erikson's most famous evolutionary stage, or the battle between the development of ego identity versus remaining in the limbo of ego diffusion, or role diffusion. Finally at mid-adulthood and perhaps after the twenties and early thirties and after the person has experienced a sense of intimacy (versus isolation) the adult grapples with the question of generativity versus ego stagnation. While Erikson defines generativity primarily as a stage in which one establishes and guides the next generation, namely children and eventually grandchildren, he also includes in this stage the more well-known relatives of productivity and creativity. He states that the ability to lose oneself occasionally in body and mind after having acquired an identity and then actually practicing such ego loss in the intimacy stage leads to a gradual experience of an intent to break the boundaries of the ego to master new frontiers. It is then inevitable that one invests new energy into that which is being generated. What Erikson does here is to parcel out the full package of autonomous self-realization of, for instance, Fromm and Maslow, along various chronological stages of development. In this way a more primitive beginning occurs already at the child stage, it is reinforced by a number of pit stops, so that "autonomy" gets beefed up along the way by successful initiations, by the satisfaction of finished products, by a sense of self, and is finally spiced up by the joy of close relationships.

At that point autonomous generation of new energy for more focused goals develops for a definitive life period for a while just as Maslow sees the full development of self-actualization as the major motivating force occurring in late adulthood.

Daniel Levinson is a social psychologist who has become well-known by his studies of prejudice in the authoritarian personality and his studies of attitudes toward mental illness and psychiatric patients. His recent book describes his insights and conclusions from an in-depth study of forty adult men from various walks of life. This examination of forty lives in retrospect has allowed him to expand the way-stations to more than was hitherto known. He has also added preparatory periods to these stages which are themselves characterized by certain reactions. Levinson sees no antithesis between his conclusions and those of Erikson's because he sees Erikson's polarities at work at the proper age ranges in his own subjects.

Levinson sketches the development of adult men with a different focus in mind, namely that based on the concept of a life structure. This must evolve for each man along certain developmental periods fixed by the physiological realities and past events. However, each man may go through these developmental tasks in very different and unique ways. This life structure is looked upon from the vantage point of sitting on the boundary between the building self and the world. From this vantage point Levinson watches the interactions and the choices each man makes. A man's life structure reflects the structure of society but it is also unique because it reflects the person's self by which he made his choices. Erikson's stages were more focused inside on the self as the self-interacts with the world, so that his stages were defined by inner attributes. For instance, he did not describe the changing historical and sociological factors in the lives of his subjects. Since Levinson looks at a "lived life" of a self among its own personal world, he feels that he can sketch the developmental process in greater detail. He therefore accepts Erikson's framework as a well-known map and fills in additional structures.

Levinson points out that his very normal subjects do not fully experience that they are adult men until they are about the age of thirty. Many of them seek out and require a mentor in their younger years to take the place of their parents. While they are officially adult at the age of eighteen, it takes many more years to overcome the feeling of being a son or a "boy" in relationship with the "real" adults in our world. This proves again how our long history of physiological and psychological dependence needs to be transcended by many successful experiences before we can truly break away and invest our embryonic autonomy into self-generated vistas. Again Levinson's study shows that the process of being more independent and self-sufficient is found at many ages. The way one shows this depends on the nature of the current developmental phase and its typical pressures. For instance, the question of independence takes new form and a more central plan at the end of the settling down phase from about the age of thirty-six to forty-one or forty-two. Levinson calls this era "becoming one's own man", in which the prime developmental tasks are settling down, advancing on the available ladder, becoming a more senior person, and speaking with one's own voice with greater articulation. This sums up to having a greater measure of authority. This period is followed by the "midlife transition" from ages forty-one or forty-two to forty-five or forty-six. During this bridging period a man comes to terms with his past and prepares for the future. One of the three tasks of this period (besides reappraising the past and modifying the life structure) is the "individuation process". As more clear-cut boundaries between the self and the environment develop, the person also develops a stronger sense of his own identity and of his goals and a more realistic perception of his world. As he then allows himself to become more individualized he can also become more separate from the world. Hence he develops a greater independence and can generate new energy from his inner needs. We recognize here what Jung said about individuation. All three, including Levinson, place these new efforts at individuation around the age of forty and agree that a stronger desire to become creative develops at this age. In this way a man's products become more valuable to himself and to others, which includes the contribution to the next generation. In other words as the person makes serious efforts at individuation his personality becomes more differentiated and complex. He also develops more effective boundaries around himself from interacting with others and the world. The efficiency lies in knowing oneself better, including limitations, so that one can marshal one's resources and narrow down on one's aims. One can also reduce the pressures of society and the demands of one's own unconscious.

Levinson projects a late adulthood era from his interviews and observations to lie between sixty and eighty-five for his subjects in which the man finds a new balance of involving himself with society and with himself. One can choose one's life more fully and with a broader perspective and also with the aid of increased wisdom. There is less interest in obtaining the available rewards and more interest in using one's own inner resources. The self becomes a stronger focus as the voices from within become more audible.

Finally, we arrive at Jane Loevinger who is a psychologist and a researcher in personality psychology. She has created an ambitious sequence of ego development. She, like Erikson, accepts the ego as defined by psychoanalysis and sees it developing in a lawful sequence of stages. At the same time she accepts the forces which Freud felt were also impinging on the ego and which she uses to augment her schema. Loevinger's approach is somewhat unique insofar as she used various personality tests to anchor her developmental sequence to actual answers from children and adults of different ages that were predicted from her theory. She goes to some effort to show that the developmental sequence suggested by others, like Erikson and Piaget, are translatable into her categories, so that there is no real conflict. According to her, the schemas of other clinicians are based on either a single source of data, or they specialize in one personality function or trait. Since she followed the dictates of science and carried out a number of studies to verify the existence of her conceptualized ego concerns at different ages, she further claims that she has thereby refined a conception of personality development without invalidating the ideas that preceded hers.

She defines the concerns of the ego as a process or structure that is social in origin and functions as a total entity. It is guided by purpose and meaning so that both consciousness or the possibility of freedom is involved besides the working of a dynamic unconscious. Even though the ego must remain an abstraction -- as it has been for all the other theorists -- it is part of the personality and becomes the closest embodiment of what a person thinks of himself or herself.

In brief the baby travels through a symbiotic state, an impulsive stage, a self-protective stage with first attempts at self-control and moves on to a conformist stage prior to the age of ten. Next in line a self-awareness level becomes a bridge to a conscientious stage which occurs around the ages of twelve or thirteen. This blends into an individualistic level which is again a bridge to the next stage labeled "autonomous". On this bridge the late adolescent acquires a heightened sense of individuality and becomes concerned with the dilemma of emotional dependence versus independence. During the autonomous stage in adulthood the previously developed first awareness of inner conflicts gives way to a capacity and a greater courage to cope with them. Reality is seen as more complex and the person is becoming more tolerant of ambiguity. Not only does he realize other people's needs for autonomy but he can recognize the limitations of his own autonomy. Self-fulfillment becomes an important goal. Finally in mature adulthood the developing ego may enter the integrated stage although not every person makes it. In this sense and in its description it is very much like Maslow's self-actualization stage of maturation.

Again Loevinger joins others who have insisted that self-awareness and concern with autonomy are important characteristics of the mature personality. Hence freedom is not only primarily the achievement of a few people, but becomes a universal orientation. She furthermore spent some time to show how the stages proposed by others fit into her scheme and that they are not in any way contradictory to hers. For instance she sees Erikson's autonomy struggle of his second stage a characteristic pattern in her self-protective stage and then differentiates the self-protective children from the impulsive ones. Other Erikson's stages are fitted into her scheme in a similar manner which again shows that both of these scientists saw and described potentially similar processes. They merely focused on different elements of it as their primary concern.

Before summarizing what we have learned about human autonomy from the scientists and clinicians, we must bring up an important argument that has occasionally been raised in the last twenty or thirty years, sometimes by very competent social scientists. They question whether the elevation of autonomy or self-realization was a crowning stage and, as a potential goal in all human development, is really a valid and inevitable ingredient in all human beings. Perhaps the researchers and the professionals hoisted this banner to the top of their theory because it represents a value from their surrounding culture and spirits and therefore unwittingly a value for them?! Let us turn to a very recent admonition of this type by a respectable and well-known social psychologist: M. Brewster Smith (Journal of social Issues, 1978), who, among many other accomplishments, was elected president of the American Psychological Association for 1978. He reminds us how other psychologists have pointed the way that the desirable values of their culture have been fused with the nature of reality. He further suggests that psychologists like Jahoda and Maslow may be surreptitiously advocating their and our values in the name of supposedly value-free concepts such as mental health. For instance Maslow's list of historical figures who exemplified the self-actualization syndrome does not include the heroes that have actualized other people's values including the actualizers of evil. Even other researchers like Levinson and Loevinger, who have picked normal subjects from their studies may still come up with empirical or analytical descriptions of merely current conceptions of mental health or of conceptions that fit our peculiar culture in which the autonomy and freedom of the individual is politically safeguarded and socially valued.

To answer this very valid point we can raise a number of issues that may weaken such accusations, even though they cannot completely prove the scientific validity of self-actualization as a universal stage in personality development. The criticism was first raised when some of the pioneers like Maslow and Fromm extolled the virtues of truly autonomous functioning. Subsequent researchers have been careful to become more aware of their own possible biases and their own roots in the surrounding culture. This was certainly true of Levinson and Loevinger who have demonstrated such sophistication in their previous research in other areas of psychology than personality development. While it is true that we can find no Japanese, Chinese, or central European investigations into personality development that come to comparable conclusions, we do have Erikson's astute first-hand observations of two Indian tribes and of pre-Hitler Germany. In all these cases he found a comparable sequence of development. In fact he used examples from all these cultures to illustrate the universal sequence of stages in the developing ego.

If we do not have any comparable observations of more undeveloped civilizations by anthropologists in the past twenty or thirty years it may perhaps be the very technological and economic level of these more primitive cultures that prevented their people from developing to their full potential, that is, to a well-defined stage of autonomous functioning. We have already tried to show how the health hazards and the requirement of hard work before industrialization had limited people's life span down from the present expectations. If truly self-actualizing behavior cannot occur until later in life, it may not be feasible to make a study of the relatively few individuals still existing at such an advanced age range in more primitive cultures. Also the increased leisure and the replacement of back-breaking physical labor by machines increased the horizon of modern Man beyond the age of forty. In previous civilizations one was "finished" or mentally exhausted by the time one had reached the age of forty and had assured a livelihood for one's family so that the surviving children could take over. The whole concept that "Life begins at forty" or that one "should make something of his life" to include later years and retirement are modern ideas that require reduction of work hours, leisure time, guaranteed retirement and a political base of freedom for the individual.

More indirect support for a universal drive toward autonomy in mature human beings comes from the events occurring in communist countries which represent another important "experiment" in human social organization. While western democracy developed and bred the values that gave rise to a concern with human autonomy and opportunities for self-actualization, in the communist countries quite the opposite values were needed and were indoctrinated as the highest good. It was wrong for the individual to think of his own fate and needs first. He had to develop a total feeling for the community, namely his town and his nation, and he had to primarily promote the advancement of his state. He had to subjugate all of his own wishes to the common good. It is clear that this value system and process is not well accepted and therefore not successful, as seen by the riots and unrest that have occurred in Poland, China, and Hungary. Nor are the dissidents of Soviet Russia an example of the success of this effort despite attempts to seal the borders against "foreign subversives" and foreign styles of life. Further evidence comes from the intense rivalries and even conflicts that have developed between the leaders of different countries. Obviously these conflicts are based on other reasons as we shall see in Chapter X. If they had truly subscribed to communist goals they would have been able to solve all territorial or ascendancy problems amicably. Hence Communism as a big social experiment has not produced a personality who shuns autonomy or self-worth. The fact that evidence for these goals emerge from their internal and external conflicts, and germinates in a society that rejects them officially is further proof that our "western-bred" concepts of personality development are not culture bound. They may indeed be universal and truly "human" in character.

After our survey of the most well-known pioneers and of the more systematic theories of personality development we recognize the characteristics of self-initiated motivation and behavior that are shared in all of these observations and research studies. We can also state with some degree of certainty that an autonomously governed self-realization is a lawful ingredient in the repertoire of human behavior and that it has scientifically-grounded antecedents as well as experiential and behavioral properties. The scientific underpinning derives from the fact that many of the people we have quoted have been trained in and have practiced the requirements of objective and reliable observations and of verification by repeated experiments. The following summary points can therefore be made:

1. While we can see an analogy of autonomous behavior in animals, it is only possible to speak of autonomy in terms of self-realization in an organism that has a self as a central reference

point. This self is perceived as a unitary collecting point for all perceptions and reflections and is an important synthesizer and organizer. This self further must gain an enduring and consistent organization or an identity, before it can act autonomously on the basis of this identity.

2. Autonomous behavior has to develop slowly. It requires extensive learning and practice in a variety of skills which then impart the necessary self-confidence to slowly counteract the long dependency period thrust on the human organism by his inheritance. It further requires a transcendence of the inevitable conflict between the security of dependence or fear of freedom and the gains from growth and from the further rewards that come with independence. It is for these reasons that major reliance and use of autonomous behavior is not possible until later in life although short spurts may occur earlier. Also primitive forays from the safe base of the familiar can already occur in childhood.

3. Self-realization can be seen as a motivating force in people or can be seen as a developmental task beckoning to the organism until he develops the motivation to engage in it.

4. Major attempts at self-actualization constitute one of the final stages in the orderly development of a more differentiated personality. It is therefore a higher or more complex involvement of the available energy. It is also a stage which is potentially reachable by human beings with proper development and proper environment. Hence we can make an analogy to a turbine which has been manufactured to run at peak efficiency; however it may only be able to do so if it was manufactured properly, if the feeder lines function well, and if all other conditions such as encasement, motor, temperature of the steam, and quantities of steam are optimum. If not, the turbine will operate at lower levels, perhaps at 75% capacity. The big difference here is that the autonomously functioning organism is not really functioning "better" in terms of output. Maslow's assertions might therefore be suspected of reflecting western values. However, we also

have so many descriptions of people from other times and other places who have functioned at this stage that bespeak of wonderment and excitement and even ecstasy. We have read novelists who have described it and we have met psychologists who have observed it in their case studies. All these witnesses describe this functioning to be "better" when they compare it with other stages. Other stages are also universally practiced but don't give off the excitement and wonder. It is as though the turbine could tell us how grand and majestic it feels to hum away at its own hundred per cent capacity. So "proof" is again offered by the consensual validation from a number of diverse sources.

5. An autonomous stage can only be achieved after one has learned and valued conformity and a sense of integration with some social community, again echoing the emergence of greater independence from a firm anchorage independency. This is a recognition of the need for others, their help, their knowledge, and even their love. Self-realization as observed by psychologists is therefore not a form of egotistical anarchy but the act of pushing out part of the self into new frontiers with a knowledge of what the limits may be, especially the limits that define another person's space and comfort.

6. Even though self-realization may be a stage in a hierarchy that has to be achieved, behavior at this stage is not completely and eternally transformed. Autonomous functioning is a process and not a static plateau, a process that occurs in waves. Behavior here can fluctuate from the self-actualizing level to other levels and may be absent for periods of time when other demands or pressures are made on the organism. Regression in the face of threat is always possible too.

7. The phenomenon of self-actualization may occur in widely differing cultures as long as a well-developed self exists in the culture. It may show itself in very different clothing, and the behavioral involvement of the self in growth is patterned to the available and allowable possibilities in the culture.

8. The feelings and experiences that accompany autonomous functioning may contain moments of awe, power, meditation, and ecstasy. These experiences have also been labeled as religious, mystical, or peak moments. They have also been described as alternative forms of consciousness. The features they have in common is that the person opens up his boundaries to new experiences or essences so that his or her self may flow out and may produce a momentary "loss of self" or "self-abandon" without the sense of having control nor the need to exercise it. This move away from safe areas may again reflect a developmental stage at which the person can afford to lose control and allow his boundary to be fluid, because he knows he can always come back to a more familiar harbor without having suffered injuries on the outside. These moments are again transitory and occasional. Zen's seductive appeal for "turning on" on a permanent level of higher unity with nature and resulting self-transcendence is a fallacy, and impossible unless it is abetted by drugs, as we shall discuss more fully in Chapter VIII.

9. There may be some special "pathology" that can develop when people never practice autonomy behavior or fail to reach self-actualizing levels. We are reminded here of the possibility of the various "non-productive" character formations proposed by Fromm, of the failures to solve Erikson's ego conflicts ending in "ego diffusion", "isolation", "stagnation", and "despair". Maslow describes people who function on the "deficiency levels" of motivation (below his "being" level for self-actualizing people) as apathetic, hopeless, or experientially empty. He sees them as lacking direction from within, requiring the search for cues for their guidance, and too much reliance on clocks, rules, calendars, schedules, agendas about what to eat, do, think, etc. (the further reaches of human nature). The more complex involvement of one's energies in searching for direction from within may create feelings of loneliness and ambiguity, hence tempt people to run and escape. These descriptions also sound like David Riesman's other-directed character. These people

are further seen as having given up the struggle and are really coasting in life, while the neurotics are people who are still hopefully struggling and are thereby experiencing conflict. These observations have added fuel to those of us who don't want to call a behavioral or emotional problem an illness or even a "neurosis". These latter problems may better be seen as "problems in living" or spiritual problems, loss of meaning, loss of hope, grief over loss or dislike of the self. Maslow prefers the term "human diminution" and thereby removes this form of behavior deficiency further from the realm of medicine. Medically oriented practitioners must give it a label of illness and then "treat" it. This conception can handle any of the crippling and inhibiting effects caused by poverty, exploitation, drug addiction, criminality, authoritarianism, character disorder, existential disorder, and psychopathy.

10. Self-actualization requires proper prerequisites in one's development and adequate fertilization when the person is still immature and primarily dependent. It, for instance, seems plausible that proper "lubrication" might be provided in childhood by parents who allowed their child to develop according to his own bent, and provided opportunities for experimentation. If the parents further encouraged the experimentation and then applauded the child's success regardless of his performance or biases, they would launch him as a separate being. The child then can develop according to his or her own needs and according to the developing self. If on the other hand parents insist that one copy their plans or ideas or a plan -- perhaps to compensate for their own deficiencies or to extend their own incomplete selves through their child -- then the child also carries alien scripts in his or her head. Similar problems would result from parents who found a child to be a plastic medium and would push him on to achievement and to perfection for their own parental gains. In either case these alien scripts can cause constant schism and tension, and those forces that may still be autonomous in the developing child must constantly compete with the "inherited"

script. Hence autonomy requires a building process and must be seeded and nurtured and reinforced. Otherwise it is inhibited and may not emerge in later life.

11. Finally, the exercise of autonomous behavior requires a friendly and, better yet, an encouraging culture broth. Therefore in a complex interdependent modern state it requires the fertile soil of a social organization and the values that favor freedom and self-expression. It further requires constraints on attacks that might take them away (as described in Chapter X). We need only remind ourselves that for instance Maslow's ideas would have been a "dangerous" and subversive doctrine at other eras of Man (as we saw in Chapter III). Just as the Renaissance society began to adopt the idea that the world is round and that we may revolve around the sun rather than vice versa, our own times may have to adapt to the possibility that autonomous functioning is a real and lawful occurrence in human nature and that it is a potential for everyone, not just for the elite. If this can be accepted as "normal", or at least possible, we will have attained a new plateau in the evolution of Man through his cognitive powers (rather than through genetic mutation).

We are therefore left with an awareness of how far we have come since the first fragile balloons of "free will". We have finally been able to give it a more realistic support and have extended its boundaries with the help of both the growing acceptance of freedom and with the growth of the science of personality. Again this awareness would not have been possible if we had looked only at individual components of the personality or of the mind. When we realize that self-actualization and growth were a process and could only be understood in terms of the laws relating to process, we can deal with them and understand them as a part of life itself. The real stimulus toward an enthusiastic investigation into this process was the constitutionally supported doctrine of the worth of Man and of the uniqueness of the individual. The latter alerts all of us to try to create opportunities for all and to help develop Man according to his potentials.

Chapter VII

PSYCHOTHERAPY AS A SUCCESSFUL PROGRAM TO ISOLATE AND ACTIVATE AUTONOMOUS BEHAVIOR

There is another arena in which autonomy has enjoyed some star billing, and which has also been supported by some scientific evidence. In the last chapter we have followed various scientists as they have sketched the necessary prerequisites and developmental stages leading to autonomous behavior. Their observations and studies have legitimized autonomous functioning as part of human development and as a form of normal human behavior. The developmental stage, however, cannot be observed directly and is influenced by so many diverse factors that their effect cannot be accurately observed over a person's lifetime. What about people who have been surrounded by a relatively fertile soil and are ready to enter the higher plateau of self-actualization, but have not arrived there? Many people in such a predicament may experience pain and a sense of deficiency. Sometimes their anxieties and depressions may make them very much aware of how far they are from the promised land of adult functioning. These people sometimes consult mental health professionals and may contract for a period of psychotherapy or counselling. Also some of the more recent systems of psychotherapy are offshoots from the personality theories already encountered above. They specifically attempt to encourage and even push the person towards greater self-mastery and autonomy. It is therefore illuminating to examine the rationale of these systems, distill out of them what they have in common, and then check over the scientific evidence of behavior changes. These observed changes over relatively short-time spans after corrective action can further serve to substantiate self-actualization as legitimate human behavior. In a way these therapeutic programs are blueprints for an accelerated spurt of growth. They can help us to see that a person can function at the more complex level if his rudimentary shoots are fertilized and the obstructing rocks are removed.

In psychotherapy, or so-called "talking therapy", the client is encouraged to reveal everything he feels or thinks. The therapist therefore has the chance to study the human thought processes and even its development at greater depth. Therapy is another new window into the workings and changes of the human mind. The therapist gains thereby a vantage point into the processes of inner experience which the philosopher of yesterday or the research psychologist may not enjoy. All three, of course, abstract from the processes they observe or contemplate, but the therapist has the chance to test and verify his assumptions again and again. It is for these reasons that personality theory has been enriched by the insights of the practicing therapist, and we have learned about stages and patterns of development, as we have seen in the last chapter. Of course, the therapist does not approach his client with the dispassionate search for truth of a research scientist. He or she has an axe to grind insofar as he or she wants to bring about relatively quickly the changes that follow from the therapist's theory and plan of attack.

While some of the newer therapies share some basic assumptions about autonomy, there is always some disagreement as to what really happens and what "works" in psychotherapy. What then are the effective leverages towards change of behavior? Fortunately, some good research into the therapy process has accumulated in the last 20 years, so that we can begin to see what these effective therapies have in common. As we shall see, the most basic ingredients very much boost our assertion that human beings can function more autonomously as part of their animal and human heritage.

The Promise Of Human Autonomy

As we have already seen, the classical psychoanalyst understood his patient as being overwhelmed by strong, hidden instinctual forces and by the frantic defenses against them. This pathological mix was acquired in universally found stages of development in early childhood. There, frustrations accumulated from the inadequate interaction with the parents and prevented normal development from occurring. The therapist therefore had a plan of action which consisted of helping the person to dredge up hidden memories from the unconscious and take a thorough journey over the distant past. On this journey the therapist would illuminate the faulty way stations of blocked impulse expression and help the patient to correct the damage. All this was, of course, abetted by an exquisite, complex theory of the human mind carried by a carefully trained expert. Insight into these distant vistas of the past became therefore the royal road to change, and the full revelation of one's relationship with parents became the map for forging new relationships, first with the therapist and then with others. One could then accept and gratify basic needs more directly without feeling guilty or having to mobilize crippling counter defensive measures against impulses.

In some of the newer therapies since Freud, the ego was more directly approached and placed into the driver's seat at the very beginning. The map with which the therapist approached the mind of his or her clients contained a much larger and more powerful ego. The unconscious had either shrunk a lot or disappeared altogether. Since these therapists had learned to appreciate the thinking and decision powers of their clients, they began to shift their focus from the past to the present. Present-day relationships and reactions became the true focus, and the client was encouraged to look for and make changes first in the therapy hour and then outside. There was therefore more emphasis on the potential for change, and on the experience of corrective action. The faith of the therapist in the positive growth potential of the human being also encouraged his client to experiment and to experience change and success. Understanding or insight became a companion of this process and therefore became a secondary ally rather than playing the main role towards change.

For instance, Carl Rogers developed a system based on his assertions about the main motive in Man. As we saw already, this motive became the maintenance and enhancement of a self-structure or ego. A counsellor trained in this anti-historical orientation would first of all approach the client with an "unconditional positive regard" not only for the good, healthy parts of the client, but also for his embryonic and perhaps hidden potential for change. His respect for the client's power would make the client the real expert on himself and not the counsellor. Instead of an interpreter, the counsellor became a facilitator. He or she would encourage the client to get in touch with the feelings at the moment, and then he or she would reflect them for the client as skillfully as he or she could read them. The client would then automatically make better choices on his own -- according to his or her built-in powers and need to enhance the self. He or she could now be able to do so because through the counsellor's reflections he or she had acquired a clear overview of all the conflicting reactions within.

Abraham Maslow saw implications for therapy in his observations on human motivation. Therapy should not emphasize the inhibition of new impulses, nor dwell on control, adjustment or self-discipline. Instead therapists should aim for a spontaneous release of feeling and for an awareness of impulses and their gratification. They should stress self-acceptance and a fuller expression of the impulses the client might find. Everett Shostrom built a whole system of therapy on Maslow's insights and called it "self-actualization therapy". Its chief function was of course to assist the person to actualize himself. It is based on the recognition that each person is unique, is looking for fulfilment and is facing a large choice of acting at each moment. Therefore, part of a man's future behavior is not predestined by his past reactions, although much of it is also shaped by one's personal history and by influences beyond one's control. For these reasons the person has a responsibility for his own realization and should not be dependent on others or blame them for what happens to him. The therapist illuminates these principles and provokes the client into looking at the possibilities and to experience them more clearly and dramatically. All the time he is encouraged to choose those that fit his goals and would give him a realization of growth. It is also illuminating to look at the 10 areas of human functioning which are measured by a personality questionnaire that Shostrom constructed. This inventory is filled out by the client before and after his counselling and has been used in many research studies since its inception to show changes in the client's personal orientation in a variety of therapy experiences. Among the 10 areas or sub-scores are an Affirmation of Self-Actualization, Spontaneity of Action and to be "Oneself"; Belief in the Worth of the Self, Acceptance of the Self despite the inevitable deficiencies; and a Constructive View on the Nature of Man. The other five areas are similar to those found in other, more traditional personality questionnaires.

The therapists that stress direct experience as corrective also emphasize will and the ability to make choices. They also developed their ideas in opposition to the view of man as a passive victim to conflicts from the instincts and from the unconscious and included systems like the "Gestalt" therapy of Fritz Perls. He emphasized the expression of feelings, and especially those that encourage the experience of physiological states such as muscle tensions or aches. Again the main concern here was for the client to discover his or her individuality and to progress along his or her inherent capacities to be active, striving, and self-actualizing. In these systems the therapist emphasized the here and now, rather than the past, and encouraged the client to experience feelings rather than know of them or verbalize about them. Again the Gestalt therapist stressed the client's inherent ability to determine his or her own fate, to be creative, and to be genuine or "authentic".

The various existential therapies all encourage the client to find and nurture autonomy and the decision-making process. Therapy is seen as an encounter of the client with new parts of himself and with new goals rather than as a treatment. Decisions about one's own existence have to be made first before insight leads to the right decisions. The goal of therapy is therefore changed from adjustment or conformity to an encouragement to make decisions and to shoulder the normal existential anxiety that inevitably accompanies this process. We even find a new emphasis on autonomy in some of the behavior therapies that have battled fears and "bad habits" so successfully with ideas adopted from the principles of learning and conditioning. There was first of all the discovery by various behavior therapists that the removal of the unwanted symptom meant much more to the client than the deliverance from a frustrating and often incapacitating evil. The disappearance of a phobia also enabled the client to feel a great relief and a sense that he was no longer at the mercy of a curse or of an "illness" that could drag one further and further into doom. As a matter of fact, this deliverance changed the client's identity from that of a victim to one who was now in the driver's seat and had greater control over his life. Behavior therapists began to realize that the experience of self-control, such as practicing the successful experience of previously feared scenes under relaxation, gave many of their clients a sense of freedom with which they now attacked other troublesome areas of their lives, or tackled new areas resulting in positive change and growth. On the basis of such findings, Albert Bandura established the principle that effective therapy has to include procedures that create and strengthen the inherent expectations of personal efficacy. Self-efficacy or mastery must be aroused or appealed to in such a way that the client can generate expectations to influence and change his self-defeating behavior, until he develops the conviction that he can adopt a new plan of action to produce the wanted outcome. Some behavior therapists have also taken to teaching their clients the relatively simple principles and practices of unlearning and relearning, in order to supply them with the tools by which they can control and shape their own behavior. Hence self-control became a goal towards which behavior therapists set up courses to teach people to control eating, smoking, drug and alcohol intake, as well as ways to become more assertive, relaxed, and less anxious or fearful.

An important movement that belongs in these newer schools with the main goal of affirming autonomy is the Rational-Emotive therapy of Albert Ellis. Ellis puts the client at the center of his own world and gives him almost full responsibility for his own destiny. He can either make himself sick or he can duck out from under his own self-defeating irrational feelings about himself and thereby become a free and happy agent. Ellis almost entirely relies on the rational capacities in Man and asks his client to do the same and use them to defeat the irrational and inherited ideas of self-condemnation and self-derogation. He sees Man as having potentially an enormous amount of control over what he feels and does. He cajoles his clients to realize this and to use it. In the beginning he teaches his clients to analyze their irrational beliefs, which had led to conflict, anxiety, or depression. He then asks his clients to use their own rational capacities to substitute more rational beliefs, which instead emphasize the person's own needs and views at the expense of old and blindly accepted standards of evaluation.

We see the same faith in the potentials for positive and autonomous decisions at work in the newer approaches to the treatment of the so-called "mental patient" in our modern mental hospitals. We used to do little more than babysitting for the deviators and rejects of society besides the administration of drugs and other physical therapies like electric shock treatment. This custodial approach seemed justified under the assumption that these patients suffered from an illness we only half understood. This view made these poor patients seem weak, vulnerable and incapable of looking out for themselves without extensive help and protection. A custodial attitude in the treatment personnel required them to hold an eternal blanket under their charges, in case they fell, and then give them extensive assistance to get them up and to remain standing. We have since learned that this attitude became a self-fulfilling prophecy because the patients learned that they could finally be accepted if they played the roles that were so humanistically handed to them adorned with the medical prestige ribbon.

Nowadays a different attitude accepts the potential that is locked up in each human being to develop and grow towards a higher stage as enumerated in the last chapter. If this faith is advertised and communicated to the patient he will get in touch with resources and strengths that are still locked up or have never been used. He will then try them out where the hospital personnel provide much more freedom and choice, including demands on the patient to determine his hospital life, and to plan for his discharge and life outside the hospital. The sequence may include a series of graded steps of greater self-determination, called day hospitals, halfway houses and group homes. This new attitude has been incorporated in the so-called therapeutic environment concept, which has revolutionized the organization and the staff-patient interactions of mental hospitals. It has been associated with greater self-government, self-determination, greater liveliness of mental patients, and also with the disappearance of the so-called zombie "burned-out schizophrenic", and with the longer maintenance of these patients outside the hospital.

The emphasis on the positive and growth-promoting forces in the human being have also been largely responsible for the proliferation of growth, sensitivity, or encounter groups. The therapeutic strategies described above are used here to allow people to expand their repertoire of action and of feeling. The significant fact of these groups is that the person with anxieties, conflicts and hindrances does not need to see himself or herself as a "patient", that is, as someone who is "sick" and full of pathology. He or she comes in and is accepted as a relatively well-functioning person who wants to grow out of a rut, become more sensitive to his own feelings and reactions and to those of others, and who may want to become more creative, assertive of his wishes and self-expanding. Research has shown that the consumers do indeed change to a more positive self-concept, if certain characteristics and behaviors prevail in the group leaders.

We can recognize an important implication in these newer therapies that are based on an autonomy-oriented conception of the human personality. They get away from the idea of "curing" a person or of treating an illness, an idea that is so prevalent in medicine by necessity. Instead of a search for weakness and pathology, they nurture strength. They focus on the obstacles that prevent people from functioning as fully as they could according to the model of growth. They are based on the idea that the human being can act like the little rocking man -- a child's toy with lead in its circular base. When it was pushed over, these therapies also promote a more optimistic concept of Man, because he is seen as basically capable of functioning and even of soaring to new heights, if he unlocks his own potentials and uses his resources. If Man pays attention to these forces, his positive qualities are reinforced and then rush him on to more creative and potentially successful ventures. Hence the awakening of hidden coping skills is seen to have a snowballing effect.

These therapies also prefer to get away from the medical model and instead label their client's difficulties as "problems in living", rather than as mental sickness or neurosis. The increasing number of advocates of this position further call their intervention or help by such labels as "relearning" or "remotivation" or "reawakening competency" or providing a "sense of mastery." They prefer to call themselves facilitators or trainers who set the client free from crippling dependency on to his journey towards self-realization, rather than as experts who supply the insights and the direction. They give back to their clients the feeling of control which the latter have lost due to internal obstacles like parental rules or to conflicts due to earlier struggles with powerful people during Man's long period of dependency. They urge their clients to find and experiment with their own autonomy and to experience these forces as real and rock bottom foundations on which to build new hopes and new lives.

Since none of these therapy systems have as yet been found superior to each other, nor superior to older and rejected models that are still in vogue with certain practitioners, it might be fruitful to look briefly at some of the most recent research on outcome in psychotherapy. Even though some of the studies show that "all have won and all should have prizes" other studies are unearthing some of the effective ingredients various therapy systems have in common. The findings of these researches support, as we shall see, our basic assumptions about self-determination and autonomy. Not only are most of the contemporary systems of therapy -- including psychoanalysis -- successful in some patient populations, but the success of some more "radical" treatments in more primitive tribes raise questions about the rationale underlying some of our western systems. For instance the elaborate preparation of the schizophrenic patient and his family by the "medicine man" and his ritualized performance of making deep cuts into the shaved scalp of the patient in some African nations, quite successfully relieves the patient from the "demons" of his psychotic behavior. In Peru psychotherapists attempt to get their patients to adapt to their fate or to touch base with spiritual values without ever mentioning mastery. In Russia remotivation through productive work gets many of their bona fide mental patients back into the community.

Studies that use placebos, or inert substances that are administered as "medications", to control pain, anxiety, depression etc., have abundantly shown that they are indeed effective in a significant number of people. Further research has shown that an important component of the placebo effect is the physician's communication of his assurance to the patient that the placebo will be effective. Treatments that have been prescribed conscientiously in various medical conditions by physicians fully convinced of their efficacy not only have turned out later to be worthless, but have also been shown to be significantly effective in reducing symptoms or the seriousness of the original condition. We have further proof of the effectiveness of suggestions and therapist's faith in pain control. Some researchers, such as Theodore Xenophon Barber, have even concluded that all of the amazing effects produced under hypnosis are not due to a special state induced in the subject, but arise from the provisions of a social contract between hypnotist and subject. Under this "contract" both believe hypnosis to be a special state and act out their respective roles by mutual agreement of benefits without harmful side effects. As the "subject" he narrows his concentration to the demands and tasks he is asked to carry out. The same tasks can be carried out by subjects in the laboratory who are merely cajoled to cooperate with the scientist for the urgent sake of advancing science. Recently clever experiments on faked acupuncture show that the same analgesic effects can be produced when it is either performed "properly" or when it is simulated without the subject's knowledge. Furthermore it has been shown that school teachers somehow influence their grade school students to improve their performances as shown in future achievement tests if they are informed that these students were singled out by prestigious-sounding, but really fake, tests to be "late bloomers" and therefore capable of extensive improvement.

All of these experiments show that merely the expectation of change or growth can be a potent enough force to produce change in the subjects. Recent observations of Jerome Frank and his associates at John Hopkins University also have shown convincingly that the transmission of the mere expectation of a therapist's faith in change to the patient has a significant effect on outcome, provided the patient also hears and accepts this expectation and gains some hope for relief. This expectation to get help is therefore one significant determinant of outcome regardless of the system of psychotherapy. In addition, a new sense of mastery and growth in self-control are significantly related to positive outcome. They can be stimulated by the therapist if he provides successful experiences, again unrelated to the type or theory of psychotherapy. This would indicate that the therapies which stress the potential for growth, for self-control, for self-realization, all can induce a related expectation in the client and get him or her to move in that direction. Both Jerome Frank and the psychologist Hans Strupp, however, caution us that such therapies may only be appropriate and helpful for people who accept such growth values and goals. Other therapies may be found to be appropriate for others -- for instance, for those who want to be dependent, or for those who like to think of themselves as mere corks bobbing on the sea of life. As we have seen already, people with different motivations in other countries may get better under very different strategies.

While these ideas may be particularly relevant for people trying to find the most suitable psychotherapy for different types of clients, they are relevant for us here for one important reason. They have shown us that a goal of self-mastery from the therapist can substitute autonomous behavior for helplessness in the client. The goal kindles similar expectations in the client, and they lead eventually to real changes in behavior that are visible to the client and to others, and contribute to a positive outcome. We thereby arrive at an independent confirmation of the existence of self-rooted autonomous functioning in the human being. In the previous chapter such behavior has been ordained as a lawful stage of human functioning from the observers of people at certain stages in their growth. Now we find further evidence for these observations and principles by demonstrating that the cessation of growth can be reversed by special psychological techniques. People who have become trapped in tensions, self-incriminations and helplessness can be freed and propelled to new stages of self-confidence. Once they have arrived there, they can begin to involve themselves in more creative and fulfilling activities.

These excursions into the art of psychotherapy have clarified the following points: It is possible to teach and encourage autonomy and to create appropriate blueprints for actions. This can be accomplished by proper modeling from people with convictions in the client's improvement, by rewarding of first attempts, and by transmitting the proper expectation. It is further possible to remove certain blocks to autonomous behavior by getting people to clearly identify the garbage they carry around in their self-perceptions, and by getting them to discover and detoxify old and useless scripts inherited from their past. One can speed the development of self-realizing behavior, if it has been retarded or reversed. It is possible to encourage people to experiment with self-initiated activities, provided one can instill faith that this will work towards change, and also organize proper feedback for the person towards the establishment of his self-confidence. One can provide or promote a solid base of security by encouraging self-acceptance. It allows a person to venture out and try new behavior associated with real satisfactions and further growth.

Chapter VIII

GENERAL SYSTEMS THEORY AS A SCIENTIFIC BASE FOR AUTONOMOUS BEHAVIOR

We could not take such a strong stand on the validity of autonomous functioning and of an ego that expands its horizon, if we could not rely on another source of recent knowledge. Contemporary Man has made great strides in unlocking the secrets of energy by penetrating the atom, and getting glimpses of the nature of heat, electrical charge, fission and fusion of atomic particles, and the processes of wave transmission. Other windows have been opened into the events occurring in the living cell, where we now better understand the composition of molecules and their complex functions that make life with all of its intricate investments possible. We not only understand the basic ingredients a little better, but we have broken the locks on the more complex living organisms and marveled at the wonders of organization that help explain physiological processes and the interactions of organ systems. From all these vantage points into the secrets of life, from its tiniest particles to its most complex manifestation in a group of people, we have recently been able to abstract some of the basic principles of life itself. These inevitably point towards the facts of life's expanding nature and to the spinning-off process, or towards autonomy as a valid form of life's workings.

These principles are known as General Systems Theory. They were first formulated in thermodynamics and other fields of energy physics to explain the transfer of energy. Almost 30 years ago they were successfully transplanted to an examination of living processes by von Bertalanffy and have allowed us to have a better understanding of the manifestations of life ever since (Grinker, Miller, Allport, others). These principles are not very hard to understand, if we compare a typical non-living machine like the gasoline engine with an appropriate illustration of a living creature like a butterfly.

A gasoline engine uses energy in the form of gasoline and oxygen, allowing them to combine in a controlled way, so that the sudden combination gives off heat. This converts into pressure that pushes pistons which convert the now mechanical push into rotary motion, that can be translated into spinning wheels via certain gears, and thereby propel a car. This nonliving system is similar to many other such systems, whether more simple or more complex. An example of the former might be the flow of rainwater into the crevice of an overhanging rock. In winter the water inside the crevice freezes and expands. Thereby pressure is exerted on the rock, so that it breaks off from the wall of the cliff and falls to the canyon floor below, -- again a translation of one form of energy (chemical) into another (mechanical). Work is again performed, except that here nothing very "useful" happens for the purposes of Man. In both of these examples there is a period of quiescence or nothingness until energy is imported into the system to make it work or move. Energy is then given off from the system until the original source of energy is depleted, -- gasoline and water -- in the two respective examples. Then the system has again reached a perfect equilibrium where absolutely nothing happens and we cannot detect the tiniest sign of change. There is neither movement, nor can energy be obtained from it.

Now we can make the gasoline engine more complex. We can put wings on it so that it can fly. We can put automotive equipment and feedback mechanisms on it so that it can adjust to various conditions such as gravity, wind, temperature, magnetic forces, etc.. It has then "learned" to fly "by itself" for a period of time. Suppose we put further feedback and sensing systems into it so that it could home in on a fueling system when its tank got empty, and effect transfer of fuel from either a flying or stationary fuel pump. It could certainly fly by itself a little longer without stopping and attaining the perfect equilibrium of stillness from which it had started. Suppose we made it independent of gasoline and allowed it to drill and suck up crude oil from the ground and convert it into gasoline with the aid of a miniature refinery on board. It would have to have a computer by then that could sort out and direct these complex investments of energy with the aid of preprogrammed memory circuits. However, we may already have guessed that this flying machine would be so big and heavy that it could not fly any more. The most important point to keep in mind is that this machine at its most complex stage still could not reproduce itself. Also, if any one of a vast number of parts inside the machine broke down, that part could not be circumvented or changed so that the machine could maintain its functions even if in a slightly different way. The machine is not able to replace or repair any worn part. Only the man servicing it can do that.

What is characteristic of this complex machine in terms of its use and transformation of energy and its capabilities? It uses energy for certain defined functions until that energy is used up. Its capacities are completely determined in advance by its internal structure and parts. All these parts must interact in a predetermined order, or the system comes to an abrupt standstill. It may be highly organized, but this organization is static and cannot change an inch without catastrophe -- that is, without a dead stop. This standstill is so complete and quiet that it represents a finite equilibrium, in which there is no organization of energy processes. The general systems theorist call this lack of organization or lack of order: "entropy". He points out that any non-living energy system always achieves a state of equilibrium of "maximum entropy" -- a state in which disorganization (or lack of organization) is at a maximum -- until the system is activated again from the outside importation of more energy, or by the outside replacement of a broken part.

Let us look at the butterfly by contrast. The butterfly starts as a single cell in an egg, which contains energy in the form of nutrients surrounding a single cell as yolk. The cell feeds upon this rich source and divides into more cells in terms of blueprints that are contained in the DNA of its genes. The blueprints further dictate a re-alignment of the accumulating cells into organs and organ systems which then align themselves to form a skin, muscles for locomotion, a brain, and a system for energy intake and transformation called the digestive system. Eventually the caterpillar finds leaves, digests them, and uses the energy contained therein to fuel its various life functions. It grows and adapts to a variety of dangers and to more positive stimuli. (Of course it could also find itself unable to adapt to some stimuli and die, thereby attaining the "perfect equilibrium" of maximum disorganization of our broken-down machine.) At a certain point the living caterpillar spins a hard outer shell to protect its next stage of existence as a chemical and physiological factory. Inside that factory or chrysalis there is a complete transformation of all the components, so that muscles, outer features and the digestive system among others are changed into novel, unrecognizable forms. Eventually a butterfly emerges, which now flies instead of crawling, eats honey instead of leaves, and engages in more complex functions such as mating and egg-laying, and perhaps migration. The egg perpetuates the organism even though the butterfly must die.

What has happened here? First of all the energy sources are imported, then transformed into simple components which are eventually reorganized and expelled in different form after the energy has been liberated and extracted. This energy is converted into different forms and transmitted to a variety of subsystems to make them go in ways that are in no way related to the original energy source or even to one another. Furthermore the whole system moves from one level of functioning to another, each being very different and mostly more complicated than the other. At each level the available energy is used very differently (e.g. crawling versus chemical change, versus flying). Also, the available energy is invested into more complex processes, so that the transformed organism becomes more "efficient". It can do more with less, since it is now able to mate, lay eggs and migrate. At each stage the components have been changed and are almost not recognizable any more, or they have taken on different functions. What has changed are their interactions and the total organization of the components and the subsystems. Furthermore the organism can reproduce itself and adapt to a larger variety of outside forces and exigencies.

In terms of general systems principles, the organism is characteristically moving away from entropy or from disorganization to a state of minimal disorganization or minimal entropy. It can change the internal boundaries around subsystems by, for instance, changing its form and its components. It also can change its relations with the boundaries of systems outside itself. For instance, the butterfly can no longer penetrate the skin of a leaf, but it can enter into the calyx of a flower with its proboscis. It can transform to a more complex stage of functioning or investment of energy, in which completely new relationships between components prevail. Therefore new laws are needed to explain the functioning at the higher level of organization. These laws have to focus on the process or on the relationship between parts instead of on the nature and functions of the parts themselves as separate entities. For instance, the vast majority of cells in my body constantly die and are replaced by new ones that have sprung up from cell divisions. Within days almost all my cells are components have been replaced, but I am still almost the "same person". At least I myself and other people still recognize me, and today expect behavior and thinking from me similar to what they have found previously.

The flux of components at a new stage are in a kind of equilibrium, but it is not the kind of static equilibrium represented by a resting engine. The living system can also eventually move to a new steady state in which some very novel adaptations or involvements are possible, which could not have been predicted by studying the components or their relationships in the previous state. For instance I cannot predict how my actions, thinkings and my life will change after the publication of this book. Either praise, attack, or neglect of the book will have effects on me and my life that will certainly change its direction in a way that is not foreseeable now. Furthermore the living system can react to much more feedback, because it contains a variety of feedback systems. They monitor and process both internal and external stimuli, and relate them to a central organ (brain) for processing and output. The result is a web of circular and corrective processes which help to stabilize the organism and maintain its organization, but also allow the breakthrough of new forms of involvement.

Putting some of these principles into different and perhaps more familiar words we can see that living organisms first of all do not function simply as the sum of their parts. New functions can emerge from the parts, if they change in their relationship to each other. They can mature through a process by which primary and embryonic subsystems become differentiated and take on new functions. Boundaries between the living system and the environment can become semipermeable, which means that a boundary like a living skin can let water out to produce sweat, but not allow it or blood to escape. In this way the organism can control what goes in and out. Most substructures come under central control in different degrees, such as the nucleus directing inside the cell, and the brain for the organism in more complex animal organisms. Different substructures can take on a variety of functions so that a certain process can start from diverse internal sources and can take a variety of pathways, and still achieve the identical result or action. The great advantage of the general systems principles is that they serve as a checklist for the kind of explanations we have to find at each probe we take into the living organism, whether we want to pick a cellular level of understanding, or peak in at the physiological level of an organ system, or study it at the psychological level.

On the psychological level we can find a lot of evidence of surplus energy spinning off into new processes that are not merely designed to keep the system functioning or to repair problems in it. This spinning-off process is, of course, a manifestation of any living system that can utilize transformation of energy (live electrical nerve impulses transformed into thinking) for more complex engagements, thus attaining a new form of organization or steady state. Growth and maturation are of course major examples of this. Curiosity or the venture into new areas for which no ready-made blueprints are available is another example of the investment of surplus energy. Curiosity takes more energy than merely reacting to something familiar or waiting until the familiar happens. Dreams have been mentioned as a necessary spill-over of surplus mental energy when there is relatively little use of this energy during sleep. Subjects who are prevented from dreaming in the laboratory develop a variety of disturbances. People who volunteer for sensory deprivation experiments in which they are locked in small cubicles without being able to move, hear, see, or feel -- or are immersed into water, usually after hours of exposure, -- usually develop symptoms of mental disorganization or show behavior usually found in mentally ill people. They literally "go to pieces" when they cannot use up the energy that constantly spins off from them, because they do not use all of their available energy in the maintenance and perpetuation of the system. Evolution and the appearance of more complex civilizations and advanced technology are further examples of transformation of surplus energy to more complicated involvements. Thus creativity and exploration fall into the category of surplus energy production and investment.

Hence General Systems Theory points toward the conclusion that novel ways of the recombination of elements, reorganizations of total systems, and the realignment of energy can occur in organisms that can lead to new -- and perhaps more complex -- levels of integration. On such a new level processes and behaviors are possible that were not possible or even thinkable before. Suppose two crocodiles had by accidental mutation developed a Man-like brain a hundred million years ago and acquired the ability to speak and think for their brief lifespan. They might perhaps have been able to explain their existence and the nature of life and the facts of evolution, as well as the forces on earth and in the water that were relevant to them. However, they would have been completely unable to describe or explain what might have happened on the earth after their death. They could not have predicted the evolution of birds, or warm blooded animals, such as the appearance of a zebra or tiger or Man, nor the fact that the latter would have been able to invent television or a spaceship to go to the moon, or use hides to make shoes. Similarly we today cannot predict what other forms of life may evolve beyond us or what future generations might invent and thereby change their lives. We might perhaps be able to stumble onto some new inventions that exist in the rich imaginations of science fiction of today, but we cannot speculate on new forms of intelligent life beyond the vague little green men with horns that might visit us from other planets.

We cannot even speculate intelligently what mankind will be doing 100 years from now. Will we have more harmonious and striving civilizations that are cruising around the heavenly bodies in sophisticated spaceships to explore our planets and galaxies beyond? Or will we have polluted ourselves into paralyzing sicknesses and creeping inactivity? Or has our seeding of the atmosphere with carbon dioxide and other gases of combustion created a greenhouse effect that will raise the average temperature, melt our polar ice caps and then inundate all coastal cities and other low-lying lands? In that case large numbers of people would have to relocate and learn to live underwater or underground. Or will we have laid waste most of civilization and decimated vast number of our cities through a nuclear war, so that just a few people are left and have to start all over again? These are some of the vistas we can entertain now, but these might be replaced by more vistas, both uplifting or horrifying as our imaginative quasi-prediction is guided by new inventions and social ideas.

It remains for us to demonstrate that these general systems principles point an inevitable finger at: 1. an ego as a valid organizing concept in personality; 2. an ego which changes and grows and can invest surplus energy; and 3. this surplus energy as the basis of autonomous functioning or self-realization, which has been described as a legitimate level of functioning by the scientists we have referred to in the last two chapters.

We have met the ego before as an important third part of the structure into which Freud anchored the forces that interacted with each other in personality. The ego for Freud was less of a center, and was actually more of a static part similar to those found in the reactive models that are typical of non-living systems, such as an engine. It is therefore more illuminating to let some other psychological observers enumerate the reasons why a potent ego is needed as a center of the organizing forces within the personality. Husserl, the European philosopher writing before large-scale experimentation began in psychological processes felt that the human being required an ego or a center that transcended the variety of conscious experiences. For him it represented raw consciousness in contrast to Sartre who felt that so-called pure consciousness was represented merely by the awareness of an object. The ego or the I that feels was really, for Husserl, a reflected object that is apprehended and constructed secondarily and somewhat artificially from the many accumulated pure impressions. Even though Husserl was primarily concerned with an experiential approach to human existence, he felt that we need such an ego as a center for our own universe. How else could we otherwise explain the so-called "existence" of the ego and its constant re-establishment? Our mental system "needed it" and allocates it to a central position that assumes a greater importance than if it were merely a secondary, reflected structure. Instead, the ego is perceived by the person and used in deliberation, becoming a directive force, even if it is not always perceived as a unity. Husserl recognized that the ego is also an abstracted concept with many faces, and can even be indistinct and subject to change. But its "permanence" and its very existence in our thoughts is due to its being elevated to a necessary directing center. It directs "pure consciousness" and helps select the best-fitting one of the many momentary first impressions. Hence the existence and functioning of an ego reflect organization and the existence of an order, which point to a pivot therein that selects and directs.

In a similar vein Gordon Allport observed that Man's break with a reliance on instinct and his greater trust in the intellect required him to develop a focus on this new level. Man had to be able to transcend the bewildering complexity of millions of ways of adjusting. He thereby joined William James in observing that something was needed to regulate an enterprise that had become too unwieldy to regulate itself. James had set up consciousness as a monitor which later became changed to a self or an ego with the chief function of organizing and focusing, thereby preventing the dissipation of energy. Hence as living organisms, who tend to move away from disorganization (entropy), we "need" an ego to organize the energy and to prevent wasted application of this energy into many randomly chosen directions.

Therefore a conscious ego becomes a source of unity for the various facets of the mind. It sets the individual apart from the environment and may even oppose forces in it at times. Its important system function is to give the person internal unity. This thesis has been expanded through an ingenious explanation of the origins of the ego by Julian Jaynes. Jaynes has delved into the records and picture of ancient civilizations to prove that consciousness and a controlling self did not exist until the more intensive interaction of developing city states made this necessary around 300-200 B.C. Before that period people lived by the "bicameral mind", or by the separate and unrelated existence of the left and of the right brain which we now understand to be relatively autonomous centers with different functions. Language and causality is controlled by the left hemisphere which is usually dominant. The more emotion and (time/space) oriented powers located in the right hemisphere originated voices and visions in ancient Man before the unification of the two hemispheres by the "invention" of a conscious self. These experiences were attributed by pre-Hellenic peoples to the voices of the gods, especially since they were often triggered by stress, novelty and change, when the dominant left could not handle an event through rational thinking. Hence the right hemisphere of the brain was the location of the gods who also guided men and women and helped plan their actions in novel situations along with the voices of rational thoughts coming from the left hemisphere. The gods from the right represented Man's volition and told Man what to do through voices heard internally. Increased trade and expansion made it very difficult to understand these two sources of thought and action among the new peoples one met, and resulted in additional stress and in breakdown of communication. Consciousness and a sense of self were then spontaneously "invented" as a new and more efficient form of organization on the mental level. People no longer heard the voices from the right hemisphere as admonitions of the gods. They were now incorporated as part of a central self which more effectively guided people and helped each one to control his or her behavior and insure some conformity. One could rely on this integrated and superimposed (constructed) self rather than listen to two, often conflicting, voices; the dominant voice of one's intellect and reasoning from the left and the voices of the gods from the right. Gods became more external and further removed from each person and could be addressed at specified occasions by a self that could choose the time and place and the form of address.

In this way people could function more smoothly. A good deal of the earlier conflict and confusion was obliterated and energy was therefore saved. If Jaynes' colorful thesis is correct, he has shown us another way in which a living system moves to a higher and more integrated level and therefore saves energy, prevents disorganization and accumulates surplus energy for new tasks.

The chief reason why I am placing so much emphasis on the explanatory power of a directing ego center and on the general systems support for such a center is to answer the attacks on the ego from the Zen world and from some existentialists. The Zen position has been eloquently stated by Alan Watts. According to him the notion of an individual apart from his society and of an ego as a separate and directing part of this individual are all illusory. There is no natural order; and consistency in behavior is not necessary apart from its function as a social rule. We invent laws of human behavior artificially to create some order and then fool ourselves by the belief that it is truth and should be our goal. There is no causality or a natural order in nature -- only probability. Order and structure of the world are really cognitive structures which we have invented inside us about our world. The ego as an entity inside the skin acting apart from society is another fallacy. If we accept the real truth that we are really part of the social and physical environment, we must conclude that we do not have any control over nature. When we feel that we know ourselves or are controlling ourselves we are really controlled by the words and the gestures of others that are masquerading as our inner or better selves. The ego is therefore not a vital function, but an abstraction that arose from social influences laid down in our memories.

Watts therefore preaches that we have to try to fuse again with society rather than maintain the separate ego as a social fiction. Denial of the ego is the first healing action in the split between the individual and the world. Disavowal of purpose and the shedding of the illusion of control comes next. Genuine liberation through Zen Buddhism comes from the detachment from the ego as a unique thing which initiates or cares. This takes a great deal of work and self-discipline through meditation. One has to stop desire and the desire to stop desire. After several bouts of self denial one comes to the eventual idea that one does not care any more. Finally one reaches the stage where the sphere of what is (the world) and the sphere of one's feelings and desires about the world (the ego) are identical. At this stage one is aware that one cannot really control one's thoughts and feelings and one can let one's mind wander. Thoughts flow in intense concentration and become detached from time. A somewhat different prescription derives from some existentialists, who start with the same indictment of the ego as Watts does. For instance, Sartre considers the ego also as an artificial and non-vital abstraction. For him it is neither real nor functioning as an entity, but is seen as an illusion instead.

These principles have also found a lot of support among some contemporary artists and their supporters and admirers. Some composers and painters have insisted that chance must have as much or even a primary influence on their so-called creations. They sometimes spend a lot of effort to exclude any of their own ideas or direction, and they play down their craftsmanship and execution. Their work may truly flow out governed by the laws of chance and are perceived by the spectators as a random fabric of colors and noises. The spectator is, of course, allowed to impose his or her own organization on the happenstance of stimuli, but he must not show his or her own ordering, or attribute it to the artist.

Rollo May speculates that this call for a fusion with nature may be a reaction against the recent proliferation of industrialization, which may have disrupted Man's relationship with nature. As we have succeeded in the conquest and the exploitation of nature and have made it more objective and impersonal, we have also experienced greater loneliness and isolation. Many people have even separated themselves from human nature and have allowed themselves to become objects that are measured and analyzed. Perhaps the writings of Watts are a valid reaction to this trend, but they seem to throw the baby out with the bathwater. General Systems Theory seems to give us a new perspective here. Perhaps the persistent recurrence of the so-called "illusory" abstraction of an ego, over and over again, is no accident. The tendency of a living system to strive for organization and to move away from disorganization is illustrated by the importance and vitality of an ego on the personality level. One can only discuss the possibility of a goal of fusion and flow with the environment, if one disconnects the psychological level of functioning from the functions, forces and properties of a living system. We shall shortly take up again the transcendence of the ego as a legitimate investment of excess energy of a well-functioning ego.

The psychiatrist Robert Jay Lifton offers an interesting functional property of "experiential transcendence", which he derives from his many observations of the victims of holocausts and how they coped with death and destruction. In his attempt to integrate his findings into a theory of human coping, he sets up the state of this transcendence as one of five ways through which the human being expresses the sense and the need for immortality against his knowledge and fear of his own death. This psychic state can be so intense at times, that time and death seem to disappear. One can even appear to fuse with nature and with the environment, so that the self seems to vanish, and one is "losing oneself". This experience not only occurs in mystic moments, but also in dance, in battle, and in sexual love, or in the contemplation of something beautiful. It can produce a feeling of extraordinary psychological unity and perceptual intensity. It can change the person, because it enriches the person with a memory of an intense experience. It can even be felt as transcendence, or as death and rebirth. Seen in this light, the Zen prescription can provide a creative form of evading death anxiety and supply a compensatory strategy. It may even present a defensive maneuver on a very high level of creativity. However, it may represent an anaesthetizing illusion to believe in a permanent state of egoless fusion with nature. It may be soothing to numb one's impending death and decline, and it may impart feelings of immortality. However, it is only characteristic of one state or one ego process, in which there is momentarily no experienced ego. Nevertheless all of us including Watts are forced to revert to a state where ego is again experienced as a directing force, because we cannot stay in such a state of suspended animation by virtue of the life and energy forces at work in us as living organisms.

After these diversions we can conclude by first of all conceding that the ego is indeed an abstraction of a process rather than a visible organ. We can also admit that there is no definitive way of defining another person psychologically with accuracy at any given moment. Everything changes all the time and our behavior is at times unpredictable and uniquely constituted. Recent experiments on self-awareness have even shown that many of us "normal" people are not always accurately aware of ourselves, because we sometimes act in opposition to the descriptions we give of our behavior, when we are specifically asked to reflect on our values and preferences. Nevertheless the ego is a valid abstraction with some accurate representation for several reasons. The self is first of all very real in our experience of ourselves. We further acknowledge it as real and meaningful. First of all we are compelled to do so, because we are obeying the living system's forces towards organization and integration. This inevitable property of life requires a center or nucleus, brain, ego, at every level of interaction to escape disintegration (or entropy). Secondly, psychologists have learned to describe a person's self-concept quite accurately after studying the person through interviews, tests and observations of behavior. The inability to predict perfectly from this abstraction is merely another way of saying that the ego is an experienced entity for a given time which reflects some degree of consistency in the middle of a great deal of complexity and change.

We can also agree with the followers of Zen and with some existentialists -- that there is no real order in nature -- in the sense that events do occur by chance, such as which zebra is killed by the hungry lion, or which animal species is wiped out by a climatic change of a fungus disease in its food supply. However, General Systems Theory compels us to note that in each living animal there is organization that tries to integrate available energy and may move it to new levels of investment. Some of these may propel the animal to more complex levels of functioning. As we are animals with an ability to think and animals with an ability to think and manipulate our environment in our heads through symbols, we also organize our world and ourselves in it symbolically and for potential changes with greater complexity. The ego is a necessary device for integrating our cognitive capacities and giving them direction and commands for change, just as the nucleus is a necessary device for directing events at the cellular level, and the brain at the organ level.

People who ask us to fuse with nature permanently or to accept a purely random flow of thoughts, experiences and artistic productions may be playing a cruel hoax on us. They pull us away from our most vital birthright of the living organism, namely his built-in tendency and capacity to organize and direct. We may thereby cut ourselves off from our built-in capacities and fool ourselves that what is happening inside all of us is not really happening. It may be a hollow victory to provide people with a sense of happiness when they no longer accept their own internal organization and the products of that organization. It is like asking us to work with one arm tied to our back and accept this state as "normal". Not only do we give up the possibility to direct our fate and our likes and dislikes, but we also forfeit the joy that may accompany a well-done integrative effort. When enough people are then seduced into the illusion of being rudderless and floating happily in the sea of nature, they are acting like the emperor without clothes.

The principles of life as derived from General Systems Theory require the ego center to assume at least two important regulatory properties. One of these is to marshal and organize the available energy, so that there is no great danger of dissolution of the system or a fatal spillage of energy. In other words the ego also would tend to achieve a maximum degree of organization of parts and in that way stimulate the production of a surplus amount of energy that is not required to maintain and safeguard the organism. The other property rests in the ego's function to allow and direct the investment of surplus energy into new and uncharted waters for potential growth, or the transformation of (ego) components into a new and more complex state of integration. In this latter function we see our friend, autonomy, emerge again. Let us, however, look at the first function of organization to see how much evidence we can muster for it before we can support autonomous behavior on a more scientific basis. This baseline function will also become a foundation for our contention later on that the development of responsibility precedes and accompanies true autonomous behavior.

Already Kant recognized that the mind operates under definite ("a priori") principles of perceptual organization, by which it reacts and selects sensory experiences and perceptions and places them in some order -- that is, in some relationship to each other. He was thereby trying to oppose the skepticism of Hume about the existence of any other reality apart from its existence in our minds. He also thereby attacked Locke's idea that the mind was like a passive wax tablet (tabula rasa) which merely allowed outside impressions to deposit themselves on it. We, of course, now accept the idea that our minds form through exposure to our world, including parents, and through learning, but we add that we possess built-in methods of accepting stimuli, processing them, reacting to them, and selecting them. Thus we do not come with preformed ideas about sin, goodness, and our origin, but we do come with certain equipment and methods by which we react to the values we hear.

Kant predates modern cognition theory with its observations about the type of mental organization which our brain superimposes on the influx of stimuli. Kant assumed that pre-ordained principles akin to mathematical formulae were embedded in our minds to perform this work. He did not realize that life as a system requires this form of organization on all levels to sustain itself. We now understand that millions of randomly mixed bits of stimuli impinge on our external and internal sensory organs every second. If we paid attention to all of them for only five minutes, we would be completely exhausted by the energy needed to pay attention, order and process all that hits us. We would be so drained that we could no longer carry on our life-maintaining tasks, and would rapidly approach complete standstill, thereby reaching another state of equilibrium where all processes occur at random or without evident organization. This state is known as death! We all get into situations where we experience "stimulus overload" with its effects of headaches, anxiety, tension, and inefficiency. Just imagine what you would feel if you had to drive through heavy traffic while having to argue with your mother-in-law passenger, and while your two kids are fighting in the back seat!

To avoid these calamities we select sensory stimuli, we scan them against existing concepts or ideas in our brain to assign meaning and thereby organization to them, and we process them further in a more efficient manner. We can then ignore further impressions about the assigned concept as redundant information. For instance, our eyes might take in a certain shape of a head, a tail, two horns and a hairy covering of a shape. Immediately our actively working scanner inside the brain has found a concept that fits these few bits of information - namely "cow". At this point we can ignore all other impressions, such as other shape features, the expression of the eyes, the smell, details of color patterns, etc.. They become superfluous. We can thereby save further energy expenditure on orientation and identification. Our brain directs the gatekeepers along the sensory trail to filter out and block such impulses. If, however, we happen to be a livestock auctioneer at the buyer's market, we might instead alert our sensory equipment to open all channels wider, so that we also begin to perceive and process the animal's gait, outline features, dents and bulges in the skin, teeth and the appearance of the fur. We would then direct our sensory organs to lower the boom on all "non-relevant" stimuli, such as the landscape surrounding the animal, the people in the scene and the memory of the champagne dinner with the blonde the night before. Kant recognized implicitly that, rather than trying to find order out there in the world, there is order in the mind, and there the order must exist, or else it could not function as an integrated subsystem in a living organism,

The study of the acquisition of language with its grammar and vocabulary also reveals how much redundant information is embedded in the communication of this important medium. The redundancy allows our organizational equipment to function and each person select out the essence he needs. It is also impossible for us to formulate only those speech sounds that are strictly necessary to perceive a word properly. Our speech equipment includes a lot of extraneous sounds that surround or embed the key elements. We in turn learn to ignore the excess, For instance, we can and need to distinguish between the 'b' and the 'p' sound. But we ignore the many different 'b' sounds which each speaker constantly varies, depending on the use of the surrounding mouth muscles and the stretching of the vocal chords. Similarly we throw away a lot of speech in our processing as seen by the fact that "filtered speech" -- or speech re-recorded and spliced together in fragments half the time it took originally to say it after every half-second has been erased -- conveys the same meaning. Also we remember only the key ideas of a one hour lecture and cannot remember what the expert said and how he said it. These illustrations show that we process all the time. In other words, we select and impose an organization on the input as it reaches our sense organs and then travels to the brain.

Husserl also needed a principle of integration, even though he tried to approach our consciousness function from an experiential (or phenomenological) point of view. He even found it necessary to postulate a "drive towards consistency" that would encompass our need to increase our experiences and integrate them. He recognized already almost 100 years ago that life is not simply a random series of events, but that - on the ego level - it assumes patterns and emerges with meanings that were placed on them along the way. He called the energy-saving aspect of this manifestation of life "protensive" or having a time sequence) and thereby foresaw the organizing forces in the cognitive area which we now study under the category of "selective perception" (perception as an actively selecting process rather than a passive, reactive process).

Our need for organization to maintain order and efficiency is also seen in the judgment and thinking function, where we process our perceptions further. We are an animal that needs and looks for labels, for causes and for explanations. We need to "understand" and fit our impressions into ready-made templates or concepts that help us find meaning and help us select further appropriate responses. In other words we create "maps" of our world in our brains which include certain people and their characteristics, certain values and rules and ideas, and certain facts about ourselves (the self-concept). We may have marveled at the attempts mankind has made in classifying and cataloguing various aspects of nature and human activity. Many of us are made happy or at least feel reassured and at peace, if we can assign a name to a strange plant, animal or lake. Of course with that label may go other facts, such as whether the animal can fly or crawl, what species it belongs to, whether it is dangerous or not, what behavior is characteristic of it and what tales may be associated with it.

Finding causes and names are therefore part of our heritage as an energy-saving living system. (As we shall see later this ability also allows us to take a vacation from causality and to escape into new and non-ordered territory.) The searches for explanations are especially noteworthy when our system is severely threatened by catastrophe, attack, conflict and other disorganization. Often our interaction with nature or with other people, and our exposure to fate is severely unshaken by unexpected or novel situations that do not call forth ready-made blueprints for explanation and action in our "map". We can indeed be severely threatened by ambiguity, uncertainty, or lack of adequate knowledge. Some people may store additional plans to take care of such surprises. The concept of a god, the idea of fate, the acceptance of human powerlessness are all examples of ideas by which we may "organize" the world to take out the sting from its "surprises". In this way they have acquired meaning and make the act of explanation not as frightening and disorganizing for us. Also one may say: "I cannot understand this event and reorganize it, but the king, God, fate, or someone is there and does it for me". This solution implies giving up one's autonomy and subjecting oneself to others for the peace of mind that such as "explanation" now provides. Of course even the most autonomously functioning person must often foreshorten his rather endless search for answers and give his perceptions such order. The very belief in one's freedom and the consciousness of acting or thinking by one's choice may be seen as an attempt to organize one's thoughts around oneself as center, and as a way of assigning further meaning and order to one's behavior. For instance people who do not feel free may die by their own hands or by slowing down their various functions. This phenomenon has been observed among captives, depressed people or widows and widowers who have defined themselves as inseparably bound with the spouse.

Perhaps it may come as a surprise to the reader if we recognize faith as a necessary and universal human mechanism that is geared towards the conservation of energy. Faith in God, or in a group, or in a doctrine, or in a national ideal or in the goodness of Man are all ways of organizing our approach to nature and to mankind. They help us in assigning meaning to seemingly incomprehensible phenomena and to the wealth of conflicting data that are not yet tied together by some verifiable explanation. They cushion shock and surprises, especially if they go against immediately available explanations. For instance faith in God's wisdom may cushion the shock of the death of a friend who was the paragon of virtue. Or faith in the eventual triumph of democracy may soften the news of a vicious crime perpetrated by a respected public figure. Our faith in the love of our friends, in the stability of institutions, in the constancy of natural events all help us in establishing a sense of order in this often so randomly constituted world. Developing and nurturing a faith is our attempt to organize that world. Faith by definition is a belief that does not rest on hard-boiled or "scientific" evidence. In view of the energy-dissipating effects of holding back with explanations, or waiting until all the facts are in, we cannot maintain uncertainty and doubt for very long without suffering the consequences of chaos or "entropy" on the psychological level. Hence we develop faiths, and anchor these by sharing them with others and ritualizing them in concrete behaviors.

General Systems Theory therefore allows us to look upon faith as a very necessary human accompaniment, without which we would not be able to contain the disarray and lack of meaning that would reign instead. While we have been attacking certain faiths in previous chapters as obstacles to human autonomy, we are saying here that a faith or several faiths are part of the necessary human equipment. This is not a contradiction. We still have the choice to pick our faith or faiths. We can and should pick a faith that does not inhibit normal human development through the stages available to the personality. Nor should this faith endanger the exercise of self-realization. Preferably there should be some agreement about the evidence supporting it. One should also be willing to subject one's faith to occasional scrutiny and to find support in repeatable observations of its veracity. We shall attempt the enumeration of some faiths later on which have not violated the potential of autonomous functioning and which can support programs for its encouragement.

When we extol the virtues of perceptual organization, of causal thinking and of faith, we may also be able to recognize an old friend from physiology: homeostasis, or the tendency for an organism to maintain a stable and beneficial equilibrium in the body. The achievement of such an equilibrium for the sake of maintaining life-supporting processes was discovered in physiology when scientists studied temperature control, attacks on disease-carrying organisms, heart action, and coping with tensions. In all of these homeostatic processes a reaction may be started by a change in the existing equilibrium until the system returns to normal levels. This phenomenon of course also occurs on the psychological level. Here too a certain stability is required if the organism is to function effectively. Coping mechanisms develop to bring the person back to a homeostatic level of stable functioning when he is disturbed by excessive change, novelty, excessive stimulation, or attack. We only need to remember how disconcerting and even incapacitating it can be if we are not able to establish some order or some degree of certainty. During uncertainty, for example, we may experience anxiety and conflict, and we may eventually exhibit the debilitating symptoms of prolonged conflict. Energy is literally dissipated here to deal with such conflict and is not available for new or even familiar ventures. We are and feel drained and exhausted. Also we can again support the conclusions we presented earlier on the need for a logical sequence in personality development. One's home must be in order internally, before one can "spin off" into new directions. Stability and homeostasis precedes any attempts at autonomous self-expansion.

In order to illustrate the spin-off of new processes from a baseline of homeostasis, we can take off with one of Rollo May's criticisms of Freud's ideas about personality. Freud's explanation of neurosis based on the operation of rigid and predetermined causes also became the prototype for many analysts for the explanation of all human experiences. Rollo May (<u>Love and Will</u>) criticizes this formulation as being too narrow. He asserts that an individual sees new possibilities when he becomes conscious of what he is doing. Experimentation introduces an element of personal responsibility and of "freedom". This idea reminds us both of Maslow's observations about self-actualization and of the general systems prediction of potential changes to ever more complex patterns of relationships for the psychological level. Rollo May illuminates the potential complexities by pointing to the human dilemma (<u>Psychology and the Human Dilemma</u>) of having the almost simultaneous capacity to experience oneself as a subject -- wanting, wishing and feeling -- and to experience oneself as an object -- being manipulated by others. Our consciousness therefore oscillates between the two possibilities, and "freedom" becomes the capacity to experience both modes. This freedom is a more complex experience of the two modes, rather than a new state that is switched on and remains. The actual incorporation of this freedom mode requires a vacillation in view of the existential problem of experiencing two modes and in view of the fact that we experience the problems of death, dependency etc. in our consciousness.

The process of arriving at new integrations within the ego, when surplus energy allows an expansion of involvements, is further illustrated by borrowing the boundary concept from General Systems Theory. James E. Durkin has pointed out that the reception and influx of, for instance, very positive feelings from another person involves the momentary break in the ego's boundaries of both people. In this way the emotions can flow between them and allow one or both to expand their ego function, by incorporating the love and respect from another human being.

The opening and closing of ego boundaries in the process of growth or expansion also finds an echo in the observations of Martin Buber and Andras Angyal. The former graphically described the opening of boundaries in the creative encounter, in which it is possible for a person to "lose oneself" in the free experience of another person without having formed any preconceptions about the person. In this I-thou experience boundaries must be opened so that the person now fully lives in the present encounter. All his input channels are then open to the other. In the I-it mode of relating by contrast, the boundaries around a person are strictly drawn and guarded. The person utilizes only the past and organizes or interprets, in order to avoid the enrichment -- and also the possible dangers -- of further involvement. In the I-thou stage the dissolution of boundaries allows an investment of surplus energy into another person. It can also lead to some exhaustion and to a "blindness" to other needs, such as hunger and safety, at least for a short while. Andras Angyal similarly observed that self-expansion is possible in a self-governing organism endowed with the potentials of spontaneity. This ability presupposes opposing forces in the living human being. One is a trend to autonomy for which energy is mobilized rather than dissipated. It characterizes the person as a self-governing entity who is able to select, choose, adapt, regulate itself and regenerate. Life in this mode is not only oriented to preservation, but goes beyond the status quo or beyond homeostasis. The tendency towards autonomy is exemplified by mastery over the environment, by conquest and achievement. The opposing trend for Angyal is the need to be at harmony with super individual units, such as society, nature, world order, a nation, or God. He calls this tendency towards fusion, belongingness or self-submersion: Homonymy. She describes a dynamic equilibrium between these opposing forces rather than an antagonism.

These complex and temporary plateaus of dynamic equilibrium are adequately explained by the change and expansion of ego boundaries, and by the fusion and more complex integration of new relationships and the self-exposure to new ideas. Hence general systems laws can explain and illuminate the various dilemmas and their resolution which different existentialist writers have described as characteristic concerns of Man, such as the concern with the meaning of life and of existence, the struggle between freedom and self-submission, and the simultaneous contemplation of other opposing forces. The struggles described in the existential literature become recognized stages in Man's development. Each one first produces conflicts between opposing questions (dialectical forces) which may be followed by a synthesis or integration. This in turn expands the horizon to provide a temporary harmony. The energy that has previously been expended on the existential struggle may now be available as (surplus) energy for a new involvement or for tackling another dilemma. Thus further growth is possible. General Systems Theory thus lends a scientific validity to existential struggles which were first proposed as explanations for the fragmentation of Man noted by the early students of personality. It does so by giving them the status of levels of development found in life processes. However, existential writers could not agree on the relative importance of the existential fears and crises, and also did not connect the human personality with underlying structures, such as brain states and physiological events.

General Systems Theory therefore points the way towards defining the forces operating in an ego that can expand, break its own boundaries, take in new complexities, and integrate them all at a more complex level of organization. Since this is not a haphazard process -- as we have seen in the last two chapters -- we can see evidence of organization and of control at work. We are therefore forced to assume and find an organizing force or center. Furthermore this ego center generates forces towards self-expansion and growth, and these forces are synonymous with autonomy. They are not blind and automatic reactions to disturbances, and they are not the built-in exertion of homeostatic control against threat. They represent the application of surplus energy into new investments, not through random squirting, but by some directed and goal-oriented exertion. This view gives human autonomy roots in the laws of life, as viewed from a scientific perspective.

However, this surplus energy can also be undirected, so that it does not require a return that might guarantee or benefit the maintenance of the organism. By its definition as surplus energy it can literally be squandered, in which case gratification may come from the very exercise of this process and from the exuberance of doing so. Maslow pointed out that self-actualizing people are not striving in the ordinary sense, and sometimes do not seem to be "going anywhere". Hence they are capable of seemingly unmotivated actions, such as found in art wonder, joy, mystic experiences and play. In this context Lifton proposes two processes available to the ego by which it can organize life and connect past with future. One is called centering versus decentering. Centering is the buildup of the self by adorning it with various attributes around a core from such areas as work, play, sexuality, relation to society, etc. This allows one to feel "at the center of things" and to feel properly located in the world. Decentering then becomes a very necessary complementary part in the process, because there also has to be a detachment from one's involvements. In this way one can encounter the new and judge new events and issues for possible changes in ego boundaries. Decentering is a temporary suspension of the integration and is synonymous with "losing oneself", but it is necessary or the self becomes static and unable to change. The second ego process is grounding, or the connection between the self and its own history including one's social and biological history. Grounding again allows decentering to occur, because the latter involves anxiety, risk and even some inner chaos. A fluid centering-decentering equilibrium can bring about the experience of transcendence and allow one to have mystical or peak experiences. Lifton who has studied the survivors of holocausts, attributes their psychic numbness and alienation to an impairment of grounding in which the present no longer "makes sense".

General Systems principles about life therefore become a model for the human personality, in which energy-production is more typical than energy-consumption. Man is therefore not merely a reactor to stimuli, like a slot-machine, who soaks up energy just to process and maintain various functions, although he can and does function on that level. A stimulus-response model such as the one proposed by Skinner or a tension-reduction model proposed by Freud are therefore inadequate. The facts of cognitive organization of sensory experiences, the selectivity of perceptions, the investment of selective energies into the environment and into relationships are all evidence of a process in the personality that contains an organizing center which also initiates direction. In other words we require a model of Man that contains an ego or self as center which also is capable of initiating on its own; that is, exercising autonomy. Hence Allport's autonomy of motives and Maslow's succession of motivational stages can fit under such a model. Similarly Roger's drive of enhancement of the self can be seen as an essential characteristic of a living process that is constantly pushing for expression, until a new level of minimal disorganization or chaos forms by "mutation". Furthermore the verified emergence of autonomous functioning in this living system justifies democracy as a proper substratum, because it allows many more people to organize their lives by their own mental powers without having to spend their energy to preserve themselves against threat, or to spend energy to repress the spin-offs of surplus forces.

Finally the very recognition of autonomy as a force in stages of personality development and the emergence of a democratic society in history as a growing medium for this autonomy all illustrate again that new stages can evolve in life, as predicted by General Systems Theory. We can again recognize further support for an organismic view of Man, insofar as we can demonstrate a succession of changes both in individual Man and in the evolution of his social organizations. These changes are a succession of levels of organization which cannot be predicted from past levels or from the components of the new level. They are not caused by adding new components to the old level. Even though we can never predict the changes, we can understand them as manifestations of life, thereby obeying principles of life and of life processes. Hence these principles help us to understand, and illustrate growth, evolution and the new combination of components at a new stage of integration. They give promise to the possibility that we can perhaps succeed in solving the very problems which we also create as by-products of newly integrated solutions, such as the bad "side-effects" of democracy that may accompany the official recognition of human autonomy... as we shall try to show later on.

Chapter IX

Democracy as the Political Base of Human Autonomy

One of the important theses of this volume is that our discoveries of autonomous functioning in personality -- like all important scientific discoveries -- would not have been possible without some important nutrient in the development of Man. One of the most important fertilizers for the various discoveries in Chapter VI was the creation and practice of political democracy. We have many examples of how an enriched soil facilitated the germination of important scientific knowledge. The increase in sea travel on more sea-worthy vessels and the need for finding more raw materials to support an expanding lifestyle in the Renaissance helped to spark and then verify the idea that the earth was round, and that it represented one of several planets that rotated around the sun. The discovery of the microscope and the growing problems with communicable diseases in increasingly complex and interdependent city states stimulated the discovery of bacteria from such pioneers as Pasteur and Semmelweis. The greater tolerance for an individualized relationship with God without the interference of an authoritarian church laid the groundwork for Darwin's discoveries about evolution and stimulated a more naturalistic view about the development of life. This in turn led to a more thorough search into Man's ancestry and development and helped to build anthropology.

Freedom in History

Besides the democratic experiments in the Greek city states of antiquity democracy as we know it is a relatively modern idea. It germinated in the freedoms introduced by the Renaissance, was nurtured through a number of revolutions against absolute rulers, and became refined through the experiences of the Industrial Revolution. The so-called democracies of ancient Greece were not really like republics in which elected representatives make the decisions. Decisions in ancient Greece were made by the debate and vote of all assembled citizen on certain days. Administrators were chosen by lot from among free citizens. This form of popular expression of opinion was possible in cities or small states of less than 10,000 inhabitants, where it was possible to convene the citizen at certain occasions. However, it did not rest on notions of equality, because only free men could express their wishes and could vote on decisions. Women, minorities and slaves were considered in a class below. The majority, therefore, had no voice and no vote, and could be ruled without ever being consulted. According to Hegel, the inhabitants only knew that some people were free, but not that Man was free. Therefore, their liberty had only an accidental and transient growth and was easily usurped by strong leaders and by invading armies.

After the Reformation and the Renaissance ushered in new religious, scientific and social concepts, philosophers began to reexamine the old ideas of divine blessings for kings and members of the aristocracy. Men like Hobbes, Locke, Kant and Hegel began to realize that rulers practiced a form of anarchy, insofar as they felt themselves to be above any law and above any legally constituted government. Even though they might claim allegiance to God, they really admitted no superior and did not accept the commands and suggestions from anyone else. Therefore, they really lived as though they were in the more random state of nature. According to Kant they lived "like lawless savages". They introduced randomness by following their own whims. Even though they superimposed their whims on their fiefdoms and organized people accordingly, this form of personal capriciousness did not allow any kind of stable organization to form within their state.

Therefore in his contemplations Kant bestowed three inseparable rights to the citizen. The first was a constitutional freedom which gave the citizen the right to obey only those laws to which he had consented. The second was equality or the recognition that no one among civil authorities was superior to any other citizen. The third was the citizen's right to political independence. One's existence in society was based on one's own powers and rights as a member, and not on the arbitrary will of another. Hegel ventured that the idea of Man's essential freedom arose in the Germanic states with the consciousness in religion that Man was free to communicate with God without an intermediary. This reform -- brought on by Martin Luther -- freed the spirit of Man and expanded it so that a start could be made in examining the purpose of the state and civil government.

Hobbes in 1650 also made the far-reaching observation that absolute liberty for each person to use his own power to prepare his life and his nature belongs only in a condition of natural existence. When Man leaves this situation and enters into a social organization, he surrenders that natural liberty for a "civil liberty", meaning freedom to do what the laws of the state do not forbid, or to omit what the law does not command. This concept introduced the idea of a social contract between people, but was still too limiting a concept for contemporary evaluations. Locke in 1690 expanded this notion by showing that democracy implies giving up part of one's power to the majority of the citizens for the sake of uniting them into a society. When one consents to allow one's elected representatives to govern, one gives up some liberty and responsibility to the society. In turn one enjoys the privileges and the protection provided by the laws one has helped to shape. In Chapter XI we shall see how this conformity with the majority is embedded in more complex moral concepts that lawfully develop in the personality in parallel with the development of self-actualizing behavior.

The French and American revolutions finally destroyed the whole notion that established regimes and social organizations were either sacred or inevitable. People developed some hope that they could build more just and perfect societies with the aid of idealism and reason. Even though the Industrial Revolution destroyed some of the idealism, the use of reason and law strengthened some of the democracies with relevant ideas that came from the contemplation of the basic nature of Man. This we shall try to elaborate on below.

Hegel saw the widening separation between state and church as a new development toward maturity in the history of mankind. In addition, personal experiences of liberty were becoming identified with universal ends, and both of them were subjected to more rational analysis. From this people emerged with a realization that their own feelings of selfhood were only assured stability if they were recognized as public goals shared with other people. Nevertheless Hegel justified the state as a supreme unit over and above the individual, and further revealed his political conservatism by favoring a hereditary monarch.

The British philosopher John Locke added a much more revolutionary concept in 1690. His essays on government refuted the doctrine of "divine right" and established the proposition that men are "created equal" with regard to authority. He therefore questioned the rights of governments to demand obedience from the consciences of men. These ideas had a profound effect on Thomas Jefferson and influenced the achievement of independence by the United States, as we shall see below. Mills added the idea in the middle of the 19th Century that it was the privilege of the human being as part of his normal functioning to use and interpret his own experience once his faculties had matured. Each person had the right to find out how his own and other people's experiences in history were properly applicable to his own circumstances and character. Other people's customs may be consulted and may provide evidence of what their experience had taught them. On the other hand, if a person merely followed the customs of others, he did not have to make a choice, and thereby neglected his own extensive endowment of human faculties. Mental powers had to be exercised like muscles to become developed and improved, and the state had to recognize these facts and provide maximal opportunities.

We see here the beginnings of the same ideas that sent personality psychologists and clinicians into the fuller discoveries about the nature of self-actualization. It is not surprising that a social climate of freedom and of innovation leads men into the discovery and fuller realization of what is already theirs, because they are living organisms functioning on a cognitive-experiential level and living according to the laws of psychology and of living systems. We are again reminded of the points in Chapter II in which we saw that proper technology and economic conditions must prevail before Man can lift his sweating brow from the toil of securing his food and his security. A further proof of the importance of necessary preconditions for the contemplation of freedom and personal autonomy comes from the experiences of many of the developing nations in our present world. Newly liberated countries or countries substantially supported and coached by Western democracies do not develop Western-style democracies. In fact, we have heard the complaint from these developing nations that human rights are a rich country's "luxury". Survival is such a crucial concern in many places that it takes first place over human rights.

The Constitution of the United States as an Example

The Declaration of Independence in 1776, the Constitution of the United States as ratified in 1789, and the Bill of Rights enacted in 1791 are amazing documents in the history of mankind. They are not only amazing in view of Man's thinking and development in this period of his history, but they are amazing also as documents that have endured and even inspired people in the 200 years since. This duration also attests to the possibility that Man, given his basic nature, may be able to fashion a complex, well-functioning society from these principles. Perhaps many of the ideas expressed in these documents can be attributed to the general revolt against irrational authority that became so prevalent in the British colonies in the New World. Perhaps they owed even more to the great men and thinkers that discussed and framed these documents over many months and years. Perhaps they owed some influence to the extensive feedback from a whole variety of reactions from the representatives and legislators of the 13 original states when they took issue with different provisions of the drafts from their respective traditions and laws. All of these factors affected the framing of these documents and the people who finally voted for them.

Underneath all this turmoil and debate at the birth of the American constitution we can find two other important sources of influence. One is the ever-present inspiration from Man's own sense of either having achieved or being capable of achieving an autonomous state of functioning as part of his basic development. This represents the thesis of this book. The second source is the formulation of some of the principles as rights and political concepts from philosophers over the ages as we have indicated above. Perhaps three philosophers are more immediately recognizable in the American documents, whose architects have acknowledged their debt to these philosophers in their writings. One was the French philosopher Rousseau whose ideas also influenced European revolutions so enormously. Government for Rousseau was a social contract between men to insure the natural rights of freedom, happiness and equality as much as possible. These were present in the natural or savage state, but might be obliterated by the wrong government. Therefore, people had a right to change their government when it violated these "natural rights". Thus he ushered in the democratic principle that people had the right to live under the government of their own choice and to choose officials that can carry out its function. Locke reiterated the idea that men had "natural rights", particularly those pertaining to life, liberty and progress. Therefore, government was not established by God, but by men to protect these rights. Consequently men had the right to revolt against any government that failed to do its duty. Finally the philosopher Montesquieu argued eloquently for the benefits that accrue when the government is divided into an executive, a legislative and a judicial function. Despite the idealistic sentiments from the philosophers, they were overshadowed by the actual deeds of the creative and autonomous statesmen who built successful governments and wrote workable constitutions out of the shambles of the revolutions. They operated within their own faith in mankind. The early philosophers cited above were not in favor of full democracy, because they distrusted the decisions coming from everybody. They worried that certain people were not ready to govern or vote. Rousseau, for instance, felt that democracy was only appropriate for very small states, while men like Locke, Hobbes, and Montesquieu were afraid that too much freedom could become a divisive force and lead to corruption.

It is not necessary here to summarize the documents underlying the American nation. We might only remind ourselves of two important segments that are relevant to our thesis regarding autonomy. The first comes from the second paragraph of the Declaration of Independence: "We hold these truths to be self-evident, that all men are created equal, that they are endowed by their Creator with certain unalienable rights, that among these are life, liberty, and the pursuit of happiness. That, to secure these rights, governments are instituted among men, deriving their powers from the consent of the governed,…" Representative government introduced the really novel idea that special people are periodically elected and then exercise the ultimate controlling power during their tenure. They, therefore, replaced arbitrary, hereditary, and permanent rulers. The second reminder is an overview of some of the provisions of the Bill of Rights, or of the first 10 amendments. They include among others the freedom of religion, freedom of speech and of assembly, and freedom of petitioning for grievances; security against unreasonable searches and seizures; protection from one's deprivation of life, liberty, and property without due process of the law; and a speedy trial by jury. Later slavery was abolished, and the right to vote was expanded to anyone regardless of race, color, or sex. Eventually all of these rights and the basic principles of freedom, equality, and due process of the law have been incorporated into other democratic constitutions of the Western world. Sometimes they have evolved into different forms of democratic expressions and into different governmental practices.

The Basic Principles about the Autonomous Nature of Man

Besides faith and belief, a number of important values were incorporated in the documents that construct modern democratic governments. One of these is the value of life itself, which is considered a sacred trust. It cannot be sacrificed to the whims of a dictator or to anyone else with the power to manipulate or shorten life. The belief in the sanctity of life is most critically applied to the life of Man. It is even often carried over to animals. While no one condemns the murder of a mosquito buzzing around one's head, we are concerned about the "humane" killing of the animals we eat or use in science, and we reject the torture of animals. We can, therefore, identify a related value, namely, the essential worth of a person and of his life. This value is sometimes expanded to mean the dignity of the human being. In this context, the achievement of the person in his work and roles, the amount of tax he pays and his intelligence are not used to evaluate a person's right to help out in the governing process. Even the pauper and the mentally retarded person living in the community -- and, more recently, the mental patient -- is allowed a vote. While this provision creates a few problems at times, inevitable evils and chances for fraud would arise if tax records, intelligence tests, or psychiatrist's judgments would be introduced to determine the eligibility to vote. We shoulder the problems, because we give first priority to the idea that human life is sacred and worthy, and to the conclusion that any man is as "good" as the next one. In other words, we value the person because he is alive. We listen to him and his needs and we give him the right to have these needs and to express them. Beyond that we give him some basic "human" opportunities to foster and express his needs, as long as they do not hurt us and others. Here we can recognize a value about individuality, or that life has its own trajectories that are legitimate and perhaps worthwhile -- first for the person himself, and later perhaps to more people and to society at large.

Equality is therefore bestowed on everybody on the basis of being born human. These formulations do not recognize any special privilege or power due to wealth or breeding. Mills already recognized in 1859 that this assumption is not only the most just, but that it is perfectly suited to the nature of Man. In other words, these values are projections of the principles of surplus energy in the living system. They are therefore reflections of our own experiences, or projections from our own basic nature. Even though men in history first attributed them to the inspiration of the gods or to their revelations, they did so because they did not dare acknowledge them to represent their own reflections and conclusions. Since everything else seemed too uncertain and chaotic, it seemed safer to entrust these principles to a god and then accept them as coming from an outside authority, rather than from the most unpredictable aspect of existence, namely from the self. We can now recognize these ideas as being rooted in the very nature of life itself at the human or psychological level.

Not only is this proclamation of the worthiness of individuality a value based on scientific evidence, it also can be seen as a stimulant to human progress and development. Mills already in 1859 pointed out that individuality diversifies and enriches both individual lives and society. As a person becomes more valuable to himself with the development of his individual capacities, he also becomes more valuable to society, or at least to people around him. His own expression of individuality may help others or solve some problems, and his increased faith in himself may provide strength and inspiration to others.

The Guarantees of one's own Freedom and of Protection from Harm

The right to one's own thoughts and feelings have certainly been guaranteed by the development of laws and constitutions. Heresy is no longer a problem, nor is it subject to prosecution or punishment. Actions are also free as long as they do not violate a law. In other words, one's actions are free as long as one does not abridge the freedom of others. Since a person is protected from the hurtful actions of others -- unlike the person living in a free, lawless association of human beings -- his sphere of safety is widened, so that he can invest himself into a whole new variety of pursuits without the fear of being attacked capriciously.

These provisions and concepts do not, however, guarantee absolute freedom, if by that we mean engaging in so-called autonomous acts that are not monitored by reason or self-reflection, or those that are attached to the immature or incomplete expression of needs. Hence in America it is still possible to lock up people for a variety of reasons, either for their own benefit or for the protection of society. Also the reasons may not at all be related to crime. One can, for instance, be quarantined if one suffers from a communicable disease. Or one may have committed a deviant act that may fall into the category of "mental illness" and set in motion commitment procedures and treatment. The big point here is, however, that such deprivation of freedom cannot occur unless it follows legal procedures. In other words, laws and rules must exist that spell out the reasons and the procedures for the abridgment of freedoms.

Another restriction is inherent in the acceptance of the rule by the majority. At the moment at which we agree with this principle we lose some liberty if we find ourselves in the minority, whether this refers to the amount of taxes, or to participation in a war or in the sacrifice of certain goods in a rationing program. However we comply often quite willingly and rationally because the whole concept of democracy and its basis in human rights is built on rational ideas. These, in turn, are an outgrowth of that phase in human development in which we are capable of employing our various powers, including rationality, for autonomous self-fulfillment. Nevertheless, we have written so many additional safeguards into our constitution and our laws that there is not as much danger that the tyranny of a majority might replace a tyranny of an absolute ruler. For instance, our guarantee of the freedom of speech and assembly tries to insure the continual expression of minority views. We even allow opposition to war through certain well-defined channels of expression, thus not coercing people to support a war. We elect our representatives often enough so that minority influence can be exerted again and again. We allow our elected representatives to make decisions through their own conclusions rather than have them abide by "party loyalty", and we keep the channels to them open enough for people to influence these representatives. We also have built up various channels for the expression and communication of minority of different views to government representatives, such as lobbies, letter writing, and media publicity. Of course, we have to maintain constant vigilance that the wealthy do not preempt the media and the channels of influence to bring about a tyranny of the minority.

Equality and Freedom as Positive Faiths

As we have already noticed the philosophers of the Renaissance perceived the growing importance of the freedoms of Man, especially his need to be free from arbitrary government. They arrived at the idea of freedom through the examination of the concept of "free will" as a necessary characteristic of reason and intellect. They compared "free choice" in nature with the limited choices established through social consent. Civil law may therefore have a limiting effect on liberty, but freedom should not be restricted by a superior power on earth. They also argued that natural laws limit freedom. For instance the laws of gravity make it impossible to "fall up". Freedom then becomes the ability of an individual to make his own choices as long as these choices are not prescribed by laws of nature or by laws of his own state with which he has consented.

This rational definition of freedom was further expanded to include a freedom to move to one's own maximum development. Mill already defined freedom in more positive terms than by naming it as the state that was merely free of coercion and limitation. Freedom instead was a ticket to individuality or the chance to be different and to go where one's talents and tastes took one -- as long as one did not hurt others. Mill's realization that individuality should be one of the important ingredients of happiness antedates the discourse of personality psychology. His proclamation that this same individuality was indispensable to the welfare of society antedates the knowledge we have gained from General Systems Theory. As we saw in chapter VIII, the availability of surplus energy from the inner forces of a living system like Man helped build modern civilization.

It is equally remarkable that the so-called truths of equality and freedom were considered "self-evident" in the Declaration of Independence. They were proclaimed on faith alone rather than on certain knowledge. The rights were built on religious principles which were at one time used to stifle such rights. Hence the whole early fabric of democratic values rested on a new faith, namely on a faith in the potentials, strengths, rationality and development of the average human being. First, democracy embodied the belief that all people are capable at some point in their development of exercising a free and rational will. Secondly, it was tied to a faith in a developing sense of autonomy that results in beneficial action for the person and for society, because it also uses rational, adult powers in its exercise. Concretely, the faith translated itself into a firm belief that human character can rise above pure self-interest and take other people and their needs into account. It can rise up to the task of government. This faith translates into a belief in the potentiality for human maturity and responsibility.

Next, this faith was translated into a doctrine, a right, and into an educational focus. There also was the realization that absolute rule and dictatorship rests on the opposite belief, namely that men cannot govern themselves, that they remain dependent children in need of guidance, and that a wise and strong father figure knows best and has the duty and the right to take control. Eventually machinery was added to take into account lapses in human maturity or the inability of some people to rise up to the levels predicted by these faiths. The impeachment proceedings in our constitution and our libel laws are examples. More recent examples are the new rules for the Congress and state legislatures in the conduct of their business -- like the "sunshine laws" -- and the provisions for censure.

Nowadays it is no longer so remarkable that these democratic values and principles were made on faith alone. As we saw in chapters VI - VIII, various observers schooled in scientific methods have substantiated that the potential exercise of free choice can lead to the betterment of Man and of society. They have established this exercise to be typical of a lawful stage in human development and the beneficial effects of freedom and equality are indeed based on the laws regarding life and human functioning. Hence the bold proclamations of these principles were not merely capricious experiments which people wanted to explore after they had gotten tired of tyranny. They can now be supported as more basic truths, because they have been found to be relevant to an understanding of Man's basic nature, and are necessary as stimulants to this nature. These ideas existed already then because people at that time had glimpses of these truths from their own experiences and from an inner consciousness of these laws.

The Promise Of Human Autonomy

There is another and important implication for democracy which derives from our better understanding of adult personality. We have seen in Chapter VI and VIII that the ego or self is an important structure that not only emerges as the required director of life forces, but is also recognized by the individual as an important anchoring focus within himself. Self-definition (ego-identity) and self-enhancement are therefore normal processes in personal growth. They require room for application and for recognition from others. It is for these reasons that we need to recognize the importance of everyone and of his drive for self-definition. We therefore need to give everyone some form of recognition for reasons quite apart from the usual religious and humanitarian ones.

George Mead (<u>Mind, Self, and Society</u>) in 1934 speculated on these processes and concluded that everyone needed to feel superior on some level in order to separate himself from others. Subsequent personality psychologists, including some of the people we mentioned earlier, were stimulated by the social philosopher Mead and acknowledged his visions as important signposts in their search for a better understanding of Man. Mead realized that we distinguish ourselves from others by doing something others cannot do or cannot do as well. We may therefore identify with an "ingroup" against an "outgroup" and wind up extolling our community and our nation. Mead hoped that this separation and realization of the self could be done on a social and non-egotistic way. If we can recognize these tendencies for self-elevation and make allowances for them and even further these tendencies, we might promote growth and an orderly progression in individual development.

Democracy provides an exemplary climate for this growth, because of its emphasis on the worth of the individual and of his contribution to society. Democracy recognizes this "selfishness", properly identified by Mead, as a legitimate claim of the person for recognition and for his injection of his needs into the public domain. Democracy provided people with a variety of avenues of self-expression, so that it even allows people to claim their superiority by either sitting atop a flagpole, swimming across 60 miles of treacherous ocean, collecting match covers, or jumping across a gorge in a motorcycle. In all other forms of government, and in communism as we shall see in the next chapter, this need for the individual to define himself as special is often frustrated and even forbidden. It is viewed as a dangerous tendency for the person to claim too much space around himself which might give him further ideas about his freedoms and needs. The best he can achieve in his drive towards self-definition is to be a member of a superior group or nation. As we have learned from history, this form of self-submersion leads frequently to conflict and warfare between groups.

The Need for Education to Secure both a General Understanding and a Sense of one's Responsibilities

The rule by a majority to satisfy its major needs is only successful if the majority of the people are involved in the government process. This means that they should be motivated in self-government and therefore need to understand the principles underlying their own government: that is, the principles of their constitution and their laws. John Stuart Mill put this idea into a slightly different perspective by pointing out how an uninformed or uninterested citizen becomes a passive audience. He felt that political power educates and stimulates people to become actively interested participants, which is not always true today for various reasons (see Chapter XII). He attributed this active involvement to the conscious realization that one has become a member of a great community which requires a certain amount of education. He is right on target with our own conclusions when he equates active people with people who have developed a stage of autonomy where they can create surplus energy and can invest this into governmental processes in a democracy. Hence autonomy can be encouraged and even insured in a democracy. The value placed on the individual life helps promote opportunities for education and for self-development which might provide opportunities to exercise the emerging autonomy. This in turn promotes character development.

There must, of course, exist some understanding of the issues that come up, so that people can evaluate the outcome, the performances of its elected representatives, and the governing process itself. Otherwise there is the danger that minorities or even a single dominant figure may wrest the process of government away from the majority and subvert the democratic principles. We have seen this sequence in operation in a number of newly created nations in the past 50 years. A Western-style democratic constitution may have been initially created or supplied by the country of previous ownership, only to be subverted into a dictatorship sooner or later. We have even witnessed the development of a tyranny with its senseless suppression of people and rights. Even wholesale massacres have been possible. In all such instances the rate of literacy was low to begin with, and the people were not properly aware of the principles, advantages and responsibilities of self-government. This is why it was also not possible to have democracies before the advent of printing and cheap books. The only exceptions were the Greek democratic city states, but here the free men had achieved such a high degree of learning and culture -- thanks to their many slaves -- that they could intelligently make the decisions at the assemblies in the marketplace.

Where democracy has succeeded, it has done so in places when compulsory education has made people aware of the machinery by which they can translate their wants into programs that can then be entrusted to their elected representatives. Further knowledge was required to influence them in a certain direction and to monitor their performance. An educational system that explains the checks and balances, and a public relations system that can spread the knowledge about issues, candidates and the governmental process are necessary, both for the success of democracy, and for the internal development of autonomy. As we shall see in Chapter XI, this growth goes hand in hand with the development of a mature morality that insures the success of a democratic government. In this way the latter also rests on an appropriate sense of responsibility and on the willingness to abide by laws and by the majority. Under such conditions it is also possible for more people to grow to stages of self-actualization and to the correlating stage of adult morality, as we have seen in Chapter VI and will see again in Chapter XI. Only then the freedoms guaranteed by democracy give people the opportunity to exercise their autonomy. The checks and balances built into the system also help people to develop a sense of moral responsibility until they can reach higher stages of moral development that also follow a lawful sequence as explained in Chapter XI. The achievement of higher levels of morality by a good number of people can prevent any excessive use of power by those who might be stuck at lower levels of moral and personality development. We shall see in the next chapter how the exercise of power without checks and balances can distort the perspective, so that the person may become blinded by power or enamored with it. Sometimes the danger arises that such people may change the whole democratic process. In our own history some of us were afraid this could be happening during the heyday of Senator Joseph McCarthy, or during the period where the CIA and the FBI accumulated more secret powers and influences. It is for similar reasons that the Watergate incident was so important for our education and for the development of an increased sophistication about the self-governing process. Richard Nixon and the people around him became blinded by the exercise of power and by their own arrested development of morality. Thanks to the timeless efforts of our press and our courts we began to understand better this fearsome possibility of what can happen if a group of individuals believe that they are above the law. Thanks to the citizen lobby Common Cause, constituents began to hound their representatives to overhaul the state and federal systems of government. They pushed for the passage of new laws and rules, to insert missing checks and balances, and to open up the governmental process to public scrutiny. The various sunshine laws about open hearings and open records and open committee meetings, the disclosure of income and influences of elected officials, and the limitations of campaign funds to prevent the inundation of fiscal power are the results. Therefore the Watergate incident and its aftermaths have strengthened our democracy and educated us to its potential dangers. It may have reassured many of us that we can survive the threats of indiscriminate power by having better safeguards and an educated alertness in the future.

Faith in Man's Freedom is a Self-fulfilling Prophecy

The most basic assumption underlying democracy is that people are fundamentally capable of making wise decisions if given an opportunity and then the practical experience. In the early days of the liberalization of absolute monarchy through a number of revolutions various people expressed the fear that such increased freedoms for a large number of people would result in mob rule or in anarchy like that of children when left to their own devices. The contrary faith in people rising to the challenges of increased freedom is of course based on the faith that a person is capable of intelligent autonomous behavior. Furthermore he can grow to the inevitable stage of more responsible self-government. In the most extreme sense Madison, during the aftermaths of the American revolution, expressed his faith in promoting a better vision of fighting for one's own freedom, if the citizens are allowed to bear arms. This provision in the Bill of Rights was for Madison a "noble experiment" which entrusted a sense of rational power and a sense of one's own motive to the people. He concluded that the more authoritarian governments must be afraid that their own armies might rebel against them and use their arms for this purpose. A free people would not do so, although we now realize the danger of creating fatal accidents and encouraging crime when people possess handguns that have lost this early symbolic meaning.

As we have already noted above, this faith in personal unfolding under freedom has now been replaced by our knowledge that people can and do develop lawfully to such higher stages of adult development. At that point they not only can use and manipulate freedom for themselves and for others; they may even exult in this exercise as an achievement in their growth.

Therefore the faith did not produce new expectations miraculously. There was more involved than the mere hope that the release of motives would push people onwards and upward to new and more complex stages of involvement. The faith stimulated such expectations precisely because the latter were rooted as embryonic potentials within the growing personality and system of life forces. Naturally the specific nature of the expectations were colored by the faiths expressed by the philosophers and statesmen who evolved democratic principles and wrote the constitutional documents to implement them. In this sense this faith in the ability of people to be free and to be able to govern themselves became a self-fulfilling prophecy thanks to the basic elements of human nature. It never became a self-fulfilling prophecy during the days when so-called God-fearing men also urged greater liberties for Man's salvation for the sake of merely humanitarian and selfless love for one's fellow-men!

There is much corroborative material on the success of self-fulfilling prophecies in other areas of human involvements in which the expectation of the reformer is based on solid evidence from human psychology. For instance we have learned that we can expect children to grow more quickly to a sense of responsibility and identity if we give them more room to experiment and if we reward them for any successes. An overprotective hovering over the child under the assumption of his or her extreme immaturity infantilizes the child and creates more dependency. Thanks to these learnings and their effects on adolescent growth we have officially lowered the voting age and the age at which a person could legally drive an automobile in some areas. Another example can be offered in our recent discovery of the true nature of mental illness as a chemical deficit and as a defensive narrowing of a world filled with anxiety. We could then encourage so-called mental patients to exercise dormant powers and abilities. We knew that these processes were either still embryonic and unused, or they had been locked away under the shield of being "sick" and playing a "patient" role. When the custodial handling of such patients gave way to the "therapeutic environment" -- namely, encouraging the patient to function more autonomously and responsibly -- they rose, on the whole, to the occasion.

This revolution in our view towards mental illness also has had a profound effect on our commitment procedures. In most states of the United States at this time the so-called mental health acts specify carefully the evidence that must be considered and becomes binding as to whether a person can be locked up in a mental institution against his will. Once he is behind such walls he must be examined very promptly by a team of experts who further evaluate if the evidence is sufficient to hold the patient or to refer him to less stringent, alternate forms of treatment. In addition a legal hearing is required within a few days at which time the commitment proceedings are brought before a court, where the patient has the right to be represented by an attorney. Once he is committed, or if he has signed himself into the hospital voluntarily, he retains a large number of civil and other rights. Thereby we are buttressing our realization that the patient may not be totally unable to govern his own affairs or that he remains a helpless victim of his "illness". In some states the patient can look up an ombudsman in the hospital in case he has any grievances. This official is not usually dependent or accountable to the hospital administration.

Many hospitals also give medical patients more credit for retaining some responsibilities and taking some initiative, because they require full information both for their own security and for making intelligent decisions about themselves and their lives. We have recognized that this counteraction to the traditional "sick role" (one gives up all responsibility and entrusts oneself blindly to the experts) re-engages the patient as an active partner in the treatment process. This appeal to equal status with the "experts" has been found to accelerate healing and recovery. Active cooperation based on knowledge and the psychological re-engagement of the patient's motivation and expectation stimulates internal physiological processes that speed healing. Here is another self-fulfilling prophecy that had its success based on medical and psychological facts. Its success was not because we "should" be more humane and personalized with sick people rather than treating them as an inert "gallbladder case". As a result we now possess "patient bills of rights" that are prominently posted in many hospitals.

We have also given medical and mental patients the right and the duty to make decisions about their treatment. We need informed consent nowadays before physicians can take out part of a person's intestinal tract, administer electric shock treatment, or prescribe a course of drugs. This newer policy goes against the idea that only the experts know best. With the increased education and knowledge available in a developed nation, the patient may well be the final authority on what is best for him, provided he gets the proper information and can exercise his adult capacities. He becomes one of the "experts". Similarly, recent decisions by the U.S. Supreme Court make the woman an expert over her own body, so that she can take the responsibility of whether she wants to mother a child or have an abortion in case she becomes victim to a physiological accident. Previously this responsibility was not allowed her when she and society had to conform instead to an abstract law giving the fetus a "right to life" akin to the right enjoyed by a thinking and feeling person.

In these last examples we also see the application and proliferation of democratic principles. If people can rise up to the requirements of self-government and have quite often succeeded in solving some of their problems over the 200 years of our nation's history, then people can dare to expand their sphere of responsibility and decision-making. These experiences also provide further knowledge about how to make decisions. For instance, it is required that people must now be fully informed before they consent to participate in any scientific experiments. Until recently a scientist could con a person to be a subject by merely flashing his scientific credentials and giving some vague assurances that the experiment would have no ill effects and would greatly benefit mankind. We now expect that most people can and should understand a scientific experiment and the risks involved, provided the investigator takes the trouble to translate his concepts into those available in general knowledge.

This new faith in the ability of people to make their own decisions is also responsible for the new views on so-called "victimless crime". Some authorities argue that we should decriminalize certain offenses, such as taking drugs, prostitution, and the production and consumption of pornography, provided no one but the consumer gets hurt. In this way the client takes full responsibility for his actions as long as the risks have been explained and publicized. For these reasons the consumption of alcohol has been removed from the law, provided the drinker does not endanger others; and we have not placed smoking into the category of a criminal act even though we have found out that it is dangerous to health and contributes to many deaths annually. Several states have, for instance, abolished helmet laws for motorcycle riders under the assumption that the uncovered operator takes the risk of incurring a definitely higher chance of injury and death in an accident. We even have neutralized suicide by no longer making it a crime under the assumption that people may have some right to decide whether to live or to die, or to be treated if we can find evidence of mental illness. All of these changes are based on the notion that adults are autonomous individuals who are responsible for their own actions. They do not need supervision or paternalistic overseers in such personal areas that affect only their own person. A paternalistic view divides the world into the weak and the strong or experts, in which the weak may also sometimes be labelled as "sick" and then treated in hospitals. As we shall see in the next chapter, this view prevails in all communist societies for several good reasons.

A further filtering down of the democratic process can be observed in our factories. Nowadays workers want to have more say over their jobs and over their working conditions, after years of better education, knowledge, and exposure to democratic principles of self-determination. Many industries have successfully experimented with limited schemes of self-government, with profit-sharing, with ways of making suggestions, and with plans that give the worker a full overview of the manufacturing process and their own place in it. Most of these schemes have resulted in higher motivation and in such effects as less turnover, less absenteeism, and higher productivity, as well as less conflict. In all such cases there has been an increase of morale of job-satisfaction. Workers enjoy a sense of belongingness and of participation because they are encouraged by their education and their democratic surrounding to develop to a greater degree of autonomy and involvement. In all of these examples we see a proliferation of democratic decision-making and a widening of people's spheres of responsibility. Hence democracy creates experience in decision-making and promotes a greater involvement of people in their own affairs. As they develop along normal channels to a stage of autonomy, they can successfully handle such opportunities. We shall, however summarize in a later chapter what we have also been warned by many contemporary observers: that it can be dangerous to catapult a person into a position of responsibility and power without guaranteeing the satisfaction of his basic needs and without giving him sufficient control over the problems surrounding him. Such premature role-taking very often drives the person into inner confusion and into anxiety which may drive him further into himself.

The Concept of the Supremacy of the Law as a Safeguard over Excess Power

It is necessary to put the spotlight once more on the legal process in a democracy. Democratic constitutions specify that no person can be above the law. This state of affairs differs from monarchies and other more autocratic governments which implicitly or quite explicitly make value judgments about people. They are graded as to their worth and some are assigned greater privileges or arbitrary powers and the ability to command. If certain roles are endowed with more privileges in a democracy this is made very clear and spelled out in the laws that these privileges go with the position and not with the person. Thus we address our president and our elected officials with certain titles, observe more deferential behavior and give them outward symbols of higher status and privilege. These signs, however, disappear when the person is no longer holding the office and returns to private life. Deference after this point is then only accorded if the person's performance while in office has earned him or her permanent respect and even devotion. The differential treatment given to the ex-presidents Harry Truman and Richard Nixon is a good example.

The distinction between respect for a role versus respect for a person is nowhere clearer than in the necessarily authoritarian institutions of a democracy, namely in its army and its police force. When I was a soldier in the second World War we were told that we saluted the uniform and obeyed the commands of the officer and not the man inside the uniform. In other words we respected and conformed to the characteristics assigned to the role according to certain rules, based on the rational functioning of a military machine. During the war the goals of defending the country against a formidable enemy required secrecy

The Promise Of Human Autonomy

and a fast chain of command. Absolute obedience to these provisions were necessary. The individual soldier took an oath to conform to these rules based on the full knowledge of the implications of his oath. It was possible and even recognized that errors in selection or because of the haste in commissioning officers in a wartime emergency that occasionally an unfriendly, unfeeling and even inhumane bastard might slip into an officer's uniform. A further filtering down of the democratic process can be observed in our factories. Here too, the goals and the rationale of the military required obedience, just as obedience is necessary to a policeman in the conduct of his duties. As soon as the officer takes off his uniform and does not give a military command, or as soon as he leaves the service, the respect does not go with him. He is then perceived and reacted to in terms of new rules or in terms of his individual behavior. In a democratic country we do, however, have procedures for appealing to special boards or to laws when the officer or policeman has used excessive or irrational authority in the conduct of his duty. Nowadays the Nuremberg laws, formulated after World War II about the limits of obedience to national or military authorities, have provided new guidelines for the individual soldier to resist when he is ordered to perform acts that go against commonly shared precepts of morality. Hence it is no longer possible to obey blindly if an officer commands one to kill or torture defenseless people. These laws have thus charted another course for human autonomy.

Therefore, no leader in a democracy can be above the law, or determine actions and privileges for himself that are not accessible to others. Consequently, Richard Nixon was finally controlled and punished although he claimed that a president could cover up evidence, and shield wrongdoers for the sake of the more important and lofty goal of governing the nation. We have impeachment procedures in our Constitution for such contingencies, and we elect all our representatives every few years. All political power is derived from the Constitution and limited by it. Such ideas were accepted by the majority and cannot be changed except by the people as a whole. Constitutionality therefore made it possible to control government and its magistrates.

The three arms of government, -- the executive or President, the legislative or Congress, and the judiciary or the Supreme Court also -- have provided the necessary checks and balances. These have prevented any one branch of government from becoming too powerful, or to usurp privileges that would cut the flow of feedback from the ever-changing mixture of majorities and minorities. Our forefathers were fortunately aware that the mere appeal to the sense of responsibility and devotion of both the people and their elected representatives was not sufficient to secure democracy. Perhaps they had a dim awareness of present knowledge of the intervening stages in personality development, before a person reaches the mature stage of autonomy and morality. Perhaps they were also aware that regression was possible, especially under the impact of new, anxiety-provoking duties and responsibilities. They must have been aware that the exercise of power can change one's perspective and can even lead to a form of humanistic blindness. Hence we can be grateful for the tripartite system of government which has worked relatively well as an "experiment".

The Problems Associated with Power

Perhaps one of the most astute insights into the dynamics of human behavior is provided by the limitations on personal power by the writers of the successful democratic constitutions. It is, of course, well known from the study of history that excessive power is not a normal way for the human being to express his needs. The more contemporary study of behavior has also supported this idea by showing that excessively dominant behavior is usually the result of disturbances in the personality. Either the person may not have developed adequate control devices and is impulse-ridden, or he is expressing important, but repressed needs in a deviant way. Or he may be compensating for real or imagined feelings of inferiority and insecurity. These forms of expressions have certainly occurred with frightening frequency and often with devastating results in the hereditary or self-appointed leaders in history. In all such cases, a leader had not been selected as a result of demonstrating some consistency in behavior and some maturity that was publicly available. The abuse of political power for the sake of purely personal needs is certainly diminished and almost totally eliminated in functioning democracies. At least it can be corrected at the next election.

However, our forefathers also had some intuitive knowledge about the social psychological influences of social roles and of ritualistic practices on human behavior. They recognized that the ascendance to a position of power and eminence required some major readjustment for the person filling the role. The opportunities and trappings of personal influence can change one's perception of oneself, as well as of one's relationship with others. The old saying that "power corrupts" is partially involved here. It is certainly true that power changes and sometimes distorts one's perspective, because the distance between oneself and others is suddenly elongated. One may then be much more isolated from the feedback of others. Despite the experience of a boost to one's ego and the new sense of accomplishment with increased power, others may boost one higher in recognition and adoration than one wants to shoulder. One may have to live up to this new sense of perceived power, until one's own sense of perspective is obscured and distorted. One may accept the omniscience that others bestow on one, or the trappings of office, and assume excessive power in order to maintain it at that artificially high level. There is also the question whether a sudden and unaccustomed rise in power may awaken the infantile reaction of omnipotence. Or does it reawaken compensatory, anti-weakness defenses, because the person is now more easily threatened, and so visible that he may worry about having to hide small blemishes? Or are old scripts about getting even with parental ogres reawakened, so that one uses one's power to create scapegoats and enemies? Also the assumption of power may resonate with one's sense of adequacy and one's sense of achievement into a magnification of newly acquired power to satisfy a personal sense of adequacy.

We may note in passing that some of the effects of power may actually constrict a person's range of responses and eliminate alternatives. In this way a person previously functioning at the self-actualization level may find many of his choices limited, especially those connected with his intense personal relationships with friends. For these reasons dictators and autocratic kings are quite heavily limited in what they can do -- at least in public. They have to worry about living up to the image they have created and in terms of the expectations of being a super person which in turn partly justifies his power manipulations.

Here is where the many provisions of our and other countries' constitutions either help the person in power to stay in good touch with efficient self-monitoring devices, or they give others and the people at large a chance to replace him. Our aforementioned checks and balances, the supremacy of the law, frequent schedules of elections, votes of confidence, and our amendment procedures are all examples of such provisions. In fact, these devices in the constitutions provide checks for the person in power himself, because he can use the feedback possible with such devices as a guide for his own behavior. In this way he may grow in the role and become more fully mature and develop his own plateau of autonomy. This fact was beautifully illustrated by the growth which Harry S. Truman experienced during his presidency into which he was cast suddenly without preparation and without being chosen to fill it.

In addition to legal safeguards against the use of excessive power in our Constitution, we have also developed new forms of more informal feedback for our leaders. Opinion polls, both public ones and those conducted privately for our leaders, are devices that sample views and values and can help leaders to assess whether they are out of line. These polls also represent effective expressions of opinion, and can be used by the people at large to become a barometer of their own views. Other devices that gather and channel feedback are letters to the editor, talk shows, the mail to elected state and federal representatives, and the more informal surveys and interviews conducted by newspapers and TV and radio stations.

We shall take up these points regarding power further in the next chapter. There we shall meet facts about power and the more salient reasons why contemporary communist regimes show evidence of failure, even though they rely on a so-called scientific theory of social organization and of government.

Chapter X

The Failure of Communism as a Further Proof of the Process of Autonomy

The time has come to take a hard look at communism from our vantage point of securing a better view of the psychology of autonomy. This psychological analysis of communism will give us further proof that autonomous functioning is a universal human stage of development, and that its suppression is either impossible or that it creates more problems for the oppressors. This hard look will also enable us to understand why communism does not and cannot really "work" that is, produce a society of men and women in which they can feel fulfilled and gain satisfaction of higher human needs. This excursion into communism can also teach us what the inevitable harvest looks like, when the seeds of autonomy are inevitably ripening within developing human beings while someone is denying them the opportunity to scatter these seeds, even though they may reside in a culture that guarantees health, life and leisure.

In the 19th Century there was new hope that Man could construct societies with the help of his newly discovered idealism and reason, which would be nearly just and perfect. The revolution in France and in America had already toppled the long-standing idea that the traditional social orders were sacred or inevitable. Many schemes for social reform were tried. There were also some small-scale social experiments in this country which were based on sharing goods and activities, and which practiced communal living. Brook Farm in New England, Oneida in New York, and New Harmony in Indiana were examples which were sometimes called "socialist" or "communistic", because they stressed equality and unity, and because they required a sense of identification with a total community. These communities failed or disappeared for reasons that have occupied many analysts since. In the meantime the Industrial Revolution had created new products and had opened new vistas. It also required a greater degree of interdependence among people, more complex social orders, and new ideas about Man. The "side effects" of the Industrial Revolution unfortunately also included ugly factories, mechanization of work, exploitation of workers and their families, and squalid slums.

These blemishes on the great face-lifting of Man's destiny occupied many social analysts, which included the German philosopher Karl Marx. He scoffed at the goal of creating societies from the communal experiments, calling it utopian. He decided to undertake a "scientific" analysis of history and focused on purely economic and political factors, while ignoring the psychological variables inherent in human reactions in the market place. The theory he derived from the study of industrial production and distribution outlined an inevitable evolution that unfolded according to a dialectic process, borrowed from the philosopher Friedrich Hegel. According to this idea, any newly established force inevitably induces the development of a counterforce. The inevitable conflict between "thesis" and "antithesis" results in a new integration or "synthesis" which represents a creative solution, until it eventually begets its inevitable counterforce to renew this process. On the historical-political scene of the 19th (and 20th) Century, capitalism, which arose as a force or "thesis" out of the Industrial Revolution, would eventually create two antithetical forces, namely the ruling classes or the owners of production and the proletariat who were the exploited working classes. Also, the low wages paid to the workers could not buy back the products they produced, so that the accumulation of surplus products would drive the capitalists to conquer new territories for their markets, thereby stimulating imperialism. The gulf between the oppressors and the oppressed eventually became so enormous and glaringly untenable that the proletariat would revolt and overthrow the ruling classes and the system of capitalism or private ownership. The new synthesis from this revolt would create a new system in which all surplus value from the work of men would be reinvested by them into the society and into their lives for their common welfare, rather than for the benefit of a few. After an initial and inevitable "dictatorship of the proletariat", the proletarians would become the majority and the state and its vigilance could relax. In this society all class distinctions would dissolve, because everyone's contribution would be equally valued and recognized. As a result there would be no more need for a centrally based government, because suppression for the sake of securing the revolution was no longer needed. The State would "wither away" as an instrument of oppression. With freedom there would be no need for a State, except as an arm of administration. It would give way to a state of communism which rested on the principle "from each according to his ability, to each according to his need". This "need" was narrowly conceived by Marx as tangible needs, including subsistence, economic security and even luxury.

This theory, here highly simplified and abstracted, held many attractions for people in the last 130 years. In an age in which science had obviously given Man very tangible benefits like the steam engine, electricity, and modern medicine, it had now equally spawned a scientifically-based theory which seemed to explain the problems that were also obviously cropping up in many places as men invented and built these fabulous machines. Many of the analyses of Marx of existing conditions seemed to make sense and appealed to large numbers of people either by virtue of their deprivations in a sea of plenty, or by virtue of their loyalty to the realm of rational ideas. Also, Marx's theory cut Man off once and for all from any vestiges of unquestionable dependency on God and on the mediators in organized religion. As such the theory was again attractive for those who felt confident enough in their own thinking powers to fashion new ideas about the nature and the destiny of Man. It gave them a chance to reject the idea which had held back progress for so long during medieval history: namely, that

Man by himself was impotent because he was an imperfect copy of a perfect God.

Marx did more than merely propose a theory. He made it attractive to the more action-oriented segment of the population by stating that this inevitable dialectic process in our era of industrial history could be helped along by the organization and planning of the workers. Hence the Communist Manifesto, written in 1848 by Marx and Engels in more popular language, became a very influential blueprint for thought and action, and has been adopted by many reform and radical movements from the waves of revolutions in 1848 on to the present. Since Marx's time communist writers have differed on the amount of coaxing and pushing that is necessary or even mandatory for the "inevitable" historical process towards a communist synthesis to occur. When we browse through the writings of Trotsky, Lenin, Mao Tse-tung, or the speeches of the leaders of communist countries and of communist parties we discover some differences of opinions on the amount of organization required, on the degree to which violent overthrow is inevitable, on the advisability to ally with other non-communist reform movements, and on the use of the parliamentary process for the passage to a communist state. However, all presently existing communist regimes agree with the basic formulations of Marx's analysis and with the aims for a developed industrial society. All of them further claim that their program of change and their future goals are based on Marx.

What is the present status of the theory and how valid are its predictions after it has been tested by repeated experiments in the laboratory of nations? Let us take a quick survey of some of the major results of the application of the theory in a number of countries: in Russia for 62 years, in the Balkan countries and Czechoslovakia, Poland and East Germany for 34 years, in China for 32 years and in other countries like Cuba, Vietnam, North Korea and Cambodia for a lesser time. On the positive side, poverty, insecure living conditions, and unemployment have been practically eliminated. In all these countries, literacy and health have been markedly improved, sometimes to the highest level achieved anywhere else. Nevertheless Raymond Aron, a

French journalist, has just written a book (<u>In Defense of Decadent Europe</u>) which tries to show that western nations have not really been aware of their superiority over the Soviet Union in some areas. According to his thesis, the Soviet Union -- despite impressive progress in achieving equality with the United States in weapons production and nuclear power -- has had to borrow most of its ideas about productivity, distribution, agriculture and other economic areas. They are behind in technical innovation, scientific progress, and the living standards of their people. In addition, they require a huge police force for control, and therefore represent a colossal failure in history. The Soviet economic system has not been able to produce the goods required for the physical and moral health of its people, and therefore does not even merit the respect of most European communist parties.

On the negative side of the ledger the evidence seems to pile up somewhat higher for all communist countries. First of all there are clear demonstrations of the momentous waves of oppression over dissident opinions, over deviant thought and behavior outside a narrow range of the acceptable, and over minorities in every communist country. These sometimes take on a bizarre and more often frightening dimensions. In Russia the fate of dissidents under Stalin and Brezhnev's leadership are well known. In addition a more or less official policy of anti-Semitism threatens the Jewish people with underemployment and other hardships, and has resulted in wholesale attempts at emigration. The suppression of literature, art, and music not conducive to the guidelines of "proletarian morality" are also well documented and result in defections at every opportunity. The suppression of small attempts to liberalize artistic and intellectual expression in Hungary and Czechoslovakia by Soviet armed forces are further illustrations. The Cambodian communist regime has slaughtered thousands of its people and has created many refugees. In China, the "Cultural revolution" enlisted the aid of students and adolescents to suppress all "foreign" influences outside the narrow party line of behavior, including even dress. All schools and universities were closed for a number of years to "liberate" the young guards for the revolutionary zeal, and presumably to prevent any discussion and contemplation of the official guidelines. Now we are faced with a wholesale persecution by Vietnam of its millions of Chinese ethnics, so that they have either perished, or been washed ashore by the thousands as penniless refugees. The world is thereby faced with another "holocaust", only 34 years after the end of the last and hopefully final one in the concentration camps of Nazi Germany. This is the same Vietnam which has fought against South Vietnam and the United States for so many bloody years under the battle cry of liberating their brethren in the South from a repressive and corrupt regime.

In none of the communist countries do we find any sign of the State "withering away". The excuse of needing time for educating the masses toward communism and for maintaining tight control against an ever-present death-threat from surrounding capitalist countries is no longer tenable for Russia and other European countries. They are almost two generations old (34 years). Quite to the contrary, the State has tightened its hold on more and more aspects of life and thought. It has maintained control over much more than economic planning and distribution -- namely, over education, information, science, art, travel, and freedom of movement. In addition, the promised disappearance of class distinctions, which propelled the workers toward change in the first place, has not taken place. Class distinctions are very obvious in every communist country. There is now a clear distinction between the rulers and functionaries and the rest of the population. It is true that the possession of property and goods is not any more the obvious distinction of the ruling class. However, they alone have the power to allot property and country homes and the chance to enjoy them. They are the first to secure the many scarce resources, such as apartments, cars, TV sets, refrigerators, and a whole variety of food and clothing. It is clear that these relatively few people at the top enjoy many privileges that are not available to others. The privileges are accompanied by the signs of recognition that leave the rest of the population as a relatively indistinguishable, amorphous mass. Recognition of most of the talent, achievement and application go against the despised "cult of personality" which is considered to be a Western abomination, and is therefore not thought to encourage the individual to forget his individuality. To become a loyal contributor to the group and its welfare, any person who is successful is led away from any sense of personal achievement. Instead, he is praised for his contribution to the goals and standards of the group and for his loyalty toward upholding and advancing the nation's welfare.

Perhaps the greatest blow to the so-called scientific basis of communist theory has been the outbreaks of conflict and even of serious military engagements between brother communist countries in the recent past. According to the theory the communist parties and governments in different countries constitute a brotherhood of Proletarians who unite throughout the whole world to shrink the yoke of capitalist oppression and who administer the world for mutual benefit under one general system. Yet Russia sent its armed might into brother Hungary and into brother Czechoslovakia in order to make them conform to the Soviet line, rather than have them develop communism along their own national preferences. The two giants in the communist world, Russia and China, have been in serious conflict for many years, first over disputed territories, then over general principles of communistic administration, and of course over the clash of their respective expansionistic efforts. This conflict has several times erupted into military skirmishes and may still erupt into a major war. Vietnam has invaded brother Cambodia in recent history and has thrown out its communist regime to replace it with an administration under Vietnam's influence. While the expelled Cambodian regime was guilty of the most brutal suppression and genocide, the present Vietnamese leadership is not any more lily-white in terms of its own record. In addition China decided to invade a sizable border region of its former ally Vietnam with a large-scale military force. Ostensibly, this campaign was carried out to "teach the Vietnamese a lesson" for being too cocksure by invading Cambodia and therefore flouting China and threatening her security. This method of pedagogy cost Vietnam thousands of casualties and widespread destruction. The cut-throat behavior of communist friends similar to the markedly power-hungry lines of former colonial empires which they have accused and opposed indicates that the rulers of these communist countries are primarily motivated by power needs. They obviously wish to extend and secure their influence. This behavior is apparently not based on Communist principles, although the attacking regimes coin new terms to rationalize that their campaigns uphold Marxian principles which their enemies have violated. This behavior led the Prime Minister of Singapore, Mr. Lee Kuan Yew, to remark in a speech that the Communist leaders seem to be motivated by greed, and are engaging in a new form of imperialism. They are, therefore, more nakedly exposed as powerful human beings who -- like the old kings and imperialist governments -- engage in plunder, subversion, and overthrow. They do so from the promptings of their own whims, rather than on the basis of a plan based on a set of principles such as Marxism, or on the basis of consultation with their subjects.

Another major flaw in the so-called scientific fabric of Marx's theory was the fact that the "inevitable events" just refused to take place in those places in which they were supposed to be most "inevitable". According to the dialectic process inherent in the history of capitalism (according to "St. Marx"), the creation of the counterforce or antithesis would be greatest in the most highly developed and industrialized countries. The gulf between exploiters and exploited would widen until the bourgeois middle class would eventually find itself among the exploited and join with them until only two classes would remain. The consequent maturing of a sense of exploitation among the exploited would lead to organized demands for reform increasingly set by violence from the oppressors who would be unwilling to give up power from their position of divine rights. The violence would polarize the two classes even further until the inevitable revolution would erupt. In none of the developed countries under capitalism have any of these polarizations taken place. Quite to the contrary, the middle classes have grown and become more influential and even tone-setting with their values and their goals. In many countries the majorities, developed through coalitions of middle class and working class parties, were able to stem and even sometimes reverse the absolute power of industrial corporations. Hence the abolition of child labor, the institution of minimum hours and of overtime, the guaranteed minimum wage, government spending on housing and medical care, slum clearance, passage of anti-trust laws, the nationalization of some industries, and compulsory safety and protection devices in factories and mines all regulated and curbed the exploitation and excessive power of employers. The revolutions have instead occurred in undeveloped and agrarian countries.

Various communist thinkers have tried to modify Marx's theories to explain some of these problems. Nevertheless the discrepancies between fact and theory, and the accumulated frustration and suppression of human needs remains in communist nations. These problems furthermore threaten to endanger the balance of the world and jeopardize peace. The first major reason for these failures of a theory and its large-scale experiments is that communism failed to take into account the facts of human motivation. Marx analyzed the relationship of men to each other in history solely in terms of the shifting relations between economic classes and the means of production. These forces determined all other interactions, including the emergence of moral, social, religious, political, and legal values. There was therefore no such thing as a basic or intrinsically human development. Personality developed in accordance with the historical period in which one lived, or the economic class in which one belonged. It was shaped by the forces of production and distribution characteristic of a person's time. If a ruling class determined the government and its laws then their beliefs, values, customs and preferred modes of thinking were also copied and became the official morality and philosophy of the land. This picture was true for the absolute monarchies and aristocracies of the Middle Ages and the feudal periods because of their ability to retain power under a religious justification.

Russian leaders and social scientists have carried on this theory to the extreme by insisting that the conditioning principles of the Russian psychologist Ivan Pavlov can explain the development of all human characteristics. It is therefore possible to create the ideal Soviet man and woman uniformly in all regions of the vast Soviet Union regardless of former indigenous cultural traditions, because of the shared economic system. The educational system based on Soviet and Marxist principles can speed this uniform personality development by devising additional pedagogic principles. (Gruen: Paper on Soviet Psychology). However, the psychology of Soviet men and women is uniquely different from that of all other human beings, because of their radically different economic system. The explanations of personality organization and development found in the West, such as those attributed to Freud, Adler, or Maslow, are not relevant to the human beings inhabiting the Soviet Union, because these theories explain human functioning as it occurs in a capitalistic system.

The economic emphases of Marxism have contributed many good insights to alert historians, economists, and political scientists to the economic bases of many better understanding of events that were previously explained purely by focusing on the leaders, battles, and the use of force. However, the attempt to apply Marxist principles to understand Man's functioning and personality has not helped to clarify his behavior. Now we understand that people are motivated by many other needs than the need to gain subsistence, especially once subsistence has been somewhat secured. Men and women do not passively copy all dominant values in order to secure that subsistence. Abraham Maslow and other psychologists have shown that people may be motivated by needs to preserve and gain status, recognition, security, belongingness, and by a drive to express their autonomy. Sociologists in the forties and the fifties pointed out that our American middle classes had become more influential in determining the dominant values and behaviors than the upper classes. Furthermore, middle class people were motivated by getting ahead and gaining status, and by cementing their place in the social and economic environment with stable guidelines of regularity, order, and inhibition of emotional impulses, so that one could easily conform to well-understood principles of respectability. In such an ordered universe each person could find his own individual paths and improve himself. The middle class were not concerned with a definition of themselves as being deprived or exploited. They were not angry at any oppressors, nor did they want to have anything to do with major change or with any revolutionary movement.

During my own undergraduate college years I was a misguided communist sympathizer for a short time in the late thirties and early forties. We were helped by our radical tutors to clothe our appeals for

The Promise Of Human Autonomy

change and for the redress of grievances in revolutionary language, peppered by the phrases and the cartoon-like stereotypes of orthodox Marxism. We were often very discouraged by the reaction. Not many of our fellow students or the workers we approached were turned on by these appeals, even if the goals were in their own interests. The appeals were foreign to their ears and to their needs of wanting to identify themselves with an influential core culture. We usually consoled ourselves that the masses were still not liberated enough to see through the "bourgeois propaganda", and that we would have to try harder. What we did not understand then is that we turned others off because we did not understand and appeal to their needs. Our appeals served much more to help us lost souls to identify with a big movement, and to unite in a meaningful bond. The movement's common vocabulary and phraseology brought us together in a cult into which we had been drawn either because of our lack of adequate information or out of youthful rebellion. Many of the causes we supported were good ones, but they were preempted by the revolutionary movement as stepping stones to future aims and to an inevitable revolution to parallel Russia's course. The F.B.I.'s sometimes frantic attempt to persecute America's communists was not half as effective as the omission in Marxism to account for human motivation, and the deficiency among American communists to understand human relations in a democratic country under capitalism.

Marx was not interested in people and their individual welfare. For him the fate of people was determined by their society and primarily by its economic organization. As a result we see there none of the many evaluations of the human life as we witness them in books and debates in the democracies. The individual is not valuable in the communist system; in fact, he is expendable. It is even perfectly all right to sacrifice the human life and the lives of whole groups of people if they stand in the way of the common good or if they either purposefully or even inadvertently obstruct the aims of building a communist society. We see this principle repeated in the purges, the executions, the torture and banishment of dissidents, and in the wholesale slaughter of unwanted segments like the Chinese millions now living in Vietnam. The expenditure of the human life is diametrically opposed to our belief in the sacredness and worth of life and in the welfare of each person, and we are attempting to live up to these beliefs after violating them in our Indian campaigns and in some other wars. In communism the welfare of the group and of the nation comes before anything else. Therefore each individual has to subjugate his wishes and needs to the welfare of the group. He gains self-esteem and basic satisfaction through the acceptance of the group goal, and through his enthusiastic application of his resources to it and to the welfare of the group. If he fails to do so and puts individual needs first, he merits the censure and eventual punishment by the group. These principles are found in educational treatises, in schools and colleges, in all youth groups, in the communist party and in work organizations. They are buttressed by many slogans from the leaders of the country. If human beings followed official communist guidelines, it would be impossible for them to achieve the stage of personality development that we have called self-actualization The very idea is heresy, and the steps required for such autonomous development would have to be changed to a very different conception of the human nature and of the "good life". This subversion of human development provides the key for an understanding of the great failures in the application of communist systems towards the solution of human problems arising in contemporary societies.

Another major failure lies in the basic requirement in communism to secure the revolution with a "dictatorship of the proletariat", before the therapeutic synthesis of true communism can emerge. The "scientific" theory requires a cadre of experts and dedicated toilers who study and know the theory so that they alone are prepared to direct and organize the new state, and who also constitute the watchdogs over the precious new ideological seedlings in a still hostile or barren soil. This elite further has the right and the duty to wield unlimited power to secure the new state, to protect it from the inevitable attacks from still smoldering pockets of enemy resistance inside the state and from the enemy's allies on the outside. It also has the power to educate the masses, so that they become aware of and skilled in the workings of the theory. This power gives them the right to exclude any conflicting or extraneous material and literally bombard the inhabitants with monolithic propaganda. Only in this way do the people learn to carry out the laws and procedures that are good for them by virtue of the theory and through the watchfulness of the elite.

Such a requirement of an elite produces two major evils. One is that it prolongs the inevitable dependency from which Man has to be weaned over an extended period of time. This has been due to his long and enforced dependency as an animal that brought a large and complicated brain out of the womb, not yet "wired" for use. The elite and its dictatorship prolongs the security of "papa and mama know best", and therefore stifles self-expression, independence, and initiative. This message serves, of course, as a "security blanket" and is further adopted from the accepted practice that one has to learn a new trade or skill from an expert. Leaning on others for one's beliefs and interpretations also solves one of the existential dilemmas by turning to a safe authority. In this way one stifles the loneliness that many feel on the trail to freedom. However, the human being pays a stiff price for this choice, especially if the choice is made by others in a governing elite. The message of depending on an all-knowing and supposedly benevolent elite tends to sap the strength of a person who is eventually capable of listening to his own voice and judgment, and who could move on to the investment of this judgment into stages of higher character development.

The other major evil is the fact that power can corrupt. Vested in an elite group of leaders it has its own distorting influence on them, because of certain psychological forces at work. Even if the leader in the position of power means well and works toward the common good, the rules he establishes become his creation and his property. He tends to isolate himself from any effective feedback, if that is not written into the procedures that govern his leadership. Feedback that is critical or reveals frustration must be seen as irrational and irrelevant because it "bites the hand that feeds". We see these principles beautifully illustrated in the development of dictators like Napoleon, Hitler, the Shah of Iran, as well as by Communist dictators. Power is all-right to use when one molds clay or in the construction of words and the building of thoughts. As soon as one has the power to manipulate people, there is this added corrupting and distorting element which we analyzed above. No better illustration of this idea is there than the successful exhortation of Reverend Jim Jones to get his congregation to commit mass suicide for the common good and for eventual salvation. The elitist leader has to be more and more controlling and stifling to maintain his power. Any mistake or slow-down must be seen as personal failure and requires redoubled and more frantic effort. He must also keep his own belief in the value of control intact, and so he has to invent new ways of justifying his control. The isolating properties of power may add fears of counteraction and of premature replacement to the leader's world, which may even culminate in quasi-paranoid fears of persecution. He may have to invent enemies to maintain his hold and thereby finish his "sacred duty". Only in this way can he gain his own sense of achievement and perhaps his own self-actualization. The spiral of increasing power is well illustrated by the age of today's and yesterday's communist leaders in contrast to the age of some of the elected leaders of Western democracies. Stalin, Brezhnev, Mao Tse-tung, Chou En-lai, Ho Chi Minh, etc., are or were old men remaining in office until death. Their age contrasts with the ages of a John F. Kennedy, Jimmy Carter, Margaret Thatcher, Edwin Heath, Pierre Trudeau, Willy Brandt and others. We have further evidence from psychological experiments on the functional boundaries around a person's world, that power tends to corrupt. Therefore it may enlarge the "skin" (defining the enclosure of the self) of, for instance, a national leader to include his national "boundaries". Hence a perceived threat to the latter might be interpreted to be a personal threat, akin to someone attacking such a leader in person.

It is for such reasons that we require a national goal of autonomy and independence as a potential achievement for every person, as we have it in the constitutions or provisions of our democracies. Even though not all people can reach it in terms of their own personal development, and even though it is not available all of the time because of still unsolved problems in the society, it is at least on the books and forms the kernel of the laws. It is therefore protected by the society as a right, and the people in it can applaud anyone who achieves this goal. A democratic constitution also adds the necessary checks and balances which regulate power and its ability to encroach on the developing potentials of people further removed from the power. These checks also prevent the escalation of power into the irreversible self-corrupting stage. Watergate has proven again that power can corrupt and that new laws are necessary to stop the possible loopholes. We shall have future Watergates, but we have also learned to trust our system to deal with them retroactively.

We can therefore assume that the pressure of compliance and the ideal of putting the group before the individual in communism is self-serving to those in power and is necessary to preserve the status quo. In terms of the dynamic forces behind the communist system of motivation and personal development, that state cannot "wither away". The danger of communism is its appeal to developed nations when they either experience a lot of internal poverty and hardship in their faulty exercise of democratic power, or if they make mistakes in the attempts to make an equitable distribution. Communism's appeal to an underdeveloped nation suffering under a dearth of literacy and know-how among its population is its promise of a strong form of control guided by great promises. Communism, therefore, can become a faith that can sweeten either economic or inner, social chaos. Communism also has served to replace a predominant or even compulsory state religion, and may fill a vacuum in the lives of people who are trying to solve existential struggles in newly acquired freedoms.

Perhaps it is for such reasons that communist countries engage in an almost paranoid suppression of all forms of religion. First of all, some religions kindle a hope for a better life as contrasted to the miserable record of some communist societies. In addition, some religions can keep alive the hope of further self-development by allowing men to maintain a very private and individualized dialogue with God. If the believers can then pray in unison and meet in rituals to reinforce their belief outside their inner selves and also outside the oppressive regime, they reinforce each other and gain strength in group support. There is further hope that prayers may be heard and answered, so that people acquire a faith in an authority even more powerful than the regime. For such reasons, religion is very dangerous to those in power in a communist country where faith has to be channeled into a so-called scientific theory of society and of Man. Religion also challenges the distorted experience of power we discussed above.

If we fault communism with a failure to arrive at its stated goals and with a failure to allow men to develop to their fullest potential, we must also remember that the Western democracies have not "worked" in the fullest sense of solving all of the economic, social, and existential problems of mankind. The value of the "Common Good" has been with us from antiquity, but it also has served as a thinly covering mask for the greed and power needs of self-appointed or capriciously appointed leaders. Barbara Tuchman's superb analysis of the 14th Century gives us a beautiful example of such a development. She describes how the many inept or criminally corrupt leaders contributed many additional problems to mankind with their own failures and faulty judgments that could not be checked except through force of arms. Communism breeds another set of leaders who act on the basis of their own greed and power, and who have lost the perspective of the Common Good. That is why I feel that we have a chance in a democracy -- with its overt emphasis on equality, freedom, and checks on power -- to promote the welfare of the individual as this has been revealed in the blueprints from personality psychology. In the next chapter we shall see how the search for a person's individual happiness also leads to the promotion of the "Common Good", because the ultimate state of self-actualization incorporates the development of a sense of morality that is truly devoted to the welfare of other people.

Chapter XI

The Problems around Human Autonomy

Autonomy has often been suspected of breeding a sense of irresponsibility. It has been accused of justifying selfishness and the individual's isolation from the social fabric around him. Self-actualization has been indicted for legitimizing a lack of concern for one's fellow man and for encouraging immorality. Again we need to visit the laboratory of scientists who have studied human behavior to show that self-actualization develops hand in hand with a more deeply based and caring morality which moves its adherents to conform to a vast majority of laws and customs. (It does so along rational guidelines that have accumulated and been tested in a society.)

We shall introduce our readers to some far-reaching new research that thoroughly contradicts the accusations we have listed above. This research has analyzed moral judgment and concern in depth and has been able to show its universal progression from a simple and expedient form of morality to a more complex and differentiated concern with reciprocity between human beings. In addition, research has shown that the development of a responsible morality is correlated with the development of autonomous behavior and with the onset of self-actualization.

Lawrence Kohlberg became interested in the development of moral principles and reasoning in children. The well-known Swiss psychologist Piaget had already discovered the various stages of reasoning in the development of the child by which the latter approaches and tries to understand the world around him. Piaget also included the judgment of the child about various moral situations -- such as stealing or considering the welfare of others when among others -- in his scheme of cognitive development or intellectual growth. Kohlberg extracted the moral judgments used in these studies and expanded them to cover the gamut of moral solutions to various ethical situations. After many administrations of a number of representative ethical choices to samples of children and adults in different nations, Kohlberg found that the preferences of each of his many subjects could be grouped into six major categories. These range from a primitive conception of justice to a highly differentiated and rule-oriented moral judgment (reference B).

On the most primitive level of ethical choice the person believes that rewards and punishments for acts are based solely on power. One is therefore obedient merely to avoid punishment. The next level is a tit-for-tat morality in which people exchange one favor for another on a more sophisticated level of moral judgment. The person on this level realizes that his safe membership in a family or in a social group is guaranteed by other people showing their concern and gratitude for his actions as long as he does the same. Further along this ladder of development the person may realize that he is part of a social order in which he can earn respect by conformity and by doing his share of the work. In this social order one is expected to keep one's word and one's bargain. At a still higher level the individual may develop the idea that the social order in his group is really based on a flexible social contract that has been agreed upon by free and equal individuals. Finally an individual may reach the stage in which his moral decisions are based upon universal moral principles that allow the person to put himself into the roles and concerns of others, such as seen in the Golden Rule. These six stages of moral judgment represent successive forms of rights and duties in which each succeeding stage is more differentiated and more universalized than the preceding stage.

Kohlberg has therefore succeeded in ordering moral judgments into three major levels each of which contains two stages of development. In addition each succeeding level or pair of stages represents a more complicated form of cognitive judgment and was found to be correlated with general intellectual reasoning. It is, of course, also well established that this intellectual reasoning progresses as the person becomes older and more mature (Reference B). On the first or the pre-conventional level moral values are based on selfish needs. A person operating on Stage 1 would obey merely to avoid trouble or to avoid the superior power and prestige of someone who can dole out punishment. An adult or a child judging his acts on Stage 2 obeys because he either justifies it by his own needs or explains it on the basis of selfish needs of others. On the second or conventional level the person is beginning to judge on the basis of society at large, or by what any valued member of the society ought to do. He is more concerned with maintaining conventional order and organizing the expectation of others toward him and vice versa. His orientation is therefore toward conformity or toward loyal support of the social order.

If a person judges ethical situations on Stage 3 he is primarily concerned with being a "good boy" or "nice girl". He or she wants a pat on the head for his or her good behavior and for wanting to please others. Obedience is tied to a rather stereotyped idea of what the majority wants and needs, and the person is conforming to that because of his need for approval. The "law and order" fourth stage is doing one's duty and showing respect for authority and for the rules. The prime motivation here is a maintenance of the social order for its own sake. In this way the person operating on this stage can earn the respect of others.

The two stages on the highest level or on the autonomous level of moral judgment define an adherence to standards and duties that are shared by others. On this level the person who decides what to do in various moral situations develops a moral theory. His choices are justified by principles or values that are stimulated by basic moral terms, rather than from the fact that one is a member of an organized society. Thus the person on Stage 5 has a legalistic orientation that deals with contracts. Duty and conformity is defined as a contract, such as majority rule, or the avoidance of violating the rights of others. There is an emphasis on the "legal point of view", but with a provision that laws can be changed through rational considerations regarding their utility. Outside the law free agreements and contracts are seen as binding on one. This stage represents the morality reflected in the American government and constitution.

Slightly different principles govern morality on Stage 6, the highest level. Here the person prefers to set up principles for his choices that appeal to universal logical rules. One's own conscience and reactions of mutual respect and trust become much more potent forces in determining one's ethical choices, rather than referring solely to ordained social rules. Examples of such principles area "Live and let live", "Love thy neighbor as thyself", the Golden Rule of doing unto others as you would want others to do to yourself, and Kant's categorical imperative: "Act as you would after considering how everyone should act if they were in the situation." These universal principles of justice, reciprocity, and equality of human rights are abstract and ethical, rather than concrete rules like the Ten Commandments. Stage 6 therefore defines the moral judgment that has been mentioned by most of the world's philosophers (Reference D) and may even violate the written law or majority rule (such as conscientious objection to war).

An example might make the judgments in these six stages clearer. If six different people each found a wallet with a hundred dollars in it, the person operating on Stage 1 would return it if he was afraid that a policeman in the distance had seen him pick it up and would then punish him if he kept it. The person in Stage 2 would return it if he was not at the moment in need of extra cash and had decided from a photograph in the wallet that the owner appeared poverty-stricken enough to need it. The person operating on Stage 3 would return it because he anticipated a reward and praise from the owner, or from police and others for his act. The person on Stage 4 would return it because the rules in the society were to return found money to the rightful owner so as to eliminate another case of theft. A person at Stage 5 would return the wallet if he felt that he was part of the society which had rejected the idea of "finder's keepers" because personal property was a right of the owner. The person on the highest level of Stage 6 would return the wallet if he felt that his conscience would not allow him to enjoy the hundred dollars because he would have substituted a selfish act for one of consideration of his fellow man's needs. One can of course make up reasons for people in all six stages if all six of them had decided to keep the wallet rather than returning it. Since this is an alternative solution to the moral dilemma, six finders operating on the six different stages would again justify this choice in very different ways.

After Kohlberg and his associates discovered that each person's answers to the large number of moral situations could be described by one of these six categories, they created a new and better way of measuring personal choices. They now asked the subjects to respond and judge the moral dilemmas that are presented as stories such as whether a man should break into a druggist's office to obtain a cancer-curing drug for his wife who was near death from cancer. The druggist had recently discovered the drug but was selling it for such an exorbitant price that the man had not been able to borrow more than half the money, and the druggist had refused to sell it even after the man had told him his wife was dying. The subject was asked to complete the story and present his reasons for his choices. The reasons and the ending are then scored so that the person's reasoning could be placed into one of the six categories.

It was now discovered (Reference A) that preferences for the first two stages of the so-called pre-moral level were predominantly found in children and then decreased until the next two stages became dominant in the reasoning and were found to be stabilized around the age of 13 in most children. The last two stages as the chief preference for moral solutions began to increase from about the ages of thirteen to sixteen. Hence these most differentiated moral choices acquired meaning only in adolescence and required an extensive background of intellectual growth and social experience. The evidence pointed to the fact that children and adults go through a sequence of steps in their choices on moral situations and in their moral judgment.

It may now be more apparent why this research and the conclusions are very relevant for the discussion of a developmental stage of human autonomy that enhances rather than destroys the basic fabric of human society. Kohlberg and his associates found (Reference A) that moral reasoning progresses in stages along a fixed sequence, so that the crystallization of the moral choices of an individual at any given stage depends on earlier attainment of the preceding stages, in a definite order. Furthermore when the person moves on to make most of his choices at another stage he is restructuring his thinking and is displacing the thinking used at an earlier stage. Hence moral judgment is a part of personal development and it becomes a visible and identifiable personal characteristic of that individual. It is furthermore distinct from intelligence and cultural background. The most important implication here is that moral characteristics at Stages 5 and 6 and the consistency of a person's choices at these (and at other stages) is primarily governed by his general maturity. The extensive background of social experiences and intellectual experiences that accrue from getting older help the individual to progress to higher stages in moral reasoning. Full moral maturity is therefore not possible until more advanced age. Stage 4 (Reference B) was found to be the dominant stage of most adults tested. Kohlberg wonders if Stages 4, 5, and 6 are perhaps alternative types of mature responses that form alternative channels of personality crystallization. Nevertheless the testing of people in a variety of cultures shows that the developmental sequence of moral judgment goes along the same six stages. Hence there is some evidence of the fixed development of moral concepts in Man along stages. This fact has already been demonstrated to take place in the realm of intellectual and abstract reasoning from Piaget's work.

Normal development may therefore lead to an orderly progression. Similarly certain experiences and cultural exposures may lead to fixation or even regression. For instance, the justification given by Adolph Eichmann in his trial in Jerusalem for his activities to eliminate the Jews in Nazi Germany all cluster at Stages 1 and 2. Similarly research has shown that delinquents score at Stages 1 or 2. Repeated misconduct is therefore related to deficits or to retardation in general moral judgment. Moral maturity on the other hand is the capacity to make decisions and judgments that are based on internal principles. For instance, some people past their late twenties were found to be pure 5 or 6 types in moral reasoning.

Some impressive evidence (Reference A) that has accumulated around the validity of Kohlberg's discovery of the orderly development of moral reasoning comes from experiments in which children and adolescents of various ages were given the opportunity to cheat without being aware that they could be checked. This behavior and similar transgressions in moral conflict situations were found to be related to their maturity and moral judgment as shown by their preferences for answers scored for the six stages.

While the following excursion into the writing of George Mead cannot be considered evidence for Kohlberg's account of moral development, it is impressive that Kohlberg's major conclusions derive from an astute observer of Man, such as Mead, who stimulated the world with his views ever since he wrote them over forty years ago. Mead attributes part of the advancement of civilization to the capacity of men and groups of men in nations to take on the role of a person who is like themselves and a lot of other people in his reactions to events, people, or feelings. This ability elevates Man beyond the level of a biological individual who merely reacts to his own needs. Maturity therefore involves a reflexive thought about others and allows for a separation of the self from others. If one translates this ability into the ability to think of one's effect on others and to evaluate their reaction to oneself, one is in the realm of Kohlberg's last two moral stages -- namely, Stages 5 or 6. Kohlberg gives credit to Mead who preferred to talk about a religious attitude rather than moral judgment and who defined it as the capacity to feel at one with everybody. This "religious attitude" may occur only for a few hours a week or only for one day during which the person takes on the "generalized other" into his views, so that it becomes part of one's concern and planning. It is also significant for our thesis and for our conclusions about the inevitable relationship between moral thinking and autonomous behavior that Mead sees a connection between the capacity of exhibiting one's own individuality and the capacity to take the attitude of others. The former capacity is more competitive as one demonstrates one's propensity for self-fulfillment, while the latter takes into account the attitude of the person whom one may be affecting in the process. Hence one can be individualized and still feel as a member of a community. The latter requires the empathy with others or the taking on of the "generalized other" which is similar to developing universal principles of moral action as described by Kohlberg.

Another independent confirmation of Kohlberg's discovery of the maturation of morality comes from the realm of contemporary philosophy. Harry Girvetz describes a science of moral behavior by comparing all the philosophers who have speculated on ethical behavior. He arrives at the same end stage as Kohlberg although he does not cite the latter anywhere in his book and presumably has not read him. Girvetz concludes that a moral act is determined by the way in which it is willed by the person rather than by the nature of the art itself. Moreover he discusses this form of principled morality as an achievement and not as an endowment. It requires both a form of personal maturity as well as freedom from poverty and slavery.

Kohlberg has pointed out that he was only interested in one form of behavior, namely in the formation of moral concepts. He was then able to claim that he found that this form of cognitive reasoning develops in a fixed hierarchical sequence in every culture. While he therefore specialized in the development of thinking processes he was also by implication dealing with one aspect of personality development. This fact has been recognized by both Kohlberg and by Loevinger, whom we have already quoted as one of the authorities who saw the development of personality topped by a stage of primarily autonomous behavior. Kohlberg acknowledges that psychologists like Jane Loevinger and Eric Erikson were even more ambitious in explaining a hierarchical and invariant sequence of stages in the development of the total ego (Reference D). The important point for our purposes is that Kohlberg again emphasizes that the pinnacle of development in his smaller segment of behavior is a form of autonomy. Stage 6 of moral reasoning makes the bearer responsible to a general principle of morality that was chosen by him from his own sense of rational responsibility and that may vary from case to case as he moves through life. His moral choices are not necessarily based on the majority view or on the laws. For instance he may choose to let his spouse die more quickly despite the laws regarding murder if the spouse is terminally ill and unable to function with any sense of dignity or without pain. He may decide to oppose his country's efforts in a war such as the one we waged against Vietnam if he feels that it subjects the enemy and his own people to unnecessary death and suffering and is not solving the problems it proclaimed to tackle.

Naturally the development of other processes in the personality such as emotions and the crystallization of the self are parallel to cognitive development. They all represent different perspectives in a fundamental unity of personality organization and stand united by their common reference to a central concept of the self. Kohlberg realizes this when he equates ego stages in Loevinger's and Erikson's systems with his six stages of moral development. For instance he notes (References C and D) that Stage 5 or 6 thinking does not stabilize until the adolescent has passed through Erikson's identity stage and beyond. These two stages and especially the latter are not reached until the late twenties or even later. As one acquires new responsibility for oneself with the development of a firmer identity one may generate a greater freedom to make one's own choices. Only then can one make moral choices defined by the last two stages of Kohlberg. Also, an adolescent may develop a cognitive awareness of principles, but only the adult can develop a real commitment to their ethical use. Only an adult carries the more sustained responsibility for other people. He therefore makes irreversible moral choices for others which Erikson called central to the development of an ethical sense that is typically found in his adult ego state of generativity. Generating new lives and ideas widens the identity of the person to include more of the human species than himself alone and thus propels the person to consider universal ethical principles for his moral choices. Similarly the person who functions at either the integrated or the autonomous ego stages, according to Loevinger, is thereby able to redirect his reasoning to contemplate general ethical principles of conduct. He can then emancipate himself from mere conformity or from an exclusively conscientious adherence to majority practice.

The main reason why Kohlberg's work and conclusions are so important for our thesis is that his discovery of a developmental sequence of increasing attachments to moral judgment parallels the development of other processes in the personality that culminate in autonomy and self-actualization. Hence we have some empirical evidence that autonomously functioning people have matured to a sense of ethical responsibility that makes them view their activities to their fellow man in terms of universally accepted principles. These principles are rooted in justice, equality, and respect for human existence. We have met this correlation once before when we found a sense of conformity and responsibility to be one of Maslow's characteristics that he discovered to be abundant in his forty self-actualizing subjects. Now there is more stringent support from experimental work on many people in different ages and in different cultures. We can thereby reject the notion with some conviction that self-actualizing people are necessarily irresponsible and selfish and are thereby impelled to immoral behavior that elevates their own creativity and need satisfaction beyond the concerns of their fellow men.

A superb confirmation of these points was recently supplied by the findings of a large-scale study carried out by the psychologist Stanley Coopersmith. In this independent research the focus was on the development of self-esteem in children and not on morality. The thorough investigation of ninety children of different ages and of their parents found that children with high self-esteem were reared under well-defined rules. Contrary to some expectations these children were more creative, assertive, and independent, even though they grew up in homes in which there were structured conditions and definite limits and standards. This information was clearly available to the children. Such limits and early restrictions correlated with greater self-knowledge, greater experiences, and more enterprising actions. Such children not only developed a positive sense of themselves, but they clearly stated their rights and privileges and that of others. Furthermore they possessed a better tolerance for the individual expression of others. In other words, firm and clear limits from their parents created clear internal definitions of one's beliefs and attitudes. Ambiguous limits, or the absence of same, force the child back on his own resources. He develops standards for which he is not prepared by his environment and his maturation.

On the other hand the child who could explore both his strong and weak points in an environment that was clearly defined and therefore manageable was then prepared to explore broader fields. In terms of our general systems model this child was able to move to a stage where he could generate and invest surplus energy. In terms of our focus on moral and responsible behavior this study shows that the beginning of creative and self-actualizing behavior was germinated in a firm parental environment which stressed firm regulation, greater demands, and therefore greater adherence to well-defined ethical standards. Again the development of a well-defined morality predates or is correlated with the development of autonomous behavior.

Further support for this conclusion comes from a recent effort to carry out a psychological analysis of the determinants of free choice in a responsible, mature individual. James Easterbrook cites Kohlberg's work and that of others to show that there is no conflict between the demands of individual responsibility and the demands of morality. He notes that the moral thinking that develops along the stages such as described by Kohlberg progresses from reliance on external control to reliance on inner control. He also notes that the development of higher moral principles produces more evidence of freely willed and responsible behavior. This kind of person does not distinguish between what is good for himself and what is good for society. He unites this pre-moral dichotomy into a single principle. He therefore understands that his responsibility enlarges to promote the development of other people as well as of himself.

Easterbrook also concludes that intellectual advancement and informed living experience teaches a person that his own self-interest is bound up with the concerns of the community and is stimulated by acts of social justice. Hence moral maturity reduces egocentricity and increases self-discipline because the latter is based on increased knowledge or on "informed intelligence". Again we are shown that increased autonomy does not lead to blind and irresponsible self-interest.

Besides providing the only fertile ground for autonomous behavior in human maturity, a well-developed set of mature principles of morality also has the powerful weight of safeguarding the survival of human societies. Recent scientists and philosophers have become aware that long-standing social ethics like the Golden Rule and the Judeo-Christian tradition have pragmatic value for the welfare and progress of the social order quite apart from their reputed origin from a god or a prophet and quite apart from bestowing the crown of "virtue" or "truth" or "good boy or girl" on the believer.

Recently the psychologist Donald Campbell argued that traditional group-centered morality or altruism may have had social survival value in numerous human societies over the course of history. He even raised the possibility that altruism as a trait may be biologically derived from some of our genes, since we can accept the almost perfect altruistic roles in social insect colonies such as bees and ants as entirely determined by biological inheritance. While this interesting speculation detaches traditional morality from theism and from God's authority it is debatable that it is merely found in some individuals as genetically inherited tendencies mixed in with traits of selfishness, or whether it is socially determined and transmitted. In the main, however, Campbell's thought-provoking analysis points to the survival value of both altruistic and self-oriented behavior. Therefore the traditional concern for one's neighbor need not be based on religious authority, but is simply a proven and well-formulated way of ensuring the survival of complex human societies. The Golden Rule therefore may be the accumulated wisdom from social evolution that has pragmatically proven survival value.

Kohlberg's scheme of development along more differentiated stages of morality also supports the value of social responsibility for the survival and stimulation of autonomous behavior. Social responsibility toward others must be worked out and defined as a foundation before avenues of autonomy can be set or new avenues tried out. Our social laws and our morality are a product of our tendency to organize our social interrelationships on the cognitive level. This idea is supported by the requirement that living systems tend to organize the forces relevant to their operation in order to minimize surprises, especially catastrophic ones. This organization then allows the accumulation of surplus energy and its reorganization at a more complex level where it can be invested in new (and self-actualizing) activities.

Such a form of social organization is already apparent at the simplest level. If I extend my activities into my neighbor's backyard he will retaliate and I will have to expect attack, and to defend myself or attack first. This process may escalate into destructive warfare. Moral thinking on the simplest level of Kohlberg's stages already takes this necessity for social or cognitive organization into account. We meet this form of safeguarding one's realm of action already in the territorial behavior of animals. Among many animal species territories are carefully defined, marked, and defended. Such marked territory is often recognized by other animals. While this form of marking one's boundaries is instinctual here, it is the forerunner of social territorializing through laws and principles. It minimizes surprises, saves energy, and has survival value. Kohlberg shows that this old way of guaranteeing a breathing space can be expanded to include more complex human activity, such as thinking. It can then safeguard action that we have labeled self-actualization. Hence morality at a higher evolutionary level as found in human beings and as discovered by Kohlberg in Stages 5 and 6 is a necessary condition before autonomy can be seriously developed and can have a chance to function. Autonomy is therefore enclosed inside moral tradition just as the animals' physical life space has territories. These "boundaries" become an internal testing ground and guarantee to each person that one's demands and promptings won't hurt his neighbors.

Armed with these various principles we can begin to understand a number of long-standing traditions and stories. We see, for instance, how the principle of ethical humanism in the Judeo-Christian tradition came about and why they have survived for so long. The Golden Rule of doing unto others as you would have them do unto yourself or "Love thy neighbor as thyself" are examples of 6-stage moral reasoning. They have contributed to the brotherhood of Man and to cooperation within communities. They enable these communities to investigate and conquer nature and to defend themselves against outside attack by other groups. In the course of such societies people matured to the stage of principled moral thinking, and some even had the initiative or the courage to proclaim the principles as general guidelines. The prophets and Jesus Christ are examples of such people. Their fame was in part determined by their intellectual vision that could penetrate conflicting traditions. If they had the ability to teach and to attract others, and if they exhibited other marks of psychological maturity such as faith in themselves, and if they had the boldness to venture forth and to say; "Look at me", and if favorable conditions existed in their time and culture, then they became well-known and revered. The reason we still listen to these people and quote them is because they reflect and highlight what is in all of us as we develop along similar psychological lines sketched out by Kohlberg and other students of personality. In other words, their teaching fell on fertile ground as defined by the principles of cognitive and emotional development. Therefore we don't listen too often to other former prophets like Hitler or Caligula.

We find further support among the famous philosophers of antiquity. Socrates described the "Just Man"; the stoic philosophers called it the "laws of reason"; Saint Thomas Aquinas called it "the natural law", while Kant spoke of "the moral law within". This law represented an inner obligation to respect the dignity of the human being and to promote the common welfare. The man following this inner conviction follows this reasoning because it appears, just to him, and because he sees justice to be the very essence of the life and health of the human soul. Locke anticipated Kohlberg's empirical demonstration when he proclaimed that this virtue is the highest perfection of human nature. John Rawls echoes these sentiments in a recent book where he concludes that there are universal principles of justice on which rational people can and should agree when they organize their society. These principles, according to Rawls, are: 1. A maximum liberty compatible with a similar liberty for others, and 2. An absence of inequalities that would be harmful to those least advantaged. Kohlberg found his mature subjects agreeing with the two principles (Reference D).

The connections between self-actualization and principled moral judgment also have important implications for both free choice and for the limits that have to be placed around it. A strongly developed sense of autonomy also includes a feeling of respect for others found in the same path of development as oneself. As one extends one's self-fulfillment wings, one's respect for one's own attempts of creativity is imbedded in the general respect for human autonomy and diversity and for the deep value of human life and human needs. Hence the autonomous person also has tolerance for the interests, foibles, and mistakes of others. He rejoices in the attempts of others to soar and exults in their successes as well as taking part in some failures of people of like interests. His choice of interests is tempered by his moral attitudes, so that he will not actualize himself in ways that detract from others or hurt them. For instance, stamp collectors or the collectors of bottle caps or even people with "silly" hobbies are not hurtful to others. Ballooning may similarly be without harmful repercussions to others as long as one does not descend over property that can be destroyed, or as long as one is willing to pay for or repair whatever was damaged inadvertently. The collection of animal furs and clothes from animal furs may be in that category until a sizable group of conservationists should arise who want to preserve rare animal species and who would be hurt in viewing the collector's display of his skins and coats. The acceptance of human diversity is another moral law that can promote both a tolerance for different human reactions and an encouragement of self-actualization.

The tolerance for diversity is opposed by the sometimes overwhelming need for uniformity in order to contain one's own fears and one's sense of shame and doubt. This is often found - for instance - in a dictatorship, and cripples moral functioning. If we are instead allowed to accept some of our decisions as partially our own and are allowed to take partial responsibility for them, we are then also able to think through the consequences of our actions. Here again we see at work the influence of a mature sense of autonomy that is then promoting higher moral thinking. Under these conditions we are not forced to depend on fate or on God or on any "inner devils". For similar reasons we also recognize the seizure of one's own responsibility as a great achievement. That is why so many people admired Anwar Sadat and Menachem Begin when they negotiated the peace treaty. We felt that they deserved the Nobel Peace Peace Prize primarily for the more valiant effort of putting aside their prejudices, the myth about the other, and their paranoia, thereby suspending any irrational envelopment in their beliefs.

Kohlberg (Reference D) feels that our governmental system is grounded in Stage 5 reasoning. However, from his research he concluded that less than 20% of the population reach that stage of moral reasoning. Today, as in the days of our nation's birth, most adults are at the conventional "law and order" fourth stage. Kohlberg adds that our forefathers may have understood this state of affairs intuitively and designed a government which would maintain the principles of justice and of broad human rights even though the people in power did not function primarily under such principles. Perhaps this is why they included the checks and balances, and guaranteed other domains of free action as, for instance, the judiciary and the press. Hence the principled use of freedom must be guaranteed to give people a chance to develop into it. Once one reaches such a stage one develops a greater sense of responsibility for others and for the world. We can see the inevitable progression here; freedom must be guaranteed so that a sense of responsibility develops which in turn provides greater safeguards to freedom and opens up new freedom for self-expression. We see again the interdependence between mature personality development and the promotion of democracy. A greater maturity and sense of responsibility can also stimulate a better understanding of people who are still wrestling with many identity and self-expression problems and are still on the road to fuller development. This understanding could lead to a greater tolerance for irrational behavior and to set up plans for the exercise of irrational behavior among the many. In this way they can express it in safe pockets where it will not hurt others.

Plato asserted that a just man would be indistinguishable from an unjust man if both found rings that would make them invisible so that they could help themselves to the possessions of others without being detected. Plato therefore was pessimistic about Man and pegged him essentially at Kohlberg Stage 3 or moral reasoning. He saw the just man only accepting justice as good of necessity. The just man, according to Plato, must however agree in his own private chamber that injustice is more profitable and would therefore think anyone a fool if he did not take advantage of a ring that granted you invisibility. Plato therefore harbored a rather pessimistic conception of Man. Similarly Kant and the

The Promise Of Human Autonomy

other philosophers before him had argued that it is almost impossible to obey moral laws unless one believes in God as the author of these laws. Why else should any person want to obey the moral principle even if it was given as an immutable idea from birth on? Through the pioneer efforts of Kohlberg and his associates we can now accept the idea that moral considerations can develop out of the exposure to social and emotional complexities. We can also accept the pragmatic evidence that ethical considerations have "worked" -- that is, have produced more good for more people. We even have some recent psychological experiments that show how cooperation and a motivation of concern for others can create a larger payoff. For instance, in an ingenious summer camp experiment (Sherif and Sherif) two very hostile and rival gangs of boys began to cooperate with each other and later formed into one group more friendly and larger when a series of experimentally rigged incidents "broke down" their supply truck, and almost terminated their water supply. The best solution to these pressing problems was to develop cooperation and a working relationship. This became the road to eliminating the existing hostilities. Other experiments have shown that people will cooperate with each other so that each can achieve his and the common aim even though a very individualized effort may give one an initial advantage but may then gum up the works for everyone (Mintz, Deutsch). It therefore becomes possible to credit normal psychological maturity with the development of concern for others and for ethical principles. Perhaps this realization reduces the reliance on a lawgiver in the sky or on a stern judge with his robed representatives in religious institutions. Perhaps we can accept that our most cherished and long-established moral principles were created by mature people and were only attributed to a divine authority to make them stick and to magnify their power beyond that of the few far-sighted men who had created them. Perhaps we can take new faith that morality is a man-made and man-supported and constantly rediscovered set of guidelines that are indigenous to Man's unique development as a maturing organism both in his mind and in his self. This does not mean that each person has to wait until, his own unique development generates these concepts anew for himself. We can rely on the wisdom of Socrates, Moses, and Jesus, and we must rely on the laws of our society until we understand them... or until we develop a sense of our own autonomy and morality so that we can help to change them if they are not relevant to our changing times.

If we take Kohlberg and other personality researchers seriously we can also modify moral principles to fit new realities of human organization. We can certainly supplant the moral values, supplied by God, supposedly by moral values which we evolve out of our mixture of historically proven trends and the creation and experimental testing of new moral principles. We have, for instance, ignored for over hundreds of years the so-called God-given commandments of "Thou shalt not kill" and killed our enemies in battle, killed and tortured our heretics and executed our criminals, all under perfectly "legal" and Stage 4 conditions. We are now rethinking the value of war and battle-killing in view of the possibility of escalating armed conflict to a suicidal holocaust. Also, in some democracies we are rethinking the issue of capital punishment and of euthanasia in view of our moral belief in the sanctity of human life and our belief in the autonomy of the individual. Also, our creativity has taken us to new brinks; such as mass extermination, starvation due to overpopulation, ravages of health caused by pollution, et cetera. We are beginning to examine the sacred right to manufacture a product without consequences, and we are beginning to hold the companies responsible that are poisoning our rivers and our air. We are limiting our nuclear power stations to fail-safe operation and we insist on disaster-planning for them as a condition for them to operate. Our moral commitment to the welfare of living people and as yet unborn babies forces us to rely on our rational capacities in meetings and conferences to come up with new solutions. Moral principles are forged in relation to these solutions. The point I want to emphasize, however, is that an acceptance of a developmental sequence leading up to a stage of autonomy has important implications for the development of principles of morality for all of us. Each of us can reach autonomous functioning and can rediscover the moral principles of history and of our times. Thereby we can make them reasonable guidelines for action. This discovery as an achievement is therefore more valuable as a sign of grace than if we had accepted the moral principles as a gift from God. Once we rediscover them we also realize that we can check and validate them, amend them, and - most importantly - subject them to negotiation with others. In this way we can reach a consensus. They are also subject to wide scale experimentation and verification or change. They can form valid moral principles for us and for our society and they can become visible and shared. This process was not heretofore possible when a small group of people set themselves up as interpreters of values handed down from an otherworldly authority. At that point they maintained the prerogative of so-called appointed religious representatives to have the answers and to have the wisdom.

A further implication of Kohlberg's description of thought on levels 5 and 6 is that this form of maturity generates a true respect for others. It is based on moral concerns for the consequences of one's own actions and those of others, and including concern and respect for their autonomy. This, then, is related to one's own developing sense of autonomy because moral and personality progressions are integrated and thus can be enjoyed as something that is shared with others and emerges from a common medium of growth. If one develops and experiences one's own autonomy, one must also acquire a sense of concern for that of others as another moral principle typical of Stage 5 and 6 judgment. A further principle that may arise is that one's own autonomy rests on safeguarding the conditions that helped it to grow for oneself as well as for other people. Any other form of autonomous behavior becomes an exercise of narcissism as Christopher Lasch showed in such detail. True autonomy is not mere self-preoccupation. It involves a celebration of its exercise as an achievement to which many people and institutions have contributed. The moral development alongside of autonomy also adds obligation to safeguard the political, economic, and familial supports.

We also yearn for and falsely worship "instant autonomy" in our American culture which has dangerous implications. Our search for instant solutions comes from our faith in our own power and in our goal of progress, and is nurtured by some recent successes in our ability to solve physical problems in amazingly short time. After winning a world war against a formidable enemy and rekindling our national optimism we shortly were able to go to the moon, solve the riddle of polio, and provide some prosperity for a large segment of our population. We began to believe the slogan: "The difficult we do today, the impossible we do tomorrow." We were therefore impatient to experience almost instant happiness, autonomy, and freedom. We have thereby failed to recognize that autonomy is a product of a long development. Too many impatient people are either under the illusion of being autonomous while they are still immature or are parroting the instant autonomy.

If we listen to the students of psychological development and to people like Lawrence Kohlberg we realize that autonomy is an accomplishment over a period of time that expresses itself in self-actualization only some of the time. It is supported by a very different sense of responsibility and morality than the expediency-orientation of the narcissist, who assumes the workability of "instant autonomy". The form of more differentiated morality also involves the ability to monitor one's thinking, as Kohlberg showed when indicating that its origin was in concern and in conscience. This monitoring can come in like a watchdog at times to check if one is staying close to one's moral principles or if one has thought them out clearly enough. It is perhaps similar to the close monitoring that is exerted over one's behavior by the psychotherapist, the surgeon, the bus driver, or the airplane pilot. For instance, the therapist may be able to listen critically and carefully to a patient unfolding a story even though the therapist's own child is sick in the hospital and he has not had a chance to get the latest report from the doctor or from his spouse. Or the long-distance bus driver will be quite able to drive his bus safely and smoothly over busy highways and through town traffic, even though he is anxious to find out whether the hurricane now approaching his own town is going to leave his house intact. Or the pilot will bring his plane and passengers in even though he may have anxious moments about meeting his wife at the airport since she has increasingly suspected that he may be having an affair with the air hostess who is also arriving with him on the plane and whom he had told that he had separated from his wife. In all such instances the major form of attention of the person in charge is beamed on his work, which illustrates one form of his functioning. Only in the relatively immature person or the emotionally disturbed person is it impossible to monitor the major focus under such distracting conditions. It is for these reasons we pick or test people for such professions so that we can insure their ability to monitor and watch their performance. After all, they have responsibility over the lives of others and we want to make sure that they can maintain a steady and secure attention.

Even though this kind of monitoring is a mental set that is expressly "switched on" for exacting work performance, it resembles in its watchfulness the monitoring which the morally mature person may occasionally cast over his actions. He will also want to check if his actions and thoughts are consonant to the moral principles that he has chosen. We see here the kind of concern at work that an autonomously functioning person casts over his exercise of autonomy so that self-actualization is anything but a selfish plastering of need satisfactions over the surroundings without regard to consequences.

It must now also be apparent that neither self-actualization nor moral concerns are instant gifts of superior heredity or endowment or learning. Nor are they merely styles of living which one can acquire early in life as one acquires the skill to play tennis or the violin. It is rather a slow maturational process and has several important prerequisites. It must be reached through a whole sequence of previous stages that may be agonizingly slow. This process may be especially frustrating to anyone of the "instant generation". The short-circuiting of development and the illusory practice of sham autonomy in our quest for so-called fulfillment creates many problems in our society which will form the major points in the next chapter.

Chapter XII

Autonomy and Responsibility: Towards a Scientific Morality

We have concentrated so far on the potential liberation of Man based on the discovery of his mainsprings of autonomous behavior. We have further pointed out that these discoveries are encouraging because they endow Man with a tool adorned with a workable morality to solve his problems and avoid the mistakes made in our past history. We have also listed the errors that accumulate in political regimes which do not recognize autonomy as a legitimate human characteristic. How can we then solve the paradox of facing so many social and psychological problems today that are much more visible to all of us and fill the volumes of contemporary writers almost exclusively? Is it not curious that we are sometimes less free in these times and that our fears and neuroses are so obvious and driving us to seek professional treatment and other solutions or escapes? Why are so many people in the so-called age of freedom turning increasingly to religious movements and even cults, or subjugating themselves to authoritarian movements with strong leaders? Why have our existential fears proliferated so that our contemporary philosophers and prophets like David Reissman, Rollo May, Erich Fromm, Christopher Lasch, and others are busy classifying and analyzing these fears or suggesting solutions?

The larger emphases in contemporary analyses and future predictions are on the dangers of conformity, the dissolution of values and of the social fabric, the sense of futility and alienation, and the prevalence of crime, drug addiction, suicide, and neurosis. It almost seems as though the existential dilemmas we have inserted into Adam are not only still with us, but have proliferated because of the very freeing of Man from the burdens of work and illness, and because of shouldering him with the heavy burden of his autonomy. In our struggle to emancipate ourselves from the long stage of childhood and from the protection of our parents, we fear an enlarged self-awareness and maturity, and we try to avoid freedom and responsibility.

Let us reiterate and clarify a major thesis that underlies this volume's appeal to our understanding and utilization of human autonomy before we re-enter the darker side of contemporary existence with its many problems. We are first of all accepting a world that is not based on an intelligent master plan which was created by an infinitely intelligent and kind force. Instead, the world is composed of a flux of forces which proceed by fits and starts and harbor no blueprints or logical theories or laws for its operation. There is therefore a great deal of chance operating in all the forces of the universe. Most spontaneous experiments in nature end in entropy, which is a complete absence of organization. This finally subsides into a quiet equilibrium until a new set of forces evolves to start another process. Only in the processes called life do we find tendencies toward organization, because life can only sustain itself if it can bend the forces of nature internally and also externally to prolong organization, reorganization, and new experimentation.

One of the important characteristics of organization on the cognitive level is that we must "make sense" of the forces in nature, including the non-living forces. Hence we constantly try to "understand" and fashion theories about our world. In this way we can understand and predict our environment, protect ourselves from catastrophic "surprises", and bend the forces of nature to our purposes and our fabric of living. We have, for instance, discovered a "scientific" form of investigation of nature, including criteria of "truth", objectivity, and repeatable experimentation that yields us some of the secrets of nature. In this way we can understand the interaction of natural forces and use them for the processes of accommodation to nature or manipulation of it with our machines and inventions for the sake of our own human needs. With this greater understanding of the "laws of nature" we can therefore maximize our own purposes and extend our influence. Thus we can extend the tendency to organize over a larger sphere and maintain a longer period of a "steady state" in ourselves and in our societies. We thereby retard and even stave off many occurrences of disorganization, and we can avoid having to acquiesce passively to random forces in a state of fearsome paralysis. It is of course inevitable that we fail in our understandings or that our technical and scientific know-how is not sufficient to forestall a problem or even a disaster. For instance, we can now protect ourselves from most lightning strikes and from gales, but we cannot protect ourselves from hurricanes or tornadoes. Even though we can predict and chart hurricanes we cannot yet do so for earthquakes.

On the human level the evolution of neurological and physiological forces and of brain structure has resulted in the cognitive manipulation of the environment. This development has allowed us communication and has brought about the creation of consciousness. The resultant psychological forces are organized by the brain's own center, called ego or self. These forces then undergo a certain predictable development to more complex levels similar in nature to cellular development, embryological development to a fully functioning organism, and physiological maturation. Somewhere near the end stage of this developmental sequence is an autonomous phase where surplus cognitive and emotional energy can be invested into the surrounding environment to create new configurations. Some of these may be useful and promote progress to the individual and may even be helpful to other individuals.

We do not, however, comprehend the implications of these new ideas about human development. Modern technology and modern medicine are so new that we have only recently prolonged human life and maximized leisure sufficiently to increase the number of people who develop to the autonomy stage. We have also only recently given them more support and an official political doctrine to allow them to practice this more mature functioning. It is therefore not surprising that there may be a lot of false starts, and even disastrous experiments with this newly recognized and proliferating power. In this chapter we therefore want to examine the problems we have created in contemporary society that may be derivations of more autonomous functioning. Despite the promise of that level of functioning, these problems represent failures because they have created more and new problems for the harmonious functioning of society and Man in it. These failures go along with our conception of the universe as a plan-less place where accident and chance is as often found as organization. There is therefore no reason why failures and blind alleys would not develop. It is for these reasons that our recent literature has been full of treatises on the problems and on the disillusionment rampant in our society. This is true especially when we compare these problems with the great promise of the official doctrine and its hope for human progress and development. We therefore want to review briefly the major problems that have popped up in recent times and have manifested themselves in social and individual behavior that has proven to be destructive or counterproductive to our peace and happiness. We shall try to tie them up in each case with our theory of human development which includes an autonomous face. We will try to show how attempts at autonomy or the unprepared stabs at autonomous behavior may have contributed to the social problem.

A. Problems arising from technological progress attributed to self-actualization

Our technological innovations have indeed transformed our lives and our very existence. We have literally changed the face of the earth and harnessed many secrets of nature for our purpose. However, these products of Man's ingenious use of his autonomy have also brought with them a bewildering new world with many new problems. The psychologist Brewster Smith talks about the need to re-establish our human sense of direction in a perilous world. He points to the paradox that clearly identifies us as the makers of this new world, but it is a world where we feel less and less at home.

One of our most celebrated recent prophets, Alvin Toffler, directs a carefully reasoned discussion towards the discontinuities and disruptions caused by the acceleration of change. He points out the hidden impacts of change and how it affects the products we buy, the cities and towns we live in, and the very nature of our friendships and our love attachments. We are here faced with the possibility that our society may break up into temporary, disconnected, and even competing subcultures. We are then shown how the over-stimulation with novelty, the overload of information, and the stress involved in making constant decisions influences our health and our life-style. The very fact of not any more being able to hand over one's knowledge and experiences and values to one's children adversely affects our ability to make rational decisions and severely strains our capacity to adapt.

Another danger signal comes from the difficulties in finding ourselves in a vastly proliferating society in which the autonomy of many inventions and innovations produce an enormous cafeteria of lifestyles and identities. "Finding oneself" in this information overload is therefore a difficult journey, and becoming conscious of oneself as a prerequisite to self-definition often produces the painful strain of having to glare at this "razzle-dazzle" over-stimulation. Various of our social prophets have written about the difficulties of standing on one's own under the onslaught of decision anxiety and of doubt. For instance, Rollo May describes with great insight the problems that come from a demand to solve our problems rationally as practiced in a democracy while more hidden and often irrational needs exist side by side. Hence many people are pushed too fast to solve social and philosophical aims before they are freed from internal conflict and before they are ready to engage in rational problem-solving. According to May, we inherited a new faith in reason from the willingness to free individual initiative in capitalism which indeed overcame some of the early problems of production, distribution, and marketing. However, laissez-faire economics have lost their efficacy and have since been used to rationalize and hide the dehumanization and mechanization of the person in the modern capitalistic state. The collapse of this confidence in the use of reason came about by the fact that the prediction of inevitable harmony in Man's economic and social relationships with the use of reason did not come true. Therefore the medieval fears that were laid to rest by the new belief in the power or in the rational capacity of the individual were replaced by a new and pervading fear of isolation. It lead to new chronic and acute anxieties.

We must here also remember that anywhere from one-fourth to one-third of our population have lived at or below the poverty level over the last hundred and fifty years and have either been barely able to maintain a subsistence level or have suffered gravely because they could not do so. This evil is a glaring demonstration that our society cannot follow up on its promise to guarantee a decent existence if the person strives for betterment and self-fulfillment. The people below the comfort line are not only unable to eat adequately or have adequate housing, but they also are suffering from poor health because they cannot afford adequate medical attention. Their motivation to be more successful is further nipped in the bud because they fall short of getting an adequate education for jobs, both because of their lack of funds and because of their reduced motivation. The psychologist Kenneth Keniston points out that the children of these people are excluded from our society and face discrimination by the majority. In this way they breed further problems for themselves and for the rest of us. He joins other political critics by blaming our system which he sees "driven by the relentless quest for innovation, growth, and profit". He feels that the system has worked well for a majority that has elevated our nation to be one of the most prosperous in the world. However, this feat has been achieved at the expense of maintaining a pool of cheap labor for the menial tasks still required.

These big deficiencies are starkly revealed when the light fades from the bright solution of yet another one of our old problems. Thus we have managed to get to outer space, travel to the moon, borrow the great power locked up in the forces of the atom, broken the genetic code, and eliminated an impressive array of illnesses that used to be the scourges of the earth. We have solved age-old problems of production and distribution. For instance, less than seven percent of our population is now growing and harvesting the food for all of us so that ninety-three percent of us are freed from finding, hunting, or growing the materials we need for our three daily meals. Even the unity of mankind without wars and a further conquest of nature now become a realistic possibility for the future. Nevertheless, more people are feeling increasingly uneasy and bewildered. The problems enumerated above, including crime, pollution, recession, sudden shortages of energy, and inflation often cause the individual to feel powerless in his own life and also as a member of the society. He becomes a victim of these evils and becomes unable to inject his voice to control his and his neighbor's destiny. He seems increasingly faced with a seeming tyranny of the machine and with a faceless bureaucratization of big government.

Rollo May (<u>Love and Will</u>) calls this a "schizoid world", because he sees a lot of people are out of touch, avoid close relationships, and who are unable to feel what is stirring them. He relates this emptiness in many lives to the lack of power in directing one's life or influencing the world. Hence the feeling of despair and futility leads to apathy, to lack of feeling, or to a psychopathic thrashing out, which become defenses against the inevitable anxiety in the face of the objective powerlessness. The inventions like nuclear power and the possibility of nuclear destruction create a sense of futility. According to May, the individual is told that he can do anything he wants, and yet he has less power in the world than in former times. These contradictions plague the person with doubts about himself which may result in his virtual paralysis and in his turning away from an involvement in the life around him.

In a penetrating analysis of the successes and failures of capitalism in the last 200 years Robert Heilbroner sees an ideological shift in government from a laissez-faire value system to one where the government feels obliged to take a more active responsibility for assuming a minimum level of economic performance. This shift has led to a wide variety of welfare functions, such as social security, welfare payments, and medical care. The spending associated with these programs not only increases the size and scope of government but generates an inflationary force. It has also generated a philosophy of entitlement, so that people on all levels of our society are assuming that subsistence, economic stability, health, education, peace, and freedom from crime and persecution are rights to which they are entitled.

The changes that have been brought about in our lives have also partially brought about great increases in the needs for minerals and for energy resources. Also the great and violent changes created by an industry trying to fill the demands have created such problems as air and water pollution, unwelcome changes in the environment, a dangerous rise in world temperature, and the accumulation and seepage of chemical and nuclear waste. In other words, the experiments to create more comfort and enjoyment for a vast number of people and the attempts to take more responsibility and concern for the security and welfare of all people has also created new problems and inequities. Where some problems are solved or when new paths are broken, new problems arise and can become overwhelming enough for a while to force some people to declare the original thrust as failures. Heilbronner advocates a major shift to economic planning to bail out the capitalistic system. To this end a great amount of energy and attention must be paid toward planning the economic processes. In this way we can create irresistible forces to monitor, control, and supervise all aspects of the economy as it has never been done before. The emphasis must be on the protection of the rights and benefits of mankind rather than correction of the erosion.

While these are ideas for possible blueprints of the future, the apparent or actual failures of some of our economic experiments have bred some disillusionment and some apathy. While this erosion in drive and optimism has not yet led to paralysis, it has resulted in a widespread jump into quick solutions or into avenues of escape from their responsibility, as we shall see below.

B. <u>Dangers lurking in the lure of autonomy without adequate psychological preparation</u>

We live in a culture that extols the autonomy of the individual as one of the highest values. Our history is rooted in the establishment of individual autonomy against the curtailment of it by an arbitrary and distant power. At one time this power was represented by the British crown prior to our revolution and prior to the Declaration of

Independence. We have immortalized this sentiment not so long ago in a popular song where we express it as "Don't fence me in". Our folk heroes have expressed it by displaying utter independence away from human control, even if we had to change our folk heroes from cowboy to truck driver, thus keeping abreast of the times. As we have shown in Chapter VI, a functional sense of autonomy develops only slowly as we gain a greater sense of security, awareness of our skills and deficiencies, and a secure definition of ourselves. This process requires a long period of maturation and goes on through an extended period of dependency which we have inherited from our evolution. For a long time and during various times in our more mature years we need to be dependent on others for some of our needs and even have to lean on the experts and other authorities for information and answers. The psychoanalyst Erich Fromm (<u>Escape from Freedom</u>) has best explained the dilemma that confronts modern Man in such a culture as ours when he is faced with the promise of autonomy and the lure of freedom while he still feels afraid to let go of his dependency and his security. This fear of letting go also produces a fear of freedom, because freedom alternates periods of isolation and self-doubt with periods of exaltation and self-confidence. Faced with need to examine old standards and be flexible in one's decision forces many a person to escape into a more subservient role readily provided by demagogues and power-hungry leaders. Hence we have our share of "authoritarian personalities" who drown their insecurity by accepting the clear standards of a movement which divides the world into good and bad people or into "our group" with "our standard" and "the others". These people flock to religious, political, and authority figures who promise happiness and salvation for a strong commitment to their values and their ways of expressing them. This form of foreshortening of one's development is often reflected in the bigot, in racial and sexual prejudice, in religious cults which require obedience, and in fascist movements.

The pursuit of the valued goal of autonomy may also push people too quickly into a state of isolation. Either some people mistakenly relate individualistic goals with cutting oneself off from friends and peers or they are so intent on practicing autonomous behavior without

The Promise Of Human Autonomy

experience in prior psychological stages that they don't know how to relate. They are then apt to turn others off. To remove oneself from the mutual give-and-take and from more intense relationship with others is really like throwing out the baby with the bathwater. Yet many people mistakenly hunt after instant happiness or instant love on these very unprepared individual terms. They are therefore not able to find either. They also become disillusioned and may become either bitter or depressed.

The tendency of isolating ourselves too early and making us afraid of trusting our still untried judgment is also reflected in the lack of concern that we often show in the face of suffering and cries for help. Most of us still remember the symptomatic case of Kitty Genovese. Thirty-eight different people in New York City witnessed from their windows of their homes how a young girl down in the street was repeatedly stabbed by an assailant even though this sequence took several minutes until the girl died and the assailant fled. None of the silent figures stirred a finger to call the police or to try to intervene and aid the unfortunate victim. Several psychologists have since investigated the question of when and how innocent bystanders come to the aid of a stranger in need of help. While they have also indicated the need to preserve personal boundaries in busy city life as a way of protecting oneself from over-involvement and perceptual overload, the well-guarded boundaries so many people draw around themselves also indicate a fear of getting involved. People become afraid of venturing out into a unmapped territory in which no guidelines exist except what one can improvise on one's own in the spirit of the moment. If we ask people to be autonomous before they have had the psychological preparation and the prerequisite opportunities for experimentation in their development, we guarantee this seemingly selfish isolation. The excessive praise of autonomy without foreknowledge and training may instead promote an absence of community feeling, and a reduction of neighborliness. It may force the individual to redraw his frontiers so that he exists in a very small psychological world.

C. The misuse and distorted use of autonomy

Again the relentless propaganda about the value of autonomy and independence has created a curious adoration of "success" as a concrete and identifiable goal of development as an independent person. Especially in America "success" is correlated with a self-made individual who moves beyond his initial station in life and proves his autonomy by advancing his standing in the community a few notches. The move is usually defined by a road that travels along well-defined positions and titles. These job placements provide visible status and economic rewards which then allow further very tangible embellishments of the status, such as specific possessions, well-marked areas of residence, and social memberships and distinctions. In order to enter the road of upward mobility to higher status as soon as possible, it is necessary to cast off from one's family of origin. One has to establish one's own small family without depending on one's relatives or on one's roots. The script calls for an elevation into status positions beyond what one's parents achieved. Following in father's footsteps would be a mark of failure. In the prevalent ideology of the first two-thirds of the 20th Century in America before the appearance of the counterculture both parents and child entered into a common conspiracy to make sure that the young man or woman "bettered himself" beyond social and economic accomplishments of the father. Various sociologists and social critics have discussed the price so many people paid for this fierce forward push under the battle flag of "independence". By cutting oneself off from one's roots and by rejecting the model of one's parents one burns one's bridges unrealistically and thereby makes it impossible to return to a haven filled with acceptance, love, and nurturance which everyone needs at times. This idea rejects guidelines that have helped in the past to pave the way from the baby's complete dependency to a greater sense of self-confidence and initiative. Worst of all, it creates a crippling sense of tentativeness and unwillingness to take up new roots, because the beacon of success requires one to be ever footloose and pull up the stakes again when lady luck moves a beckoning finger around another corner. Hence a person on such a treadmill does not want to define himself too securely and does not want to cultivate lasting or deep relationships. These may hold him down when he finds another opportunity to move upward. At that point his old friends may become unwelcome baggage, or the basic satisfaction he may have experienced with them may tarnish the new goal and keep him stationary. Such wallowing in the old pleasures may invite "failure". The critics and psychologists who have investigated the effects of this upward mobility attitude on personality have pointed out how such an attitude invites deep-seated insecurities and brings about an often dangerous orientation to sit loose and remain tentative. The prevailing sense of loneliness and alienation in segments of our culture, especially in the middle classes most attracted by the banner of upward mobility, has been attributed to this unwillingness to settle down with a definite value system or to relate on anything but a superficial level.

One of the over-the-counter remedies that have sprung up to cure some of the resultant insecurity and up-rootedness have been the various sensitivity and growth of encounter groups. Typically they offer a sense of sharing under the watchful guidance of a more-or-less trained leader. In this way the unfamiliar release of feelings and the sharing of one's basic reactions toward others is controlled so that it does not get out of hand. Then these unrehearsed feelings neither plaster others like a shotgun nor boomerang back on the sender. In addition these groups typically develop a sense of trust and of cohesion on the basis of their open sharing, which is also helped by the artificiality of the groups. They provide a sanctuary away from the "real life", since everyone has entered into the contract of open sharing, and everyone has contributed time and money to make it work. There is some evidence that the learning about oneself and about the effect of releasing and sharing feelings carries over favorably into the "real world" of the participants, although we are aware that the frustration of "re-entry" sometimes outweighs the "high" experience during group meetings. We also know now that there can be real casualties in encounter groups. The proliferation, the excessive promises, and the social meaning of these groups and their function as cults have been ably discussed by Alvin Toffler and Kurt Bach.

One other effect of the misuse of autonomy in the upward mobile core culture is the abdication from the more independent judgment that is based on a firmly developed self-confidence. Instead, the adherents to this middle-class ideology cannot trust their own feelings or needs any more. They deaden their inner voices by stressing order, regularity, and the poker face. If one can organize one's environment in a defensive way, there can be no surprises, especially when one may have to turn inward and trust one's own feelings. Or one has ready-made masks to hide behind if an old and unwelcome voice from within blurts out or emerges when one is not on guard. The resultant need for conformity and for keeping up with the Joneses has been well documented by the sociologist David Riesman. His concept of the "other-directed personality" describes the behavior that stills one's own sense of direction, and focuses instead on what others do. In this way one sails in the direction from where the wind is coming from, and is mainly influenced by fashion, advertisements, and the popularity appeal.

This old middle-class ideology has been heavily dented by the counter culture coming from the beatniks, the hippies, and the Woodstock generation, with much justification. However, their multifaceted revolution has not provided definitive answers, so that we have only increased the cafeteria of available lifestyles. Even if the choices now include some healthier fare more in line with the proper sequence of personality development it also has bedeviled the decision by proliferating the choices.

The major issue here is the misuse and exaggerated emphasis on one aspect of human self-actualization. We have seen in Chapters VI and X that an autonomous phase in human development imbeds the exercise of creative and initiating behavior in a lot of prerequisites and correlates. For instance, a sense of trust and competence for the adequate practice of one's skills is necessary as well as the reinforcement by others. A sense of identity as a secure, anchoring place is another essential foundation. The immersion and full experience of close relationships with others provides an important satisfaction and nurtures emerging maturation of intimacy needs. Finally a highly developed sense of morality and a willingness to conform are required to secure a tolerance from others of idiosyncrasies arising from one's experimentation with autonomy. These experiments can then also be judged adequately by the originator in terms of his moral standard rather than being exploded outward like buckshot from a shotgun.

It is therefore a misuse and misunderstanding to wrench the inventions of autonomy and other self-initiated behavior from its emotional and developmental base. It is false to elevate these as the highest good without preparation, and make these the sole indicators of one's successful development. This distorted emphasis focuses purely on independence in terms of difference and novelty, no matter how artificial or irresponsible or unplanned it may be. Any good actor would then learn the proper role and any psychopath could gain recognition merely for being "different" or for being "unique". Recently the psychologist Edward E. Sampson has again pointed out that an individualistic and self-contained ideal in its excesses leads to alienation and estrangement. People are offended and turned away. This exercise isolates people from each other and separates people from the nutrient soil from which we were cast in the first place. Sampson further points out that we are not yet able to cope with the increased interdependence that has developed in a complex technological society. People tend to avoid the basic human bonds and turn inward. This withdrawal from an important source of human satisfaction also makes it harder to sit down together to solve our common energy and population problems, so that this procrastination becomes another casualty of an exaggerated adoration of individualism.

Another consequence of an exaggerated concern with freedom and self-development is that it banishes previous rules regarding personal relationships. Some of these may have been so elaborate and unnecessary in the past as to cast social intercourse into very rigid boundaries. However, the complete removal of all guidelines is again like throwing the baby out with the bathwater. It therefore becomes a scary reaction to approach another human being or to declare one's need to be closer if there are no limits and no guidelines. Due to human need and social demands people are eager to relate deeply and to commit themselves to others. However, without some commonly shared guidelines the involvement turns into quicksand in which one can sink quickly and disastrously. These consequences are, for instance, more glaringly apparent in sexual relationships and in marriage. Sexual involvement has been redefined as a right and a form of free expression of the autonomous man and woman. It has therefore almost become an end in itself and is no longer identified as an activity that can change in meaning and in depth and can undergo a change in development from being merely an adventure or thrill to being an expression or other human emotions and involvement. Again the lack of commonly shared principles regarding marital and family life may plunge many people into unions for which they are not prepared and for which they do not share common expectations. Hence this spirit of experimentation and tentativeness may contribute toward our high divorce rates.

As Rollo May has pointed out, freedom is not automatically bestowed on one just because he is bopping around in an empty sea of free choice. Even though more people can now experience autonomy, we still have to learn the basic "skills". We have to identify the ingredients and learn the secret of steps. Once we are armed with this knowledge we can begin to monitor our own behavior and differentiate sham substitutes merely labelled "autonomous" from the genuine article.

D. Danger from the false promises of "instant autonomy".

Under this heading we are really expanding another misguided use of our belief in autonomy. We have become spoiled by some of our successes in the technological and scientific realms. Crash programs brought about the atomic bomb and the exploration of space and led us to land on the moon. Similarly, devoted effort has almost eradicated some of our worst diseases like smallpox and polio, and has contained other scourges of mankind like malaria. It has caused headway in such killers as cancer and heart disease. Our ingenuity in planning and engineering is enabling us to bridge seas and to tunnel the mountains or to send our satellites into the sky to facilitate communication. What has taken our forefathers decades and sometimes centuries to solve can now be catapulted at times into a few years. These successes have instilled the hope that "The difficult we do today and the impossible tomorrow".

Also, we have developed an exaggerated faith in the engineering skills and expect them to solve all human problems "instantly". We have already met this mistaken faith in Chapter XI, when we discussed the slow development of an autonomous moral character. This optimism for quick solutions also has affected the area of human relations and personality development. We now expect "instant happiness" and "instant autonomy". Everyone under this banner is entitled to try his wings and is guaranteed success without having to have any of the certificates of prior education.

The exercise of this guarantee of uncritical self-involvement can lead to some conditions resembling anarchy. It has, for instance, been most eloquently expressed in the mental health professions by the psychologist William Schutz's prescriptions for his encounter groups: The leader of such groups should follow Schutz's model and give over the reins completely to the participants. If they want to go crazy or hurt each other or act out sexually that is their responsibility. It is based on their built-in autonomy. The leader divorces himself completely from any responsibility and only concentrates on "being a good leader". This abdication of leader responsibility to people who may be too sick or too handicapped or too unprepared to take it without proper judgment is decried by many mental health professionals as a dangerous ticket to disorder and to casualties.

The latest thinking of the psychologist Carl Rogers also follows the "instant autonomy" route for the society at large. Buoyed by his experience of personal growth of clients in his work with growth groups, Rogers now advocates "open forums" in families and schools in which the children and the students have equal voices to set the goals and to choose the techniques of education. He feels that the prevalent rules of the culture and of the past are of little value because they represent the answers of others and are not echoed by the immediate participants. Society can therefore contribute little to the growth of any given individual. Even though Rogers has an extreme faith in the wholesome emergence of self-actualization in the young and the virginal, his reliance on untrained and unchecked seedlings may also result in danger and anarchy.

Another "instant autonomy" is the so-called creative imposition of various cult "treatments" upon people who are not able to function autonomously and thereby become problem cases. Peter Schrag describes in some detail many of the pseudoscientific treatments we apply to deviant groups such as the excessive chemical control of abnormal behavior, psychological misuse of tests and of behavior modification. In our haste to cure the ills of society we may get hold of esoteric concepts and techniques. Sometimes a distinction between freedom and devious forms of control get blurred in the process so that we then replace morality with a system of pseudoscience. We even at times "treat" unemployment and poverty as though they were signs of "maladjustment".

A final word on the effects of "instant autonomy" leads us to a very recent work by Christopher Lasch. He starts out with indicting our society for becoming increasingly dominated by narcissistic individuals. He cites two major reasons for this trend. The narcissistic personality becomes more conspicuous and rises to eminence because we elevate "beautiful people" to prominence and parade them before the camera and the news media. They thrive under this attention and become role models. These people are further not admired for their accomplishments, but for themselves. Naturally they begin to bask in this love and live out the fantasy of their so-called success. These people then fight the restrictions of society and hit out against its basic structure, because they then decide to follow their own rules. The "here-and-now" takes precedence over the future or the past. Like the clinically diagnosed narcissistic types these people elevate freedom of the individual's impulses as the highest good. This penetrating analysis by Lasch shows what a prostituted worship of self-actualization can do. Under this short-circuited redefinition of self-actualization any new and startling behavior is "beautiful" whether this is a fine voice, or a hip-swinging crooner, or a big crook, or a grouchy sports star. People with such "accomplishments" typify the illusion of "instant success" and "instant happiness", so that we accept fool's gold for the real item. This form of worship is premature because it is done without understanding. The label of self-actualization makes the behavior acceptable even though it is counterfeit.

Lasch attributes this development to our mass consumption society where narcissism can become a way of survival in the jungle of capitalist social relations. Hedonism and self-absorption then become escapes and are wrongly classified under the psychiatric labels of the mental health movement. Further illustrations of narcissistic behavior under the banner of "instant self-actualization" are found in the increase in crime and terrorism, in so far as many young people opt for instant gratification and extinguish their concern for the welfare of others. It is certainly found in the increase in drug addiction for which the not-so-distant Pied Piper song of "Turn on, tune in, drop out" is still audible. It is expressed as a worship of crass individualism and a lack of concern for others in the Gestalt prayer, attributed to the psychiatrist Fritz Perls: "I do my thing and you do your thing. I'm not in this world to live up to your expectations and you are not in this world to live up to mine. You are you, and I am I. If by chance, we find each other it's beautiful; if not, it can't be helped." The true meaning in this popular "prayer" as excess individuality has been aptly analyzed by Greening. We also see this lack of concern for others reflected in the increase of venereal disease and in teenage pregnancy because instant sex gratification had become a tangible substitute for intimate relationships.

E. Problems associated with greater self-awareness and with lack of guidelines

Descartes in the 17th Century beautifully illustrated how the exercise of autonomy can be a lonely corner where one must rely on one's own adjustment and where one harbors doubts. He showed this by describing how the atheist must even doubt the theorem that the sum of the three angles of a triangle are equal to two right angles. The atheist can only rely on his own judgment here. For Descartes any knowledge tinged by doubt cannot be "true science" in contrast to our modern concept of scientific truth as an approximation, constructed from statistical averages of many observations. For Descartes only the belief in God adds the stamp of absolute truth on all beliefs.

Rollo May (<u>Search for Self</u>) agrees that we accepted without question what our elders told us many ages ago. We even chose our spouses, our jobs, and the education of our children on the basis of judgment from others. Nowadays people search more for what they want because of the emphasis on freedom, self-reliance, and autonomy. This development also creates doubts and a feeling of emptiness. People don't know any more what they feel and do not know how to go about discovering their feelings. They furthermore do not experience their own desires. Since we are also thrown together through our living conditions and since we experience greater problems from this interdependence, we are forced to become aware of ourselves. Hence we search more frantically for the existence of our own selves. In this fashion we have created the "age of anxiety". The end result is a reaction of futility or despair; we feel powerless to direct our own lives. We may then resort to drug abuse or to apathy. If a person feels that his wants and emotions do not really make a difference, he gives up wanting and feeling.

If the recognition of autonomy as a stage in development and as a goal can create new anxieties and a fear of the unknown, it may in turn restore the wish to become dependent and to become unaware again. The idea is essentially Erich Fromm's thesis when he analyzed why we still do not have genuine political freedom in an age in which we have separated church and state, enjoy universal education, and practice democracy. We may be afraid of freedom and may want to give it up again to a dictatorship, to a majority, or to a demagogue. Fromm also indicts the cut-throat competition in capitalism for creating a fear of freedom. The complexity and enormity of the system also breeds a sense of isolation and a sense of meaningless, alienated insignificance. Hence the individual cannot develop to the constructive character structure in which self-actualizing behavior is possible. Instead, the person escapes into submission to a leader or into compulsive conformity. These two characteristics define the "marketing personality" character which is unique to capitalism. This character type takes his cues from the fact that value is determined by consumer goods in the marketplace, and consumer goods therefore become models for desirable personality traits.

The Promise Of Human Autonomy   XII

Uncertainty in the face of demands for awareness and autonomy may well be responsible for the increase of religious movements and cults. Here too we find a strong inspirational leader, a definitive and well formulated set of values and principles, and a concrete guide to proper behavior. Alienation may also be reduced by forming communal living arrangements. In such groups and movements one may be able to exchange one's individuality for the security of the community. The self may become diminished by acts of self-sacrifice for the good of the community. Since the latter provides reasons and rewards for such acts, one may acquire feelings of euphoria associated with self-sacrifice.

These is no finer illustration of these principles than the wonderful poetic fantasy which Dostoyevsky invents and narrates through the voice of Ivan in <u>The Brothers Karamazov</u>. The story describes the events that take place when Christ decides to reappear silently among a crowd in medieval Spain the day after a hundred heretics have been burned by the Inquisition. After being recognized and surrounded by a crowd begging him to instill new faith he is imprisoned to be burned as a heretic the next day. While he is waiting in his cell the Grand Inquisitor visits him and berates his coming back and spoiling their accomplishments of converting Christ's gift of freedom of the soul into a promise for Heaven and eternity. The rulers who "corrected and improved" Christ's teaching knew the truth, but kept it a secret. Feeling that people could not take freedom and the lack of control, they instead gave them bread, solace, and the crutch of dependency. They therefore became conscience and law for the people. They allowed them to sin and to be weak and then helped them in exchange for strict obedience so that the people adored their leaders as saviors.

Another escape from awareness is reflected in the fear of innovation and the deprecation of modern times. People with these views may reject any innovation and any sign of independence and may even persecute them or join movements that support such programs. Such people may yearn for "the good old times" and become our conservatives and even our reactionaries. Everything of old -- whether values or material things -- is magnified in value and resurrected as a rare find. One of the finest disparagements of the "good old times" was Barbara

Tuchman's detailed description of the "golden" age of chivalry and of Camelot. In 14th Century Europe there was first of all a complete absence of organization and loyalty at the highest places. In their place we find nothing but constant wheeling and dealing. Treachery and greed reigned supreme among rulers and aristocrats who were mired in luxury and pomp. The clerics, the pope, and the whole structure of the Catholic Church were corrupt and sinful. Most of the clerics raked in money by the bushels for selling pardons and dispensations. Marriages were undertaken for the purpose of making and breaking dynasties, while "love" was reserved for mistresses only. Looting and a scorched-earth policy was the rule in the frequent wars, while armed bands and brigands swarmed the countryside between wars. Due to the toll of troublesome diseases like the plague and many other medical problems, only half of all children survived. Women in the childbearing range of 20 to 32 who were not of noble birth could only have an average of five children. Due to early death, half the population was under twenty years of age. The three major evils of pillage, plague, and taxes produced a widespread consciousness of the prevailing wickedness. The rulers and the institutions failed miserably to solve the many problems. Everyone was absorbed in mutual hostilities, class wars, and brigandage. The emptiness of the military pretensions of chivalry and the falsity of its moral ones slowly caused it to die a painful death. Eventually the resultant reactions of loss of control and of faith pushed people toward rebellion which then brought better days in subsequent centuries.

We can conclude that the difficulties residing in the humanistic model of self-actualization is that it does not offer final answers to the riddles of existence. The questions which Adam had asked himself and we have inherited ever since still have to be tackled anew by each one of us on our own level of development. These questions have to be subjected to our own unique, if tentative, solutions. There are no ready-made solutions. No expert, no authority, no dictator, no communist theory, and no religious dogma can give us a valid blueprint. The search each one of us must make is a lonely journey which may be raved by anxiety. When we rely on our beautiful gift of reason, even that can be evanescent and easily replaced by another vision.

Chapter XIII

SUGGESTIONS FOR THE FUTURE

In the last chapter we have piled up a monumental mountain of problems that we seem to have accumulated in our contemporary society and that are partly inherited from a greater emphasis and use of autonomy. Not only do we have to contend with "future shock", "the culture of narcissism", and "the age of anxiety", but we find ourselves saddled with a fear of freedom, a sense of alienation and of disillusionment. We see our false idols "instant happiness" and "instant autonomy" crumble before our eyes. This sad and tension producing reminder of problems comes after we have illuminated the discovery of autonomy in human behavior and its roots in the processes of life and its anchorage in morality. And we must quickly add here all the gleaming achievements of our technological genius that have transformed our lives with marvelous machines and inventions. What do we do now with our rags as we view the basket of riches? Is there a way out or is it inherent in our unpredictable nature that we wait and muddle through until we either arrive at another plateau or at a golden age, or that we perish in a holocaust?

What I am proposing is that we speculate further on the insights we have harvested at the dawn of the age of autonomy. Perhaps we can recognize from our knowledge of human development and mental functioning some tentative and perhaps experimental solutions to the big questions facing humanity today. Perhaps a smoother functioning of human autonomy can become a goal and an achievement like marriage or having children. Nobody expects to get married before the ages of sixteen to eighteen and nobody expects to have well-developing sons and daughters until later in the twenties. Perhaps we can begin to think of autonomy as developing as one gets older. Maybe we cannot really use it for solving some of our social ills until later in our own development. In the next few pages I shall therefore make some suggestions as to how we can use our new knowledge about life, human functioning, and human development to tackle some of these problems.

To recapitulate our argument for the proper uses of autonomy we have established that the human being functions under the same principles as any living organism. On the psychological or cognitive level he requires an ego as the organizing center for the ideas referring to himself so that he can navigate among the interactions with others with a compass called the self. This self requires values and a faith and is also capable of irrationalities partly determined by unconscious motivation. Like all processes in nature this human being has his ups and downs, many of which are not predictable nor under his control. He goes through stages of evolution including one of self-realization in which he is better able to use his rational powers and his moral judgment in new and more creative directions. He can perhaps make a fresh attempt to resolve some of his inevitable existential doubts. First of all, these doubts have to be recognized and accepted just as we accept that human beings have illnesses, develop colds, get sore feet, and suffer from indigestion, as well as being able to perform feats of physical prowess and have long periods of good health. Perhaps then we can know how to recognize our good and our bad cycles and to diagnose them. We can then make allowances for them. We can also reinforce some of the good ones, encapsulate others, and develop remedies when bad ones don't go away.

Let us for a start pile up the good things we have learned about Man at the beginning of our search for the solutions of the big problems facing mankind. We have learned that autonomy can be recognized as a stage in the development of Man after his long period of enforced dependency. This stage is characterized by the tendency to use energy left over from mere maintenance and need-gratification to reorganize his self-structure for new involvement. Thereby people can involve themselves with new goals and with creative experimentation. This stage comes relatively late in the total life span although behavior more characteristic of it begins to appear in fits and starts at earlier times. In this stage the special capacity to reason can be used differently and more creatively. Then Man is more apt to reorganize his judgment about moral issues so that he is also able to recognize his interdependence and especially that his own self-actualization depends on safeguarding this very opportunity for others. This concern for the community is most fully developed in a democracy and is nurtured by laws of human rights in this political organization. Our technological creativity has provided us with a longer lifespan and more leisure time, both of which are needed to fully use the stages of development and to try new involvements. Finally we have learned that all men and women can experience periods of irrational functioning and can regress, at which times we either give them a wider berth or isolate them temporarily from hurting others.

My main thesis therefore is that Man has risen above the adversities of some natural catastrophes and some diseases. He has begun to understand sufficiently the principles of his nature and of this social organization in large societies so that he can tackle the problems still plaguing him today. We have numerous examples of how men and women have overcome obstacles in their own private lives. Franklin Roosevelt's fight against his permanent paralysis from polio and Helen Keller's triumph on her handicaps of being blind and deaf are examples. As a psychotherapist I have felt fortunate in having the opportunity to witness how human beings can change from self-defeating behavior and badly incapacitating scripts to more positive and rewarding attitudes and behavior.

From the many examples I can remember, two will be presented as illustrations of the power of human beings to rise after they have strengthened their beliefs in their own hidden responses and enlarged their coping devices. In this way they may change the whole environment for more extensive navigation and for greater satisfaction. One example is of the thirty-five-year old wife of a comfortably situated high school principal who was a respected and even beloved member of his community. During the thirteen years of their marriage his love-making had to be accompanied by a rape-like attack that stopped short of physical injury. This woman had accepted herself as a weak and resource-less person who had to submit to these attacks in order to deserve the material and status rewards that were heaped on her by the marriage. After she acquired a much more realistic idea of her strong points and her ability to decide for herself, including the right to have a voice in her own pleasure, she started a new life after a divorce. She finished her education as a competent librarian and was able to make a modest living to maintain herself while alimony provided for her two children. She found new roots in her own very different social circles and developed new satisfactions. One of them was the development of a living arrangement with another man, very different from her ex-husband, with whom she created a life of more genuine sharing and affection.

The second example is a suicidal twenty-seven-year-old airplane ticket clerk who had been reared by a very fearful and insecure widow. She forced him to be strictly obedient and self-sacrificing, without giving him any basic recognition, affection, or guidance. This man when he was a boy of 13 had a brief sexual encounter with an older man who seduced the boy through his own brief interest and genuine concern for him. The boy's resultant guilt was maximized by developing a minor venereal disease and getting secret treatments for it. His subsequent life became a living hell which he felt was a punishment for this horrible sin. He managed to do that by conducting an ascetic life of self-imposed isolation and self-negation. The resultant deficiency in many social skills and his lack of social stimulation led to his being asked to withdraw from a training program in physical therapy. This prompted him to consider suicide as a way out of his depression. With help he eventually developed a new sense of his strong points and was able to take a different view of his early digression and develop a better understanding of his mother's role. He then could put his former life and its "sin" into better perspective and was able to face himself and others again. He finished his training and found new involvements and satisfactions.

My experiences as a therapist therefore supply some of the reasons why this final chapter can be written. If people can come out from behind such handicaps as some of my clients have, there is hope that many other people can build a better future for themselves and for all of us, using new building blocks and better maps. At the same time we can also learn to accept the irrationality of Man, and make allowances -- even institutional allowances, as we shall see later -- fit into our view of nature as a process rather than as an inevitable progression toward perfection, which is doomed from the start.

Perhaps from the very beginning we should realize that there never will be and can be final answers so that mankind can "live happily ever after." The very processes of life itself, of moving to new and different integrations of the primitive energy forces into new structures, is into one of experimentation. In this process "survival of the fittest" is one of the determinants of endurance. Each more complex and energy-saving integration may create its own problems, just as it creates new solutions. Also this reorganization of living forces goes on in an inert state of nature that holds many a riddle to our survival. We can, however, use the tools of our reason and our powers of analysis to discover more of the laws of nature and the laws of life. In this way we can see some progress in our humanistic goals and can achieve an occasional high that calls for a real celebration as on Independence Day.

Before we tackle these issues in some detail there is one final word - and an answer to the cynic. Admittedly there may be limits to our knowledge about autonomy and self-actualization. Furthermore we may not have the kind of proof about our existence and lawful development of the behavioral phenomena we presented in Chapter VI, VIII, and XI. Nevertheless, these ideas are available as blueprints for some solutions to our problems. So why not use them? Perhaps we may fail more miserably if we ignore them, and we may not fare any worse if we try the following conclusions based on these concepts even though we find that they are "all wet".

A. <u>Living with a world of chance rather than a "master plan"</u>

Perhaps the very first task is to face a very hard possibility. It has already been stated by many philosophers and has been implicit in this discussion so far. There is no master plan for the universe and there is no destiny or preordination. There is no blueprint locked up in someone's vault that needs to be either pried loose or x-rayed for occasional glimpses. There are therefore no "laws" that were invested by an all-wise master engineer that govern every process in the universe forever. Nor is it feasible to hold the very opposite point of view of the world as a "jungle". In other words it is not a dog-eat-dog world where the strong triumph and gobble up the weak and unwary, whether this implies the strong meteor, the strong lightning bolt, the strong lion, the strong tyrant, or the powerful crook. It is not a world in which evil and brute strength necessarily triumph at all times, for that would imply the presence of another master plan.

Instead we must learn to accept the world as a very neutral place in which randomness and undetermined change prevails. The meteor glances off or disintegrates in the atmosphere, or falls on a populated place inhabited by intelligent creatures. The lightning either hits a tree or a family in a hut nearby. The lion either kills a zebra or an older antelope for his next meal. The bullet of the rioter either hits the innocent bystander, or harmlessly lodges in the masonry a few feet away. The cancer-producing substance wears down the resistance of one person exposed to it, while it is unable to penetrate the defenses of a second person. We were given a clear window into the haphazard conditions men and women still had to contend with in Barbara Tuchman's insightful description of the ravages of disease, greed, brigandy, and corruption that prevailed in the 14th Century.

The next important principle on our journey out of uncertainty is that living systems impose some order and some organization on the form and material they enclose and take up within their living boundaries. Hence within each cell there are signs of a plan that repeats itself in other cells and that can be stored, learned, and communicated in special structures or in collections of tissues. Man is a living system and has a very complex storing capacity for plans and for enlarging these in his brain. Since we are also functioning on a conscious or cognitive level on which we think, feel, and communicate, we also impose this need for organization on this level. Hence we have a need for order and for lawfulness. We often desperately need to believe in a "just world" even if the world without our influence is random or neutral, that is, neither "good", nor "evil". Our need for order and justice has produced an impressive array of laws, rules, and values. It has introduced constitutions, governments, courts, and science with its laws about nature. For our survival, we require this order to minimize surprises, and we take pride and pleasure in unlocking the secrets of nature and regulating the flow of goods, services, and human interaction. This control also satisfies another characteristic of living systems insofar as it allows us to function on a "higher" (more complex or efficient) level of integration where we can take our energy away from self protection and maintenance of vital needs and reinvest it into other and newer ventures. These in turn enlarge our horizon. In other words, we are able to function on a higher stage of development including the stage of self-actualization.

The implications on the social level are that we try to impose order on a world that is inherently not a "just world" -- that is, a world in which goodness is rewarded because of the existence of a master plan. Our need for order produces a drive for justice and the expectation of lawful retribution. This need then becomes a self-fulfilling prophecy as our attempts become more successful. According to Tuchman's account, there still was not much justice in the 14th Century. Any ruler, feudal lord, brigand, or mob of peasants could engage in warfare, pillage, rape, plundering, the razing of villages or houses, or imposing of crippling taxes. Various killer diseases like the smallpox, diphtheria, plague, tuberculosis, or polio could still strike rich and poor alike without rhyme or reason to the people living at that time. Clerics and merchants could amass fortunes and influence at will and through corrupt ways while hiding behind religious or feudal principles. We have come a long way since then. In many countries laws and strong institutions govern a majority of the activities, eliminating many of the excesses that were rampant in the 14th Century. A greater knowledge of interdependence also regulates the exercise of corruption and of naked self-aggrandizement. Many of the scourges like taxes are now under the influence of majority opinion. Many of the killer diseases have now been practically eliminated or can be treated effectively.

When we give up faith in a master plan and in an inherently just world, we may momentarily face a frightening existential void, because we are giving up a seemingly safe anchorage in a soothingly safe harbor. However, this letting go may only be temporary because it forces us to come to grips with our own power of reasoning and our own resources of autonomous functioning, even if they are rusty or well-hidden. The enforced process of rummaging around may allow each person to take stock of his powers and resources and thereby discover the "capital in the bank" as well as the liabilities.

This total stock-taking must also include a realization that we are passengers on a huge spaceship who have fortunately evolved a consciousness and rationality. We have also as animals engaged in organizing life processes, gained a foothold on this spaceship, and are beginning to understand it and perhaps steer its course. We not only have acquired a working knowledge of the technology and how to harness some of the forces of nature for our own ends, but we are also learning to understand each other so that we can steer the spaceship with a generally agreed plan rather than fighting with each other about direction and control.

When we take stock of our human pluses and liabilities, we must list among the former our sense and utilization of autonomy, our rationality, and our evolved standard of morality. Some of these accomplishments we have achieved without really trying. In other words, part of our foothold on earth has been accomplished by "muddling through". Other results have been due to more energetic management and planning. We have some liabilities. In the last hundred years we have lived through two disastrous wars, we have experienced one holocaust in Hitler's Germany and another in Cambodia and Vietnam, and we find a number of social and psychological problems in the most "developed" societies.

The Promise Of Human Autonomy

However, we get glimpses of further control of these problems and of the randomness in our world. We have overcome big crises and fantastic odds in our history. We know that we can sit down and plan and think a little more and thereby tip the balance against randomness and more in favor of a more "just" world. This will be a world in which we can maximize the satisfactions and predict the rewards and the punishments according to our view of justice.

It has been said that we have gone far enough in the ladder of evolution in view of our large and complicated brain. At least it is not possible to foresee and imagine the mutation to a new species with a super-brain. We can, however, evolve, and with the aid of our brain, so that more complex human beings and societies can develop with knowledge and extensions which our brain can produce. Survival of the fittest becomes therefore replaced by survival of the ideas and inventions. Just as the microscope and the telescope have become extensions of our brain and the computer an aid to cognitive manipulation, so our knowledge of human psychology can become the manipulating device for creating a more fertile social environment.

All these efforts go back to a recognition and use of autonomous thinking and a recognition of its full maturity at the end of a developmental sequence. Only when we are really facing this form of functioning as a reality can we detach ourselves from the belief and search for a master plan, even if the latter may be more comforting and soothing at times. When we really begin to rely on ourselves we are forced to sit down and plan together. Then we also recognize that this process will have its setbacks and that it may produce unpredicted forces that need new solutions. All we need is a belief and faith -- of requiring "order" on this long-range planning level -- in a more orderly and predictable world. At the same time we must give up our hope of discovering the "truth" and in getting ultimate answers. As long as we accept the possibility that we can approximate the truth or make slow progress in our search for laws and answers, we will go along with the true state of nature. All we need to do is to look into other and older sciences and see how those concepts of matter have slowly been replaced by new ideas -- sometimes very revolutionary overthrows of the concepts of matter. Such ideas then allowed the inclusion of new facts and produced a larger harvest of the control of these forces. We are therefore capable of producing "laws" by which short-range predictions are possible, and this is also true in the psychology of personality. I am proposing that we use the insights that we so far enumerated earlier to let go of older ideas about the nature of the world and of Man and thereby build a better society.

B. Implications of relocating control of a random world into the individual for his orientation to life

We already find two recent books that approach the understanding of individual differences and of child development from the vantage point of locating (autonomous) control in the individual. They provide excellent prescriptions for the view that gives the person some sense of direction in a world that is subject to chaos without it. The psychologist Leona E. Tyler in a recent treatise on individuality bases her presentation of individual responsibility in all phases of human existence on the central idea that reality is constantly created and recreated. Citing Whitehead's term "creative advance into novelty" as a basis, she points out that we live in an unfinished universe that also is forever incapable of being completed. She accepts Whitehead's thesis that any event in the future is only partially conditioned by its antecedents. It must, however, wait for its complete determination for the next occurrence because that and each recurrence imposes a spontaneous new element. Tyler therefore accepts the idea of "continuing creativity" in the universe, which does not require the notion of a creator. On the human level our reality is constantly being created insofar as we select and organize what we turn to. Tyler thereby injects a sense of autonomy into human action and reaction, which she refers more to a general free will rather than to the specific meaning we have given autonomy or self-actualization as a well-defined stage of personality development. Here it means that each person imposes constant activity and possibilities on his environment and "creates" his reactions very much like the artist's attack on his inert materials. Only with these assumptions can Tyler discuss individual choices and perception, development, personality, and attitudes and thereby clarify the person's reactions in these areas as they emerge from various psychological studies.

Another recent book tends to communicate to parents how they can educate their children to live effectively in the world as we have described it. The Psychologist Karen Akhoj summarizes the various prescriptions for good character development in children by suggesting that we instill an attitude in our children that has the following contents: (1). One can to a large extent play a part in creating and forming one's own life. (2). One must make one's own choice. (3). One is responsible for oneself and also for others to a certain degree, so that one must share -- but not take on full responsibility. (4). It is important that the child learns that there are limits to self-realization and to unfolding, because: (a). there are forbidden acts, and laws exist that specify punishment, and (b). one needs knowledge for the reasons behind these laws so that one understands their existence; and (c). every person experiences that there is a large and well-stocked reservoir of alternatives for unfolding.

I would like to add here that we would like to harness the creativity that is here seen as a central factor in any human reaction and as a beacon for training the young child. Creativity is also a random process and cannot be programmed, by the very fact that autonomy implies choice rather than reaction. Creative problem-solving can also be directed to social problems, and creative acts by individuals must be monitored to maximize good outcomes. We therefore need controlled creativity to solve problems that may have been triggered by uncontrolled, "Eureka-like" creativity. For instance we need creative solutions to deal with atomic bombs and with their manufacture and storage. When engineers and scientists are asked to construct equipment to extract a new source of fuel from a hitherto untapped source, they work together on this problem. Others coordinate the ideas that come from a variety of different teams. Similarly the excess energy that is available from people operating at this self-actualization stage can be channeled to solve social problems. We further need policing of the creative "sparks" that have been given off by inventions and discoveries, so that they do not hurt more people than they help. For instance, the scientific community and then the courts have taken a new look and taken some guidelines to deal with the discovery that one can change genes through a further understanding of DNA. These guidelines took into account the danger of creating new organisms that might be disastrous to mankind, such as bacteria that might usher in a new disease. We already accept such policing and inspection such as imposing a quarantine for measles and other communicable diseases, the manufacture and sale of TNT, the control of drug dispensation, et cetera. In all these cases we accept the restriction on the basis of our rational understanding of the principles behind them.

A further implication of the capacity of the individual to create his own world, rather than merely react in a world that contains the promise of perfection, is a modification of the goal of happiness. It is an illusion to strive for eternal happiness and harmony, or hope for it as a long-lasting reward. Happiness should be seen as a peak of a normal human process that may also contain failure in its valleys. It is therefore necessary to prepare the person for the experience of isolation, rejection, and failure as normal human events. He should savor success and love as experiences to be treasured and remembered. The gambler already accepts the possibility of wins and losses and of their succession. If our expectations about the world and about our personal sphere of existence are changed we can be more realistic and strengthen ourselves toward the development of new choices.

We must teach ourselves and accept that there can be no "lasting" or "eternal" peace, which had either been pictured by idealists or offered by those psychologists who promise this emotional reward if we only learn to behave and feel properly. There will be inevitable breaks and discontinuity and even threats. If we have set up more extensive negotiating and planning machinery as a tribute to our gift of reason we can cool down a potential threat to our and to other's peace, before any fatal explosion occurs. This process is tried with increasing success for people who try to jump from buildings or for people who hold hostages. As we will discuss later, we are using this process in labor disputes and in some national conflicts already. If we could use it to safeguard the peace of one or two individuals we could expand its use to guarantee the peace of the world.

We are all aware of the solace that people derive from their religious beliefs and their faith in God when real calamities hit them, like an incapacitating sickness, a failure, or the loss of a loved one. Even if the event is terribly disrupting and does not seem to "make sense", it must make sense in relation to the plans of God, who still loves one and listens to one in one's misery. It is similarly possible to derive genuine solace with the belief that the world is more random and not directed by the master pilot. One can accept the calamity as a "natural event" that "makes sense" as a random occurrence or one that defies human understanding. The full acceptance of indeterminacy carries with it the tolerance for a certain amount of disorder and uncertainty as a given characteristic of the world and of life. While it requires the more difficult reliance on one's own reason, it is also a better map. I have been a witness to many nagging doubts that have tortured the believers among the patients I have consulted in the hospital when they try to answer the question "Why me?". We of course need to educate people toward a reliance on their own reasoning and to develop a sense of trust in this source of strength. Witness here the experiments that have been made in child development which show that training the child to think is often superior to training in rote memory. These practical applications to our orientation stem from our central thesis that we have to accept, stimulate, and use autonomy because it is an important characteristic of living systems on all levels of functioning. We therefore cannot any more afford to depend on abject Aristotelian causality that is based on a structuralist interpretation of the world. Such an orientation could include the answers from any oligarchy, dictatorship, creator, or other more powerful than us. Instead we might remember that intellectual activity originates and is monitored by the left brain, while non-verbal relationships and emotions are determined by the right brain. If we accept these divisions of functions we can learn to understand how we supply our own answers and monitor our own reactions. It is becoming increasingly hard to ignore his kind of evidence from one's own brain in answering some of the principles that derive from a just world based on a master plan. Many good people die early and have terrible misfortune. Some evil people succeed, live long lives, and seem to enjoy themselves. There is further abundant evidence of some crooks and corrupt or evil nations being able to "get away with murder". It therefore violates all observations and considering all the grief and poverty in the universe to think this world a "good creation". We therefore require a good deal of free will and a chance to draw our own conclusions about what we observe. We even have to give ourselves the opportunity to make mistakes, and even violate the common good at times, as long as the act or the consequences make sense. The Christians invented an afterlife in which divine retribution will redress an act by someone who took the "freedom" to sin or to be good. Instead, however, evil must be seen as a series of choices that define a continuum of consequences. In this way our choices can become more intelligent.

A good example is one's outlook on the phenomenon of aging and of eventual death. Aging carries with it a loss of strength, a diminishing of abilities and of functions, and a diminution of opportunities for new involvement. It also brings with it some reduction of health and the loss of friends and relatives. The typical reaction has been to dwell on the deprivation, loss, and the experience of sadness. The reaction of "never again" is buttressed by the hope of a new life after death. This implies a perfect state that requires a hope for restitution toward perfect functioning again. Let us substitute a conception that we are a part of nature which is mostly random and constantly changing. Over much of nature we have no control, and there is no eternal sameness nor finite principles governing it. Nature also dictates that living organisms get older and weaker and lose their functions and eventually die. One cannot reverse or change that. Since this process is inevitable one need not feel ineffectual and sad at being unable to stop it or slow it down.

However, I do have a choice as an autonomously functioning organism with some small power to organize my world and to make some autonomous decisions about it. Therefore I have the choice of whether or not I dwell on the sameness of my being and the restoration of my losses. I can instead dwell on what I have had and do have. I did enjoy sport X, hobby, friends Anna, Jim, and Tom, and moments in my work. I had such and such specific experiences and have positive memories of them. I therefore do have a choice of dwelling on these in my stream of consciousness. I can even lift them out of the stream and put them in slow motion and then play them back repeatedly. I can even spend loving care and energy on them. How great was moment A and occasion B! I can savor them and congratulate myself that I had the chance to experience these events or these relationships -- even one with a person that may now be fading away. No one can take away these reminiscences of one's luck and of one's choice. I therefore have the power to choose and to magnify these thoughts. In the same way we have the choice to feel guilty or inferior, as well as the choice to accept the more positive view. In other words we can identify "old scripts" and reverse them. We also have the power and the autonomy to do so, as rational-emotive and transactional schools of psychotherapy have already stated in their principles.

The answer to those who feel that they could not live in a world without order and without guaranty for reward is clear. We ourselves are powerful enough to affect the order of some events and we are also able to experiment. We can experiment with a creative and even with a tentative investment of surplus energy. We can become like the scientist who makes an assumption about a corner of nature and then sets up an experiment to see if he is right. He can either verify his theory or modify it or reject it for another one. In that way he creates some order and gains some satisfaction from having seen his own efforts resulting in some answers.

C. The need to educate for autonomy

If we can genuinely accept the characteristics of behavior found at a stage of self-actualization, we can begin to educate the citizen to look forward to it and to know what to expect. This education requires knowledge about the steps that lead to such a stage, the prerequisites and development, and the expectations that are realistic. Among the latter we would have to include the fact that self-actualization is not an all-or-none phenomenon. It occurs more frequently at a certain stage of development but does not fill the individual's life exclusively or forever.

We have already started to include some of the training in our society. Education at least tries to teach the basic tools that are required in our society to identify one's niche and one's strong and weak points in one's life. It teaches us the tools that may be necessary before an individual can realize his goals and his needs. We also educate for democracy by stressing the principles and its provisions in our schools and in the media. In some school systems children are taught how to think rather than merely to acquire ready-made knowledge. In addition we need to provide opportunities for creativity and to provide rewards for creative, self-actualizing activities. The latter should not be so strongly focused on the more accidental accomplishments of a voice, a pretty face, or the ability to act. These are more skills and tools than the results of individual effort. We need to include more recognition for creative acts that are not merely rewarded by a great deal of notoriety and financial reward. The parenting of a happy and developing child should be elevated as worthy of attention. So would be the building of one's own house, the creating of new business or service, the accumulation of a loyal and devoted following of clients by a self-involving service person or professional.

In addition we need more formal education for morality and for the development of a feeling of responsibility. Kohlberg and his associates have demonstrated that college students who took a course on political and ethical choices, taught in a Socratic manner, moved significantly in their moral development. The gain in complexity of moral reasoning along Kohlberg's six stages was measured before and after on Kohlberg's specially developed test of moral dilemmas. The students in his courses marked up a genuine change on their test scores as contrasted with the scores of control groups. This study has since been replicated in other universities with similar results.

We can also construct a guide about the minimum characteristics of self-actualizing behavior, which would utilize the behavioral manifestations that have been described by Maslow, Allport, Loevinger, and others. These behavioral descriptions can be used as a guide for the population. In this way one can check oneself and one's behavior and create more curiosity about how to grow to such manifestations. Each person can decide whether he can occasionally afford to rely on his own judgment without leaning on an authority, or at what point he can rush his need for dependency away to try and rely on his own hunches. He can ask himself if he might have acquired some immunity for the kind of obedience demanded in the Milgram experiment or for the conformity responses acquired in the Asch-Crutchfield experiments. These questions should be answered by checking whether this independence is genuine or whether it is the expression of an anti-social rebel or of a reject. A person, for instance, could ask himself -- or check -- whether he has acquired the "idiosyncrasy credits" which the psychologist Edwin Hollander felt were necessary before a person in his investigations could afford to deviate from the majority and "do his own thing". If the subject demonstrated genuine acceptance of the goals and of the social norms of his group in prior associations, he was more apt to earn these credits and retain his acceptance and even his status despite more independent behavior. While I do not advocate any widespread testing or self-evaluation with psychological tests, I do want to make the reader aware that the psychologist Everett Shostrom has constructed a test called the Personal Orientation Inventory. It measures several of the aspects of Maslow's self-actualization phase and is based on self-report. It has been validated in its widespread studies on youth and growth and development.

In a more general sense I am wondering if we could not develop the promotion of autonomous behavior as a national goal very much like athletics became a national goal for very young people in the Greek city-state of antiquity. Suppose we received some conclusive evidence from medical and health research that tennis-playing would solve most health problems and banish many illnesses. It would suddenly, become very important that everyone played tennis and played it passively well. Beauty-conditioning would be promoted in many schools, and parents would encourage their children to do the exercises and muscle preparations in order to set them up for this conditioning. There would be a proliferation of lessons and of special classes. Films and talks would all be freely available. Tennis courts would be built by the thousands -- even with taxpayer's money -- and opportunities would be created for everyone to play. Under these conditions we could conclude with some certainty that most everyone could play a good game of tennis by the time they entered their twenties. The vast majority could not do as well as the stars but better than most present amateurs except for the mentally and physically handicapped and the accident victims or people with diseases. There would still be stars and experts playing but we will assume that the society was not geared toward winning games. Instead it would be oriented to good playing as a national and social goal. Everyone would know the right position and steps of development to good players status. Everyone would talk about it. Training programs might be accredited and checked. People could test themselves for certain proficiency standards that are generally acceptable and that identify the "good citizen" who prizes his survival and health. A faith would develop that every person could reach this standard after a certain age and with proper training and preparation. People would be helped to reach this standard and might even be subsidized if they encountered obstacles. If this fantasy is too outrageous I might remind us that we already take a lot of related interest in baseball. What I'm here suggesting is that we could organize the same preoccupation with autonomous behavior as a national standard!

We might become so conscious of the prerequisite and stages in the development of self-actualizing behavior that we could also become our brothers' keepers and help others along the way. This help and concern is further predicated on the more widespread recognition of the value and importance of moral judgment at Kohlberg's stage 6 level, since we would expect a proliferation of this in a society that promotes and values the underlying emotional maturity. We would furthermore become more concerned with promoting the development of maturity because there would be more widespread recognition that functioning at the self-actualization level would help everyone and not just the practitioner. We might thus become actively involved in assisting people and families who may be working under obvious handicaps and might either despair and become casualties or reach for "instant autonomy" from mere frustration. If they do the latter they conceivably could hurt themselves and innocent bystanders or unsuspecting victims. The help needed would therefore become a very pragmatic and rational endeavor instead of mainly charity and humanistic concern. Welfare and mental health clinics would be based on this small pragmatic consideration rather than being motivated merely by "Christian" concern. It is of course quite conceivable and even inevitable for this active concern and help to become enveloped in genuine emotions of caring, sympathy, and even love. Again, our roots in living processes with this push for organization propels us to invest our behavior with surplus energy, such as hope, faith, and love. These in themselves are not merely the frosting but become necessary lubrication or promotion of new ideas and new steps. A further consequence of the proliferation of assistance is to underline and magnify the social sense of responsibility that is the necessary cement for holding an interdependent community together. It will provide the opportunity to exercise this sense of responsibility which would in turn support and strengthen the moral principles that underlie autonomous personality development and give it a firm reality.

One of the first prerequisites for providing an active breeding ground for the development of autonomy is to safeguard the economic and social conditions that provide a fertile soil. It is obvious, in view of Maslow's theory of motivation, that people who have to be primarily concerned with the satisfaction of basic and safety needs cannot free themselves to look beyond toward self-esteem or self-fulfillment. The psychologist James Easterbrook has further reminded us that prosperous people have three advantages that breed the kind of initiative that is related to a personal belief in autonomy. They have access to money, they can avail themselves to better education, and they pick up more of the abilities and even the dispositions that are required for independence and enterprise. Poor people instead put stress on luck, power, and status and do not consider independent judgment or self-control as important. Instead of "free will" they develop a fatalistic outlook which further contributes to their failures to plan their moves with the aid of personal initiative. Their social experiences in a deficient environment produce such beliefs while a belief in "free will" must be supported by environment without such wants and frustrations.

As has already been indicated, a more widespread knowledge about the meaning and development of autonomy would create a greater sensitivity to autonomous behavior and non-autonomous behavior in our society. We would be better able to diagnose our friends and neighbors. Based on the idea that the early detection of cancer is more curative, the detection of obstacles to anyone's preparation for more autonomous behavior can lead to efforts to help oneself or to help others. It would also enable all of us to recognize behavior that may look like the products of genuine initiative, but is really a short-circuited attempt to mimic autonomy or even a harmful compensation for lack of progress and for major emotional frustration. We have no problems now to identify vandalism, destructive motorcycle gangs, and a lone sniping spree of, for instance, a Lee Harvey Oswald as narcissism or primitive impulse expression. Nevertheless, some of us may show more misguided admiration for famous outlaws in American history like Billy the Kid. When we examine the behavior of people like Elvis Presley, Janis Joplin, and Evel Knievel, we are not so sure we should admire or pity them, unless we know more about their lives and become more sensitive to emotional development in general.

D. <u>Faith as a necessary organizing force for Man</u>

In our discussion of living systems (Chapter VIII) we have pointed out that a faith, or several faiths, are very necessary devices for Man to organize the multitude of social and ideational stimuli that bombard his working brain all the time. Since we constantly impose some form of organization on all levels as a vital characteristic of a life process, we also impose such organization and meaning on the cognitive, the ideational, and the emotional level. We cannot deal with the onslaught of perceptual stimuli without imposing concepts and other cognitive meaning on them. Hence millions of visual waves become "chair" for us and much energy is saved because we do not have to process all the millions. We only have to process a few of the energy waves that resonate the "chair" concept in our brain so that we can ignore the rest. Similarly we superimpose "lions are fierce", "strange dogs can be dangerous", "America is a large country with a democratic constitution", "God made this universe", etc. for other huge masses of stimuli and thereby short-circuit our processing of them. We also can thereby eliminate or shrink a great deal of our effort at analysis, which leaves us free for other reactions.

Faith in lions, in dogs, in Man, and in God are all similar organizing devices that superimpose meaning and order onto a series of phenomena. The fact that our faiths are accompanied with ready-made responses in thought and action saves further energy, because we can translate these behavioral tags on our faith into actions very quickly and then go on to another activity. Let us, for instance, take the commonly shared faith of western man that the sun rises every morning at a predetermined place and sets again in the evening at a predetermined time and place. This faith is based upon our knowledge of the solar system which in turn is based on the many repeated observations of scientists who have studied sun and stars in the universe. If we do not see the sun on a cloudy morning we do not worry about it, because this faith sustains us keeps our belief in the stability of our world intact.

I am reminded of the morning I woke up in a San Diego hotel while attending a scientific convention and saw from my window the sun rising above the ocean. After the first joy of watching a beautiful spectacle I had a sudden reaction of alarm as I remembered that I was at the westernmost edge of the United States where the sun sets but does not rise in the morning. My "faith" kept me from panicking, but I remembered the event a few times during the day so that I shared it with one or two others and made some inquiries. I finally discovered that the hotel was located on a peninsula that was bent around like a crooked finger and that further configurations of the coastline at that spot were such that my hotel window was actually facing the east. It was also facing a body of water that separated as from the main coastline of California.

It is inconceivable how much thinking-time and even panic would occur if we could not sustain a multitude of such faiths, and trust them without further checks. For instance, when we open a bottle of cola drink we have faith that it will contain cola and taste as we remember it should taste. Just imagine the next time you opened a cola bottle you found that the liquid had a nauseating taste, or the next bottle a beautiful follies girl stepped out! A world that refuses to be sustained by faiths would be a very capricious and frightening world. One would have to spend many precious moments stepping gingerly with every move and testing out any "old" move to make sure it did not explode in one's face. We spend that much effort of investigating, experimenting, and thinking when we actually find ourselves in new territory such as walking around in a mystery tunnel of an amusement park.

We henceforth develop a number of faiths about human beings, their interrelationships, and our engagement with the world in general. We draw -- just as faith in the sun's orbit -- on knowledge and experience that have accumulated in our heritage, since we are aware of our finiteness and our inability to predict much of the world on our own. We are thereby reducing the existential panic that lurks in our awareness of being a tiny influence in a tiny corner of the world against a mammoth onslaught of impressions and facts. Panic, anxiety, and disruption require energy, much of which is wasted. This may result in deficiency insofar as we cannot tackle other and new areas. As living organisms we have a "need" to minimize and control this chaos.

For these reasons faith in a theory or dogma about Man and his relation to the world is a very necessary part of our equipment. It takes away the sting of fate and of capriciousness that we have discussed as being synonymous with the often random and unpredictable nature of the universe and therefore of Man. Consequently, no man can live long or efficiently without faith. Even the confirmed atheist has one or more faiths. "The world is a dog-eat-dog jungle" is also a faith albeit it is one that keeps the believer on a watchful alert, ready to jump at the next attack.

This need for a faith is also supported by most of the people we have quoted earlier, although they may have emphasized different considerations than the derivation of faith from the baseline of general systems theory. Faith and reason, in a vision of truth, is for Fromm a

The Promise Of Human Autonomy   XIII

hallmark of the history of science. The faith of a scientist in his hypothesis or in a theory is rooted in the confidence he may place in his power of thinking, observing, and judging. Fromm distinguishes a rational faith as one that forms an independent conviction coming from one's own "productive" (self-actualizing) observation, while he recognized the characteristics of an "irrational faith" to be the acceptance of a "truth" because an authority or majority has said so. Gordon Allport has also observed that a person needs a faith to surmount the difficulties of a frequently unpredictable world. The intellect experiences inevitable failures despite its extensive abilities, so that the person has to build defenses against this kind of failure. Rollo May attributes the source of our recent anxieties to the newly developed confidence in technique and gadgets rather than retaining our confidence in the human being. An oversimplified faith in mechanical power takes us away from the belief in the dignity and complexity of the person. A proper faith in the person and his essential freedom could alert us to the characteristics of Man and thereby reduce our uncertainty and anxiety. Abraham Maslow pointed out that the ego can and wants to transcend and lose itself, such as may occur in peak experiences. We must therefore provide opportunities for this spin-off, including opportunities for developing transcending faith. Finally Jerome Bruner has pointed out that people who are engaged in "mythoclasm" -- or in the turning away of the myths that have failed them -- find themselves constructing new myths in a secretive manner.

Hence all of us need a number of faiths and even an organizing and therefore a "super-faith" as a map to the world of thought and feeling. The reader has undoubtedly discovered by now that I have a faith in the potential rationality and growth of Man. Such faith becomes an organizing and ordering principle. It can even have a disclaimer built into it that might either turn the person back to the drawing board with a "too bad" reaction upon this confirmation. Or it can contain "amendments" so that this confirmation can be "taken care of" or explained as "exceptions", and thereby keep the central faith intact.

If we all developed our own individual faiths we would on some levels of common problem-solving get into a "Tower-of-Babel" dilemma.

That is why it is important that we do sit down in a human society and agree on some fundamental faith that cannot make us work at cross-purposes and thereby defeat each other. The latter would happen if people with a faith in the essential goodness of Man are trying to work with people whose faith is that the world is a vicious jungle. We may have to amass data that invalidates some faiths that would hinder such cooperation. Once we can draw the boundary around such a commonly shared faith -- as we have, for instance, done in our Declaration of Independence -- we can then define a much larger range of faiths that can be held by individuals or groups individually. Within this large range we would put those faiths that could not interfere with the life and values of others. For instance, the faith in the medical and psychological value of certain nature foods and the faith that unidentified flying objects contain curious inhabitants of other galaxies, are examples here. Many people who hold the latter faith are active in a network that pays attention to new evidence, supplies attempts at explanation, invests time and energy into experimentation, and searches for more evidence. These people in no way challenge or endanger the wellbeing of the majority. In fact, they may stimulate many with their ideas and may be responsible for new ventures or inventions that benefit us all. This is quite beside the possibility that their faith may even be verified.

The contention that even the atheist has faith is well illustrated by a friend of mine who tried to defend his atheistic beliefs to his religious fiancé. When he admitted that he was not without some belief that could not be supported by facts or accumulated evidence such as his conviction that Man was basically good, she burst out with exasperation: "Why can't you call <u>that</u> God!" Hence we need to have a working faith about Man and about the many forces in our surroundings that are "larger" than us. There is no way to escape the forces that are beyond our own determination. They are constantly around us, whether it is the wind, the ocean, the migration of birds, the crowds at a football match, a cathedral built by thousands, a gang war, or an international war. The important point in our thesis of autonomy is that the faith we select and make our own should not be controlled by the state or by a dominant group such as the church in

The Promise Of Human Autonomy

medieval times. The Catholic church still holds sway over a good deal of the thinking and action process of its parishioners. Even here there have been many reforms of freeing the believer from thought-control of a central authority, and more reforms will have to occur, since there are powerful changes taking place in many countries where Catholics have increasingly decided to follow their own practices that are not along official lines. Similarly the Jewish sects have broken off from the mainstream of Judaism, so that there are now at least three distinct major Jewish denominations, all having rather different conceptions of God and of the proper religious practices. At one time in history we needed a very powerful God because of our own lack of power over the environment, nature, and other human beings. We let this God determine everything, even our thinking, and we let him sanctify our government and our values. Kings were hereditary and sanctified by the deity. In this way an act of disobedience to a king or to a sanctified official was a violation of God's law. Then we began to need God less as an all-powerful and autonomous regulator. At that point we were able to relegate him into a force toward which each person had a more personal relationship, except that some ministers, priests, or rabbis may still be seen as powerful and semi-autonomous intermediaries, especially if they have a great need for power themselves.

Faith in God and in religion as a guiding force is not in the way of people who are trying to solve common problems with a shared faith and theory as long as it can be monitored for the kind of excesses that might lead to an inquisition, a state controlled doctrine, or to the requirement of following a power-hungry cult leader. It must therefore be subject to checks and balances which already exist in some religions. The big danger is that boundaries might be closed in an emergency such as a war in which both nations exhort their citizens to fight and sacrifice for their cause because it is also the cause of God. Autonomy can usually be guaranteed by insisting that individual believers chart their own relationship to God and can change it as they meet new life experiences and develop new thoughts. It is of course also true that many if not most people need at times a reliance on authority and prefer to depend rather than rely on their own judgment. The churches and the belief in God fulfill a need for dependency on an adult level along well-established tracks. For many this dependency is an antidote against confusion and randomness, and thereby guarantees a faith and constancy.

The important conclusion in our recognition of the need for faith is that practically all human beings need to identify with something bigger than themselves in order to deal with their relative lack of power and control in a vast universe. We need this identification besides developing a self-identity first of all because of our long history of dependency. We need it further because of the painful consciousness of our existential dilemmas such as our mortality, our short life-span, and our lack of influence in a huge world. The resultant fear and isolation is not just due to "age of anxiety" but due to human nature itself. As much as consciousness has brought us great riches and moments of great pleasure and even ecstasy it has also produced universally shared moments of intense loneliness. Our social nature and origin practically requires us to identify with a group for a cause. It has been pointed out that even the hermit identifies with a group so far as he defines his own existence as "not belonging".

Therefore many of us feel a sense of awe when viewing a natural wonder like Niagara Falls or even just the sunset or a stormy ocean. We are similarly awed by someone like the Pope. Thousands may travel many miles to participate in his celebrations, and thereby sense and share this feeling of awe. Mass rituals have been designed to awaken this awe and give it meaning. Hitler understood this human yearning only too well, and forged it to his own sinister purposes. Most religions understand it and provide services for the sharing of awe, besides having their doctrine to help out in uncertainty. Man is then given a chance to submerge and yet feel powerful again. The identification with a universal idea and with a big, powerful organization can be soothing, strengthening, and nurturing. These institutions also help to re-establish the parental bond on a more adult level. I am therefore not arguing against faith or about providing and nurturing this faith. It is very necessary as a human characteristic. We can, however, provide a rational cause for satisfying this need to have faith for identification and for the sharing of existential awe. We can even build services and other rituals around a faith in Man's development and growth that contains moral principles of conduct which are worthy of adult morality and which echo the best of the Judeo-Christian tradition over its long past.

E. <u>An attempt to design a religion and a church</u>

As we have noted earlier, Martin Luther introduced the idea that Man can and should establish his own dialogue and relationship with God so that he does not require an intermediary like a church or its priests. This idea caught hold in an age fermenting with other ideas of Man's greater freedoms. Nowadays it is customary for a person to pray to God by himself and maintain a dialogue and a very unique relationship with him. In view of what is known of the tremendous variety of perceptions and cognitions about sheer events, we can also assume that each person pictures and defines God very uniquely. I would therefore conclude that there are as many gods as there are believers rather than there being one God.

As an illustration let me describe my God when I was a young boy and a teenager. The picture and His behavior in relation to me is still very vivid to me. He was first of all an older man -- oh yes, He was a man - with white hair and a white beard covering the upper part of his neck. He had bushy eyebrows and stern, dark eyes. The most noteworthy aspect of his appearance was that He was stern and would get very angry and even point an accusing finger at me. He never smiled. He was more forbidding than gentle, and you would never dare to ask Him a question. He was very powerful and all-knowing. He watched everything I did even when I secretly bent down to see if I could catch a glimpse of the bosoms of our maid as she was kneeling down to scrub our floors. I was taught that if I accidentally and painfully stubbed my toe when walking it was a punishment from God for some earlier transgression which He had seen and remembered. Hence this God of mine was somewhat forbidding and very powerful and also became a fine ally to my parents who were not able to be half as strict. For about a year in my seventh and eighth year I had recurrent nightmares about Him, which I later realized were consequences of a castration threat delivered by our family physician -- also a rather stern humorless man -- who had been set up to this act by my parents after they found themselves unable to stop "playing with myself". My dreams would start with ominous signs in a foreboding landscape until the frightening climax, at which time the face of God would break through the clouds, looking very angry or pointing His finger at me threateningly. At this point I would wake up in terror. I am quite sure this god is very different from that constructed by other people.

Let us analyze our beliefs in God even further. Let us visualize a reasonably successful person with a moderately good base of self-confidence, who believes in God and prays to him regularly. Suppose further there is no God or that God exists but decides to answer no prayers nor interfere in the life of a person by providing any help. Suppose that this fact is known to the person we have described. Under these circumstances it is still alright for him to pray, because it is a meaningful act for him and he derives a feeling of strength and belongingness. For instance, we were told that President Jimmy Carter prayed daily to God for guidance and strength, and perhaps we would not have wanted him to stop, or the country might have been in worse shape than it is! What really happens, when a reasonably confident person prays to a god who does not interfere or answer, is that this person reaffirms his own faith in himself by applying to something bigger than himself. It stills his fear of being such a small frog in such a big pond. His feeling of being small and insignificant is being diminished by allying himself with a big cause that is moreover benign and all-friendly. It would be absolute chutzpah for him to think that he could rely on his own capacities and sources for the strength he needs to "do right", or to ask the boss for a raise, or to ask the dental assistant of his dentist for a date, or to undergo a hernia operation. He just is not quite sure and "big" enough to feel he has the resources in him to make such decisions or to face a difficult experience all by himself. He needs to appeal to something "bigger" that is fortunately readily available and shared by millions and has a long line of tradition behind it. It is also buttressed by tangible institutions and even by magnificent buildings and respected priests, ministers, or rabbis.

The Promise Of Human Autonomy

Despite our inevitable development toward a sense of identity and toward greater self-confidence in our autonomy, we feel so small on many occasions. This happens when we are struck by faith, when we face a powerful Niagara Falls, when we read about a big disaster somewhere, or when our "best-laid plans gang aft agley". This reaction of insignificance is part of our consciousness and is one of our existential dilemmas. It is also very much rooted in our long history of dependence when we <u>were</u> small and insignificant. A child gets this feeling all the time! It is therefore inevitable that we re-experience such states and that we want to -- and need to -- escape or at least reduce the bad feelings of helplessness, anxiety, and even panic. We have been fortunate enough and inventive enough to produce the institutions and the religious belief system with its rituals to take care of such incapacitating feelings and to share them with others for an even more meaningful and constructive purpose than a mere defense. The self-avowed atheist is taking a big load on his own shoulder and is considered almost too cocky by others who gleefully predict that "he will get his comeuppance!" The myth "there are no atheists in fox holes" perpetuates the belief of the majority that no sane person could long exist without a faith in God or a religion.

All of these considerations tend to spell out a human need for a "religion" or faith in some enduring quality of mankind or Man's relation to others, and also in a faith in the force of nature that unites mankind and takes away some of the existential pain of isolation and smallness. We come back to a social and moral need for this faith even though we have found the faith in the deity to be often irrational or to form an obstacle in the road toward autonomy. We have shown that much of recent history and the developing thought of many have diminished God from an all-powerful controller of the world and a guardian of the afterlife who must be appeased or thanked or implored for help. We have shrunk him to a much smaller voice inside which has also become very private and even protected from scrutiny or discussion. Perhaps beauty or the image of Man and his positive values can even take the place and can become objects worthy of awe and of worship.

These contentions have again been supported by some astute observers of the human scene. For instance Rollo May feels that religion is neither good nor bad in itself. It is only "bad" if the adopted beliefs and practices provide an escape from Man's freedom. However, he considers it beneficial if it strengthens the person in his own sense of dignity and worth and provides him with the confidence in his values. He can then develop and use an awareness of morality and his own sense of responsibility. Gordon Allport also observes that most people incorporate faith and hope in their values and in this way become "religious". Religion is more than one defense against anxiety and doubt. It also provides a forward orientation which assigns the person with a set of meanings for the experience of knowing and being. Erich Fromm also observes Man's need to belong and thereby feel less insignificant. The monk in his cell is not alone because he has his God with him. The chance to belong and to block the sense of smallness provides meaning and direction, because it also satisfies the need to belong to a system or to a group. Hence as we gain freedom we also feel the need to unite again, which may remind us also of Andras Angyal's observations about the balance between autonomy and homonymy.

We can readily see how comforting it can be to so many people to attribute failure, misfortune, illness, and even death to the will of God. The atheist who attributes it to the randomness or the vicissitudes of nature and who accepts the possibility that there is no explanation is in a more lonely position and is bereft of the support of the majority. He cannot fall back on powerful institutions and make use of great buildings, clerical personnel, and rituals to help him express his faith and give him support of others. This sense of isolation was so well-expressed by the heroine in a recent novel by Mary Gordon. The heroine found herself automatically praying to God after she had thrown over the traditional belief in God of her strict father and his priest friends, and had embarked on a new road of autonomy and new experiences. She reflected that she had no right to the comforts of her old religion after she had given up its stultifying rigors and its duties. She was glad she had chosen the world of her new friends who had not created a very fragile "world of impossible goodness".

While I am both aware of human need for a faith and a religion and am also aware that so many religions, derived from the idea of a master-builder tend to inhibit autonomy, I am suggesting that we are capable of evolving a new religion. It could also be a religion with a very broad base. It would first of all attract people who would not want to hang on to an idea that the world was "created" by a master-builder, but that it proceeded more or less by fits and starts. It is moreover a world that has Man in it who is capable of organizing things, living creatures and other people, and who has achieved so much through his cognitive powers. However, Man is still very insecure, lonely, and even frightened at times. We have followed Adam in his fantasized soliloquy as he expressed our fear of failure, our lack of judgment, the irrational moments of being powerless or alone or living for such a short time, and of letting go of dependency and of the unknown. We will therefore always be saddled with these existential storms brewing out of our consciousness.

One could build into this religion all the successful practices of traditional religions that have helped Man to overcome existential dilemmas. Furthermore, practices can be established that take care of other needs such as sharing and the need for community. One could incorporate many of the positive striving characteristics of Man. Various denominations might therefore develop out of a basic new religion that was catering to these different needs, such as one to the need for fellowship and social sharing, another with an expression of strong emotions in order to bind and rationalize strong irrational and emotional currents and to sanction them as being proper. Such a new religion would require big and attractive buildings for meetings and for providing a visible center for its various activities. It would need an organization and officers who could be democratically elected or defined as career choices that require certain training and preparation and a selection procedure. There would have to be machinery for collecting monies and services to insure its operations. These operations and the income would have to be monitored by some people independent of the leadership and would have to be open to public scrutiny.

There would have to be times set aside and occasions for services, such as those already held in churches and synagogues on Sundays and

Saturdays. These services might contain songs and passages extolling the abilities, achievements and strength of men and women -- as well as the weaknesses and doubts. They might express various faiths: faith in the goodness of Man, in adult ability, in rational reasoning, in coping, in compensation for inadequacy, in inventiveness, in creativity, in helping one's neighbor, in community work, in the Golden Rule, et cetera. These occasions for services would tend to reaffirm one's own faith, to release relevant knowledge, and to see this shared with many others as a form of security and reinforcement. This church would have its own "saints", or men and women who have advanced its faiths and helped mankind in various ways over the ages. These might include philosophers, social critics, scientists, explorers, artists, doctors, novelists, and poets, as well as "little people" who have suddenly become prominent in history because of some inspiration or heroic acts, like Joan of Arc or the Dutch boy who kept his finger in the hole of the dike. We would then elevate people who have contributed great ideas or pieces of art and literature or music, or scientific advances, like Rembrandt, Shakespeare, Beethoven, Gutenberg, Galileo, Darwin, Freud, Einstein, Martin Luther King, Aristotle, and of course people like Jesus, Elijah, and Gandhi. This church could have its special holidays commemorating people or special occasions in the history of Man -- some of which fitted appropriately into the religious faiths -- such as Independence Day, the discovery of steam, the discovery of the first bacteria of a disease, the defeat of a tyrant like Hitler, the birth or death of a person who advanced democracy or the greatness of Man. We could reaffirm our faith, give thanks to these pioneers, and build and strengthen our human community around it.

In similar fashion one could consecrate in this church important milestones in Man's development such as confirmation, marriage, and death. Appropriate rituals would borrow from the central faiths of this church and surround the occasions with meaningful musical and verbal accompaniments. Baptism or the celebration of the beginning of a new human life can be consecrated in a meaningful way, perhaps similar to the beautiful ritual in a Unitarian church in which the minister hands a white carnation to the parents to hold over the baby to signify his or her innocence and pristine beginning, which the parents can stimulate and fertilize. This church could also commemorate victories over some arch-villains like the defeat of Hitler, or the death of Stalin, who had held back the development and freedom of mankind. It could commemorate the martyrdom and death of victims of persecution, or people who held fast to their ideas against a dictator. Also, this religion could institute something like "prayers" or especially well-constructed sentences and paragraphs that people can say to themselves to shore up the faith and help them face the world and their loneliness, misfortune, grief, et cetera. These prayers would not be said to someone out there who might listen and hopefully respond, but they would be said to oneself so that one can hear oneself clearly and thus gain new strength, resolve, and courage. This exercise involves some education -- perhaps from the church -- regarding the real psychological meaning and function of prayer. A parallel may be made in the acceptance of this prayer to the cognitive rehearsal of our plan of action in which we all engage often in a silent dialogue. This rehearsal and reinforcement nature of prayer is especially powerful if it is either shared with others in a service or is shared with many others in the world as an official product. In this way many people can reawaken hope and the tendency to try again after a setback, and it can result in taking new steps. The various "customs" of this religion would of course change over the years, with different concerns, different values, and different usages. One could institute a conclave every ten or less years to see what should be changed in the services, prayers, holidays, and administration, and why. There should be machinery so that the members of the church have input into these decisions and can be consulted by special "ballots" or "amendments".

This religion would recognize the need for both emotional and mystical experiences and would build and maintain rituals to allow this to happen. It would also concretize more vague aspects of the faiths and would allow communication of people with each other in an exercise meaningful to them and expressing important emotions. These would be elicited and channeled in ways that would be gratifying rather than frightening and would at the same time be satisfying the "community feeling" or the need to belong with each other and to share with others. We now already have small sects like the humanists who try to set up alternative faiths built on ethical values. However, most of these are rather esoteric to have a mass appeal, because they purify their ideals of all practices of sharing an emotional expression. However, the new church should not merely copy the more "successful" practices of traditional religion, but should put them on a new footing by consciously recognizing important human needs and cater to them. We need this religion in a democratic society because it can stimulate a sense of freedom rather than smother it, and it can be a proper repository of our moral values.

There is therefore no reason why we could not reassemble with a new faith and celebrate together. It is a beautiful but not unrealistic vision to see us fill the magnificent cathedrals of yesterday for a celebration of human autonomy. These cathedrals in themselves represent some of the greatest triumphs of Man's achievement and creativity. There is nothing really to stop us from hoping that one day we can sing in unison in these temples and proclaim Man's hope for rationality and for the more general achievement of autonomy. We can use them for the commemoration of important milestones of past accomplishments. It would also add great strength to a congregation if they knew that others with like minds were congregating in other places of worship at the same time. Such a rebirth would of course help in a proliferation of moral principles that are found at higher stages of personality development. In this way age-old principles of neighborly love and a sense of responsibility for others would be strengthened so that one could rest on a firm base in one's own search for values. We are now sorely in need of a reawakening and reinforcement of these moral principles.

I feel, for instance, that this yearning for ethical principles is one of the most important concerns that have motivated the "born again" Christians. These are worthy people who have searched for meaning in their interaction with others and for moral yardsticks. They have seen the vast cafeteria of goals and values with some trepidation and they may even have tasted of some of the more "forbidden" fruit therein.

The Promise Of Human Autonomy

Most of these people are young and middle-aged adults who would be entering or are in their psychological maturity and even in their autonomy phase. They are turning back to the good values and the good morality of the Judeo-Christian tradition. Moreover, they are "choosing" this morality on their own, prompted from within by being stimulated from Kohlberg's Stage 5 and 6 reasoning. They "convert" in an emotional moment when many others are present and with the help of a leader who personifies this goodness and concern and even self-sacrifice. He or she echoes their stirrings and values. The leader and the ritual and the multitudes of others rationalize and pave the way to a convinced acceptance of a moral code. This in turn legitimizes these inner promptings in the face of contemporary confusion.

It is not accidental that so many religions have stressed similar ethical values, such as concern, commitment, service, cooperation, and sometimes self-sacrifice. The Ten Commandments that outlaw murder, theft, and jealousy, and urge us to love, respect, and show concern express these sentiments. Of course one answer is that the existence of God and his universal truth inspired these common ideals. The coincidence may also be due to the fact that we human beings organize our social world again and again along similar lines because we share a basic human nature. Also, this code of laws underneath the social organization of the past has had obvious survival value and has therefore pragmatically proven itself as workable and as "worthwhile".

This development is a welcome one indeed. Now let us imagine that we could marshal these good and moral promptings from within in a larger movement that contains rituals, self-commitment, and even new identities. These in turn would anchor these moral values in oneself as a manifestation of a mature human being and in a historical tradition that has withstood the test of time and that carries with it the hope of solving some of our problems by tackling them rationally. If the old authority of God and Jesus is removed, the tremendous amount of energy invested in church services, prayers, and religious commitment can be harnessed to a sense of community routed in rationality, and then could be put to work on the pressing social problems of our times.

F. The need for re-discovery of Man's rational powers as a potent tool

We need frequent reminders that we have pushed "evolution" forward in huge steps by virtue of our marvelous brain capacity alone, and not because we have mutated into a succession of "master races". Perhaps it is important to keep in mind that this power of rationality is a tool that needs to be kept well-oiled and has to be honed out of the finest material. If we can accept the progressive development of a more rational use of thinking and of judgment with the onset of psychological maturity, we can employ the kind of rational thinking that goes with physical and psychological maturity at moments of inner harmony. We can then use it to solve our problems. This new recognition would replace the acceptance and the tuning-in on any cognition or judgment that emerges from a human being regardless of where he stands or what is happening to him emotionally and socially at that moment.

We already call for the programmed use of reasoning to solve some of our most pressing problems of the day. For instance, Robert Heilbroner advocates central economic planning as the only chance to support the capitalistic system and shepherd it through its present crises of inflations and to cushion it against further crises. We already have substituted much planning and centralized discussion in the recent past on a variety of social and economic problems for the old laissez-faire orientation of the early "free enterprise" days of capitalism. Changes in tax laws, the determination of rates on money-lending, the creation of jobs, unemployment benefits, antitrust action, regulation of advertising are among the many examples of centralized action that either resulted from extensive discussion or planning on the federal level. Much of this has arisen from similar debates in Congress before a law was passed. Heilbroner anticipates that only careful planning will get us through some of the predicted environmental disasters like the greenhouse effect in the atmosphere, the contamination of water through poisonous waste, and the danger of nuclear waste products. These and other problems will require an unprecedented degree of monitoring and of control.

This planning in a capitalistic system would move us closer to what is called state planning. While economic planning from a centralized government is the goal of socialism the planning envisioned here is not meant as a program for socialism necessarily. It is, for instance, possible to intervene in "private enterprise" with a number of laws and regulations that do not replace ownership, but insure that this practice does not inconvenience or even hurt others. We see this already reflected in the regulations that govern the fare structure of airplane and utility companies, laws governing the insurance of deposits in banks, and laws about false advertising. These need to be extended to laws governing safety not only of mines and asbestos manufacturing but of companies dealing with nuclear power. Laws also have to regulate the disposal of waste products just as we have laws about the additives of foods and the marketing of drugs. With these laws, the initiative of private companies and of entrepreneurs is indeed restricted but not eliminated entirely. The range of their actions has shrunk, and we ask the entrepreneurs to join us with their own sense of morality and concern for other people's welfare. This proliferation of rational planning built into the base of morality also implies the toning down of our worship of competition. Much has been written on the evils of unbridled competition as an old form of self-actualization, without seeing that there is a stage in development that presupposes earlier bases. We therefore need to accept the idea that self-actualization is not the same as competition, for the latter implies the survival of the fittest, so that the success of one person's self-actualizing behavior extinguishes the hope for the other person to do the same. Golden Rule thinking precludes this tendency and gropes for a condition in which the opportunities for autonomous behavior are magnified.

The use of rational planning in a problem-solving atmosphere involves, of course, people with strong views, who have chosen certain solutions, to sit together and listen to each other. On the face of it, the need to listen and even modify one's views seems to go against the very exercise of autonomy and freedom that we have advocated. It is certainly perceived to be such by the companies or groups that are behind their representatives and feel committed to their view and their solution which in turn become the property of their representatives. If we, however, remember that the genuine use of autonomy at a later stage of maturity rests on a prior development of concern and of principled morality, we can also understand that the representatives in any planning meeting may also be able to adopt a problem-solving set, rather than an attitude of defending their own autonomous ego. Under a problem-solving set people have been able to reanalyze a problem in terms of the wider perspective of having a number of opposing solutions rather than seeing it more narrowly defined as only allowing their own solution. This larger perspective then allows the participants to become once more creative and think of new solutions or expanded ones that incorporate part of their own with those of others or even into novel solutions. We may be able to amass further proof that the moral judgment on Kohlberg's last two levels is a superior force for solving problems and disputes, especially after further experiments have been made. If we then ask people who use these moral principles in their social functions to sit together and to tackle problems, we might be able to guarantee a good amount of success.

In such discussions and in all problem-solving attempts there have to be, of course, some "losers". Ideas and solutions have to be rejected or modified. Would this process not produce defeats that leave scars on the majority of participants and thereby defeat their self-actualization attempts? Would it not diminish their autonomy with disastrous results? There are two answers we can give here. One is the recognition that is already built into the democratic process that in every election there have to be "losers", and that in every decision there has to be "minority opinion". For instance, the losing candidate in an election accepts the possibility of loss and may not consider it a defeat of his autonomy. His choice of running for office and his campaigning activities may be sufficient reward for his attempts to express his autonomy. Experimentation with autonomy involves taking risks but also involves the existence of a sense of responsibility. With it goes the acceptance of a moral principle like the Golden Rule. Similarly a person who invents a terrible new weapon can still be "recognized" and can even feel proud of his inventive power even if the weapon can never be built or tested or even used.

This process of using rational problem-solving has been especially well demonstrated in discussion experiments in the psychological laboratory and in small meetings in which the participants were limited to the few protagonists immediately concerned with the problem. The small town meeting, the city council, the boards of most American institutions and of social and cultural agencies are examples. Along these lines Barry Commoner has recently suggested that one of the solutions of our energy problems is the decentralization of our energy generation. If we let individual towns and factory complexes build and plan their own energy plant with local resources that are based on renewable energy sources we might stimulate inventiveness and we can use the heat that is produced better locally. Economist E. F. Schumacher has amply demonstrated that infinite growth toward bigger economic enterprises does not fit into our world of experience. He has also shown how smaller economic enterprises are sometimes much better fitted to the problems of developing nations. They even sometimes work more toward the basic satisfaction of men and women in our western world where bigness has sometimes become synonymous with "progress" but has led to big problems instead.

These people have argued against greater reliance on large organizations like corporate and federal agencies, even though these may have the immediate resources and would be technologically able to surge into the vacuum. Control of the economic system by these giants loses out on the sometimes more creative and efficient talent of local brains. This neglect of talent creates the apathy and the feelings of isolation in the constituents who are ignored and who have become dependent. In this way the use of autonomy is inhibited. It also creates the danger of reawakening the idea of "Papa knows best" with its dangerous centralization and corruption of power.

There are a number of areas in our society where we have already instituted a new faith in rational power when there was none before. In Chapter VII we saw how the emphasis on rational problem-solving in psychotherapy has replaced insight from an expert to a weak ego that is inundated by irrational forces from the unconscious. We have placed much more emphasis on the rational powers of the growing child in our principles of child rearing so that the old notion that "Children should be seen but not heard," has been replaced by giving the child as complete information as he needs and can assimilate. We allow him more to reason with us and to explain himself even if he has to mind our limits. We now are apt to reason out the world and our commands with him and to teach him to think rationally so that he can also tackle complicated tasks much earlier than our grandparents allowed us to tackle. We now appeal to the rational powers of the hospital patient and even to those of the dying patient by giving him more information and facts. The results here are of creating a more efficient team, including the patient among the health professionals.

In industry a number of experiments initiated by social psychologists have shown that giving the workers a genuine chance to inject their own observations and to help in the decisions on changes or on efficiency-saving devices almost always increases morale and its behavioral correlates. If you leave everything up to the "experts" you do not always get superior solutions and you may produce dissatisfaction and even unrest. Another area of application is the peer review system in the review of grant applications to the federal department in various sciences. Senior scientists review and discuss the proposals for scientific research or for rare treatments for health problems. They pick the proposals that seem to have the most merit and the biggest chance to succeed. This system has worked relatively well over the years and has been accepted by both the scientific community and by federal departments as being superior to the old process of having bureaucratic chiefs make the sole evaluation and decision. Alvin Toffler proposes a similar panel of involved people to judge new inventions. He proposes frequent assemblies of citizens to decide on the kind of world they would like to live in and help to shape, rather than to be pushed and shaped into a world that is changing more quickly every day with superimposed inventions and social changes.

In addition we ought to take a more active stand in our society on the superiority of rational methods and on the use of planned discussion for solving problems. The principles of restoring to rational discussion in a fairly neutral atmosphere by people who have proven their ability to function on such levels should become more universally accepted. It further needs to be ritualized and taught in our educational institutions and through our media. The use of force in settling problems and disputes needs to be contained and even outlawed. It certainly needs to be labeled offensive and stupid rather than be admired as a macho survival of our old folk tradition where the cowboy and outlaw and the person with a gun were important symbols on the road to political and psychological independence. Nowadays it is still to customary and too widely accepted to grab for a gun or for a bomb when one cannot immediately get one's way or when one cannot settle a dispute quickly enough. Tragic examples of this suicidal policy have come to us from Lebanon, Northern Ireland, Iran, Vietnam, and from the gangs in some of our own cities.

We are beginning to see a slight turn of the pendulum in the admiration that has been generated when some international leaders have used rational powers to solve recent problems that might otherwise have resulted in armed conflict. Millions of people admired Egyptian President Anwar Sadat and Israeli Prime Minister Menachem Begin when they engaged in an age-old problem before them in the neutralized atmosphere of Camp David. In this place they did not resort to floodlights or on the power bases of their home support. This admiration was acknowledged by the award of the Nobel Peace Prize to these two leaders, because they were able to solve some of the most sticky problems and work out a peace where before emotions had mainly reigned. Similarly our admiration goes toward Jack Kennedy and Russian Premier Nikita Kruschev for solving the Cuban missile crisis with rational means in 1962. This form of reasoning oneself out of a crisis certainly stands in contrast to the arrogant and vainglorious thinking with which Kaiser Wilhelm II of Germany ushered in World War I in 1914.

We therefore need a new "Age of Reason" and not just the resurrection of the old Age of Reason in which reason was truly emancipated and used in art, literature, and science. At that time we glorified reason -- with some justification in view of its long slumber during the Middle Ages -- as though it were a new toy. We celebrated the products of reason with a shout: "Look what a great and beautiful thing we can do." I am calling for an Age of Reason in which we use reason and cultivate it as a problem-solving device, and where we can place new faith in it as a gift from our evolutionary development. We need to use it more as a developing capacity that can become a useful tool by which we have already solved many dilemmas in the past and can do even more so in the future. We can and should do this despite our realization, with the help of Freud and others, that we also have dark and deep emotions that can well up and spoil our attempt at solution. Of course we also realize, alongside with these psychologists, that our emotions also conjure up very nice experiences and some that are even very beautiful.

We need to employ reasoning power in conflicts and problems rather than resort to force, and we need to build consciously machinery to use and harness reason. We can no longer invest it merely as a luxury, as we have nurtured it in isolated "think tanks", or in little ornamental side sports like the "Center for Democratic Studies", and other debating societies. These are privately financed and left to a few people with the indulgence that they may "do their thing", just as we allow thousands of motorcyclists to go off into a place in the desert, or allow stamp collectors to get together and "do their thing" as long as they don't hurt the rest of us.

What we need, of course, is the recognition that reason from mature and relatively disinterested individuals is perhaps the most valuable tool in problem-solving. Not only should we use it but insist that others use it -- with a moral force of a large majority that can legislate and impose sanctions if necessary. We therefore need a convinced force of people and their leaders that will compel the use of mediators in disputes on such questions as energy and pollution and crime, or even in the United Nations disputes that pit nations against each other. We may have to glorify reason and create symbols and festivals for it and make it a compelling and almost sacred thing. It is therefore not enough to celebrate small discoveries in science or to house scholars in universities but we have to honor ordinary people who have helped settle disputes and have solved vexing social and economic problems. We also have to recognize that each one of us cannot always use reason, because it resides side by side with emotions and with needs and with unconscious motivations. In other words it resides with all of the heritage of our animal nature and with our long development as dependent children. For these reasons we cannot create an aristocracy of reason for which only the people displaying it are valuable while the rest of the people primarily not using reason are despised. We need to retain our tolerance for all of our psychological and human nature, but at the same time cultivate reason as a valuable tool and make it the prime force in settling our problems. This can even imply that we recognize "up days" for the people that we nominate or choose to be in positions of bargaining to solve disputes. Perhaps they themselves can declare their "unreasonable days" when the process takes too long because they are still human beings underneath.

G. Mediation as a vehicle for reason

The most well-known method by which the use of reason is substituted for the emotional debates of those on the filing line is the process of labor mediation. It was first used by King Saul in the Bible and then met again sporadically in history. It was finally used more systematically in the disputes between union and management in the American labor movement. When the two sides at the bargaining front of a labor-management dispute cannot agree and are heading for a strike or a more violent cut-off of the bargaining process, some union management contracts provide for enforced mediation by a disinterested third party. Both sides have to agree to let it go to this step. Both sides can usually also agree on the mediator. Under these conditions many an issue on wages, on working conditions, and on grievances has been settled by arbitration. This idea has also been used increasingly in other areas of social strife, far removed from the working place. Thus we have instituted and institutionalized ombudsmen in some criminal proceedings and in some mental institutions.

We have also witnessed two instances on the international scene where mediators have been used successfully. One incident refers to the increased hostility of Chile and Argentina over the long debated sovereignty of three strategic islands in the Straits of Magellan. As the rhetoric mounted and as both nations were mobilizing an increasing number of military forces to go to war, they both were able to resort to rational thinking at the last minute. They called in a mediator to the dispute by appealing to the Pope. A papal envoy is now at work trying to learn the ingredients of the dispute and to familiarize himself with the points of view of the protagonists. While a final settlement has not yet been announced it has become clear that this resort to mediation has cooled down the conflict considerably and has almost certainly precluded the use of force.

The more famous international mediation is, of course, the forging of a peace treaty between the old and bitter protagonists of Israel and Egypt. President Jimmy Carter proposed himself as a mediator and was finally accepted in this role. In addition, the two rival leaders, Anwar Sadat and Menachem Begin, also accepted their new role as reasoning participants in a mediation exercise in which they both hoped to come out with a solution. The world knows of the outcome of that exercise and the eminently successful role of President Carter as a mediator.

The expressive reaction to mediation is best summed up by Moshe Dayan in a recent interview: "Altogether, it was the most important and expressive experience of my life of all my sixty-three years. Here were three of the world's leaders together in one place at one time with one motivation. It was a high moment in history, with men, instead of using weapons to make war, using words and ideas to make peace."

It goes without saying that mediators should be mature individuals who have the ability to take the role of the "generalized other". They should show evidence of being able to function at the higher stages of moral judgment where principles of morality replace mere conformity to the majority or to laws. They should be able to take roles and have empathy for others which means that they should be able to function at a step in personality development where they have surplus energy to invest outside their own interests and needs.

H. Making allowances for irrational behavior

It has already been alluded to that we have to allow for and even honor the inevitable journeys into irrational behavior. We have to do so alongside the elevation of rational powers as a shiny tool for the new age. This irrational behavior is a frequent occurrence of people at the beginning of their ascent into personality development, and is also the mark of an arrest or a regression development. It also is the not infrequent companion of the most maturely developed individual. Besides our heritage of explanations from clinical and personal psychology, we also have abundant evidence in our midst which comes from so-called well-functioning people who are not easily tagged with a diagnostic label from the satchel of the psychiatrist. Two of the most noteworthy examples of more mammoth proportion are the holocaust in Nazi Germany which resulted in the murder of over six million people, and the mass suicide of the followers of the People's Temple in Guyana in 1978. These grisly events are a stark reminder that it can happen now. Seemingly intelligent people who have gone through adequate and even good education and who have shown evidence of being civilized in an industrialized country can spawn and maintain a lust for power, an abject obedience, or a disregard for all human rights. We almost need these reminders as a constant warning that some people in our midst can openly espouse evil.

We have already done a good deal to accept irrationality that does not hurt others and would allow a time and a place for its eruption. We have given up our persecution of this behavior as acts of the devil or the work of witches. We accept and understand the psychological and very human forces that produce them -- sometimes in all of us. We have institutionalized and sanitized some of the traditionally more destructive outbursts of impulses such as hostility and rage. Boxing matches, stock car races, and other sporting events full of violence have become safety valves for undeliverable expressions of anger. We even make folk heroes out of football players and boxers who risk injury and even invalidism for the sake of the clamoring thousands -- and for adequate payment. We give people like Evel Knievel a safe corner where he can roar over a canyon with a motorcycle, and we allow the promoter of such events to reap his profits from the multitudes who come to witness it for various motives of their own. We allow people to express and experience fear and even panic in controlled and short-lived moments such as in the roller coaster and the horror movie.

It may become necessary to set aside more such opportunities for impulse expression and for irrational behavior, where we provide a safe and recognized corner. In this way the innocent bystander cannot be hurt. For instance, there is a group of men and women in New Orleans who play very realistic war games on a Sunday in an uninhabited area. They wear uniforms and all kinds of protective devices, simulate guns and other war machines, and define death or casualties so that they can count noses at the end of the day. In this way they can see which of the two opposing teams have won the pre-set objective of the "war". According to the story about this group in a recent issue of <u>Newsweek</u>, there have been few injuries and no deaths. Perhaps more such opportunities should be available in large population centers to give the many people with needs and fantasies to stalk and dispatch a human prey a realistic enough chance to experience the chase and of being chased. Perhaps areas for "playing war" have to be provided like the area of desert near Mojave where trail-bikes can crisscross and destroy the ecology at will. The "weapons" and machinery that has to be provided can be rented by a group or individuals for a fee. In this way they are "off" for a Sunday afternoon or for a weekend.

Perhaps we need "slugging corners" in every baseball or football arena where spectators get into fights over the game. Perhaps they can be herded pushed by police and attendants if they want to assault each other. If these slugging corners have mats and other protective devices such spectators may go there with the knowledge that they may not get hurt too badly, or they may go with the knowledge that they can get hurt very badly, but they take the responsibility. Once they are in such an arena they are aware, from common knowledge and from big signs posted at the entrance, that they are no longer subject to laws relating to murder and assault and that they can likewise not sue another participant in the corral. The latter provision is already observed on ski

The Promise Of Human Autonomy

slopes or when people parachute from rented planes. The proprietors of these establishments or contrivances warn the fans that they must take the risk of injury when using the facilities, as long as the ski-slope operator has marked and labeled the slopes, and as long as the airplane owner has provided a safe plane.

Since we are saddled with needs for dependency and for nurturance from our heritage as immature children we perhaps need to provide more opportunities to follow the leader and to give ourselves up to a stronger force. Most adults yearn for such opportunities at times, and psychologists have even found evidence of psychological and physical disruption when a person represses all of his dependency needs as unworthy and as guilt-provoking. If we make opportunities available and if we institutionalize them we give a lot of people the chance to indulge for specified times and to gain some sense of satiation. In this way we do not force people into cults or movements where their dependency forces them to give up all attempts at self-determination, or where it leads to the aggrandizement of a power-hungry leader or to disaster or both. Perhaps we can institute "Follow the Leader" games in appropriate areas and buildings where a number of options are available for the management that "plays" the leader role. Assurance would be given that most of the clients in search of a dependency experience would not be hurt. They also would be given the choice of having a dependency relationship in a general area of their choice. We already practice such games on a number of occasions, such as social events or rituals in some fraternal or business organizations.

Also, everyone has occasional needs to be a leader or to feel superior. George Mead already observed forty years ago that this can hopefully be done on a social and non-egotistical level. In this way it does not get translated into the deification of the ingroup and the rejection of the outgroup. Again we may need to provide more systematic opportunity for the expression of this "need for superiority" or for the need to separate ourselves as something visibly apart from others. Perhaps our vision of "Follow the Leader" games for adults would incorporate a chance for such people to become "leaders" for a day or for an evening. We already give in to this need by devoting many pages of our newspapers to the accomplishment and to the milestones of local citizens. Perhaps we need special bulletin boards where we can post the names of people who have made a mark for themselves.

We also have to allow the safe expression of excessive needs for power and prestige without allowing these needs to where they can hurt and subjugate others. We have learned to curtail the use of power in a democracy by building more checks into the operation of our leaders. Nowadays we monitor and illuminate most of the relevant political and economic activities to prevent excesses. We have also built in many safeguards so that people cannot use economic power any more in the way earlier entrepreneurs endangered others in sweatshops or company towns or in unsafe premises. We still have to provide opportunities for people with power and with related money needs to feel somewhat distinctive from others. There are still scarce and expensive items available like Rembrandts, diamonds, Rolls Royces, and villas that do not detract from the welfare of others. Feelings of power can also be obtained by steering airplanes and trucks in simulating games. Various devices at amusement parks and shooting galleries also provide such opportunities.

I. <u>Realization of the relationship between autonomy and interdependence</u>

Western ideas of human rights are frequently seen as one-sided by many third world countries. Our emphasis on individual freedoms contrasts with traditional views in many of them, including Communist countries. In such countries the rights of the community are placed first, and due to the goals of the community, become the most important goals for the citizen. We have shown in Chapter X how the collectivist ideals of interdependence and of placing the welfare of the group before that of the individual are predominantly practiced in societies where the individual has given up the right to make his own judgment. He has also abandoned his right and his ability to decide on the values of the group. Instead, he must conform to a leadership that is supposedly more schooled and more farsighted to be able to make the goals and to decide on the strategy. In Chapter XI we have seen how a sense of interdependence and of a moral acceptance of conformity to community practices can also develop in the growing individual. Hence it can also develop in an individualistic system that promotes and encourages that growth. We have, of course, also demonstrated that in wartime and in local disasters the citizen in our own society can also put their efforts into community goals.

Conformity to community standards and cooperation with many common goals is of course a very necessary development before a society can function. It is a necessary prerequisite for the growth of individuality. This dual process requires a more widespread realization of the interdependence of conformity as foundation for the exercise of autonomous behavior. It requires the ability to have empathy for the parallel development of others toward their self-actualization, or a clear picture of the "generalized other", as George Mead has so eloquently described it. This ability would then eliminate any extreme ways of asserting one's own goals and would certainly outlaw terrorist activity, sabotage, or nuisance attacks.

First of all need to learn to unite ourselves again with others in interdependent and supportive groupings to practice and experience that important base in our development. Perhaps that is why so many people enthusiastically volunteered in the beginning days of the Peace Corp or in Vista protects. A chance to work with others and share with them can then become an opportunity of experiencing our inner strength and one's capacity to give and to relate. This experience in turn becomes an excellent milestone on the road to further self-actualization, as we have seen in Chapter VI. Also, many of us engage in very cooperative and conforming activities during many hours of the week without feeling squashed or restricted in our individual unfolding. For instance, the players in a symphony orchestra are very willing to submit themselves to a conductor who at times almost appears to act like a "dictator". The players don't mind because they also exult in the final product and the favorable audience response in which they had only a small share. Similar cooperation is willingly practiced by the members of a sports team. On the more extended level we see it performed in a factory or office, in a union, and finally in a democratic country, where the majority of the citizens support the laws and support many of the policies.

Perhaps this is the answer to the psychologist Edward Sampson who worries that the psychologist's ideal of self-actualization is merely the echo of the cultural ideal of self-contained individualism, and then takes us away from collective problem-solving and away from training in interdependence. Interdependence in a dictatorship is based on the maxim that "father knows best", and the "children" must depend on his wisdom which then also becomes the group ideal. Dependency, conformity, and the disappearance of new solutions or creative contributions are the result. We therefore need not only recognize individual contributions, but we have to make allowance for their input and create opportunities and institutionalized channels for their expression, dissemination, and discussion. We certainly do not have to preach that people should remove themselves from a sense of membership and belonging to the group as a prerequisite to individual development, which Sampson fears as the ultimate goal in an individualized society. He anticipates that the individual bred on self-contained individualism may eventually defy the group from which he has first separated himself. Why could we not recognize that the embedded-ness in a group, together with the accompanying feeling of loyalty and concern, is an important developmental step that must be reached before there can be occasional spin-offs of self-actualizing behavior? The latter should never be considered a total state that eventually predominates during all hours of the fully developing person. It is much more realistic and very much in line with the discussions of Erikson, Maslow, and Loevinger to contemplate a self-actualized family <u>member</u>, symphony <u>player</u>, etc. If he or she is conceived as being <u>entitled</u> to moments of self-actualization, he or she can also be given help to "do his thing" at certain moments. Again the cooperation rests on the realization that the helping group members may need this friendly encouragement themselves at other times. This implicit support is also needed for the inevitable feeling of loneliness when an individual casts himself off and tries new thinking and behavior as Fromm has shown so convincingly.

The Promise Of Human Autonomy

We have glaring examples of where people have short-circuited the pain and doubt of these moments of loneliness and have chosen to give up an autonomous functioning altogether. Supporters of Hitler in Germany, and the followers of Jones in Jonestown have suffered horribly for their return to a "safe" dependency. The mental health professionals who have studied the multitude of young people who are currently enrolled in a number of religious cults also report that these converts have stopped growing entirely and provide pitiful examples of deficient individuals who are operating at very simple psychological and physiological levels.

It is therefore necessary that we teach the facts of human development and spread the ideas of both self-actualization and cooperation. In this way we can illuminate the steps in the sequence of stages and we can demonstrate the interrelationship between group membership with its cooperative behavior and self-development with a goal of some autonomous behavior. Such widespread dissemination of the principles of child and adult development in our schools and in our media provides well-made and clear maps for our population, so that they understand the road, the rest stops, and the obstacles.

J. <u>Reinvestment of autonomy as a stage of human personality with human emotions.</u>

In the past decades of the 20th and 19th Centuries we have based the idea of human rights and of human dignity on religious, humanitarian, and ethical grounds. The main thesis is that we must and should base these rights and ideals on new grounds. It would no longer be "nice" or "God-fearing" to give life, liberty, and happiness to people. There are first of all potentials built into them as living creatures who are operating on principles of living systems. Secondly, these ideals are potential growth points in psychologically developing organisms, insofar as they are expressions of behavior at a lawful stage of development. Hence the individuals are "entitled" to these ideals as their birthright. We have also been saying that the need to give the human being of the 20th Century the opportunity to express these rights is more urgent than his mere acquiescence to nature. The achievement of these rights and of the accompanying stage in development is now very necessary for the very survival of human life on earth. The very self-actualizing behavior, that was available as excess energy invested into new creations, has brought about conditions that threaten the life and survival of all of us. I am, of course, referring to the condition of overcrowding resulting from the interdependence of complex machinery with urban development and to the many inventions such as nuclear energy, polluting chemicals, etc. that threaten the existence of all mankind. We have no more choice but to recognize the self-actualization stage and use it to solve these many pressing problems creatively and intelligently. We require the knowledge of how self-actualizing people can function in a rational manner. We also require the knowledge of the underlying basis of morality and of group loyalty to insure behavior that solves common problems, rather than proliferating new ones.

For these reasons of emergency we have to become cool and pragmatic in our exposition of self-actualization values and their connection with morality. We divorced them temporarily from God, from religion, and from "goodness". We even divorced them from the more humanistic prescriptions toward living more fully or toward a state of "being". We don't say that these ideals don't count, but we are emphasizing that these feelings were already stimulated by and imbued with the very same considerations with which we have more empirically built our thesis. The people who start from ethics or from religion are basing their conclusions on the same facts, the facts of life, and of human psychology, but attribute them to other causes. The dissection in this essay was done to give us a clearer picture of where we came from and where we may be going. That does not mean, however, that we have to be cool and calculating in our approach to human values and goals. It does not mean that we have to get rid of great moments of emotion and of peak experiences that were associated with the older sources.

We have indicated before how very human and how very necessary it is for us to clothe our more cerebral left-brain with feelings and with very idiosyncratic expressions. We therefore need to "create" our own emotion, including our own feelings of awe, of happiness, of mysticism, of closeness, of fellowship, and of ecstasy when we experience and apply new solutions, and when we watch the growth of our efforts and of our society. These feelings are inevitable human psychological characteristics and can become great and creative additions to our cognitive judgment. The exercise of autonomy, the glorification of healthy personality development, and the exercise of moral behavior can all be clothed with feelings. They can furthermore be created anew by each person and they can be embedded in rituals that sanctify and encourage shared feelings among people. These feelings are personally meaningful and even reinforcing. They are very much like the celebrations of confirmation, of anniversaries, and of other milestones, or they can be expressed as private experiences of quiet intensity, exultation, awe, and veneration.

K. Principles underlying autonomy as better answers to the existential question

When Rollo May reminds us that Man has the capacity to know that he was determined and that he must choose his relationship to what determined him psychologically and culturally, he also reminds us of one of the most knotty existential questions that we have inherited because of our gift of consciousness. May gives us a choice of either abdicating consciousness or devoting some thought to such necessities as our impending death, our old age, the limitation of our intelligence, and the forces from our background that condition us and limit our horizon. We have enumerated some of the main existential questions of Man by having a fictitious Adam pose them to himself in the first chapter. They boil down to three main questions we all have to ask ourselves, according to the psychologist Seymour Sarason -- and sometimes over and over again. The first is how to dilute our sense of aloneness, since we are inevitably alone with ourselves. The second is how to maintain a tie with a community, since we need others, and the third is how we can justify our continued life since we know we must die.

As we have indicated earlier, we may be much better able to accept the cycles of pleasure and misfortune in our lives if we can accept the randomness and the lack of order in nature. Our sense of defeat and hopelessness when we experience sickness, misfortune, or failure can be reduced if we give up the illusion that there is a perfect order in a master-created universe in which the proper goals are happiness and harmony. If these are supposedly only available by following the rules of the master-builder and by knowing and achieving the proper stages, then set-backs, or the failure to get there, must be especially discouraging and discombobulating. In more simple terms, we are thereby setting up too high a level of aspiration. We have thereby "inherited" an unrealistic achievement orientation that sits like a millstone around our neck and drives us on or drives us to guilt or despair when we can't measure up. If we are unhinged from this old "parental" voice, then we can take a fresh look at nature, at ourselves, and at our relationships. We can look at it as it is and not as it should be.

Then we can be more magnanimous and recognize that cycles and setbacks are inevitable and we can value our contributions here. Hence the acceptance of a random nature and of the laws of life can make for more equanimity. It can also allow us to exult more in mankind's own progress and in our progress in it. We can really then begin to take some credit for our ability and our tendency to organize and to direct.

This kind of orientation can help us answer Sarason's questions and can reinforce the answers Adam gave himself in his soliloquy. For instance, his joy in finding an hour of peace because his invention cut down his working time can be buttressed by the knowledge that he has superimposed his organizing power and his surplus energy on the inert fortresses of nature and thereby has achieved a new integration. His fearful contemplation of being out there alone and of facing so many uncertainties can be tempered by the realization that this is a normal psychological process and is a result of his long dependence (in the Garden of Eden) for him. His lack of understanding about his own nature and the reactions of others can be tempered by the idea that we know something and that many things are also unknowable or completely determined. These things go hand in hand with the other fact that we do have some "free choice". Also, our need to know is a very normal human expression of the organizing tendencies in living processes by which we try to minimize surprises and disruption and try to strive for more efficiency. His reiteration of the famous existential question of why he is on earth and what his role is and why he is on earth for only such a short time can again be tempered by remembering our human need for order and causality. After all, we are a living system and this is our way of organizing and ordering the cognitive input for more efficient orientation. A response like "Here is this old friend again," may dispose a person to be more tolerant to the nagging question and tolerant of the possibility that one has to face the ambiguity of "There is no answer." One may also have to accept that this question may be related to a counter-belief in an ulterior purpose and to a larger consciousness or plan of beyond and that this meaning in itself may be a creation of Man and of his sense of powerlessness. Adam's exultation over his rational powers and his awe at the dark emotions that occasionally welled up from inside of him certainly find echoes in our discussion of the development of people to maturity, in which rational thinking is employed on a new basis but does not remove the fact that we are also "animals". In other words, as living systems we may express energy on many different levels. Again emotions and so-called irrational feelings need to be accepted as normal and as welcome companions, and as way stations. We can further support Adam's realization of greater freedom by virtue of his and his family's creative acts and of their increases in knowledge. We certainly can see that the knowledge we learn as we grow and as we use it and extend it takes us further away from the long dependency that our peculiar evolution has enforced on us.

Adam's conflict when he compares the acquisition of a bigger faith in his control and mastery with his realization of his own insignificance in the enormous universe, can again be reduced by taking away the need to assign a meaning and a purpose to this universe. At that point each person simply exists, and he then has the option of developing along the required lines and achieve greater levels of complexities, or to go more slowly and become more like the inert grain of sand that gets buffeted about as best as it can. The former would call for celebration and a sense of exaltation, while the latter may be a form of coasting or may require some form of treatment. However, even the latter way of "existing" in this universe is possible, and characterizes many temporary solutions or coasting periods for which there are human rationalizations and even man-made feelings of satisfactions. Adam's fear of the unknown can be answered by the knowledge that uncertainty is again a disrupting occasion for the living forces operating on the cognitive level. However, we are potentially capable of applying a thinking capacity that can either find a direction, or apply a foreshortened and possibly false meaning on the future, or face the uncertainty as a normal reflection of an ever-unpredictable world. Finally we can only apply Adam's reliance on his own sense of the right and the just as signposts of his knowledge of his responsibility toward others. We have learned that this form of reasoning develops in us more securely with age, experience, and with the realization that we depend on others and vice versa. We can take some faith that these principles have similarly developed in others as a sign that they are "real" and that they have proven themselves as workable for human conduct over the ages.

L.

As we human beings develop along our path from dependency to greater independence, identity formation, and finally autonomous behavior, the road is full of potholes and other dangers. It is therefore important to insert a brief reminder of what these dangers are. This reaction is perhaps like the warning signs, for instance, "Curve ahead," that are placed on roads to prepare the motorist to be vigilant. For instance, the psychologist Fritz Redl warns us that we should not give up autonomy and independence to some leader who claims that he is willing to take the responsibility including that for our own actions if we agree to follow him. Such leaders may personalize our conscience and unhinge our own sense of responsibility by various "tribal dances" in which we put on uniform and wear other masks. In these we may commit ourselves to behavior that would otherwise make us feel embarrassed or guilty. Redl calls this a phenomenon "the superego in uniform", and shows that the wearing of the uniform signifies obedience to the leader and conformity to a form of behavior that is temporarily acceptable even if it is basically evil.

There are other dangers to watch out for as the individual is embarking on his journey to psychological treatises on mental health or in psychological prescriptions for better living. We need only to remind ourselves briefly of some of them. One of them is the development of excessive guilt about one's own actions and reactions. This is often associated with a tendency toward self-denial and a feeling that one is not deserving of either rewards or of pleasure. Another related problem is the feeling of unworthiness and inadequacy from which basis the person either selectively ignores or strenuously denies his own strength and positive points. An offshoot of this reaction is the feeling of unworthiness that one has not moved further on the road to perfection or because one has not reached an impossibly high standard of accomplishment. Usually such standards are unknowingly copied from others and then are made our own by borrowing them. The longing for security can induce a search for strong authority figures to substitute for parents. A corollary to this reaction is the need to restrict the independent movement of others by supporting laws and practices that single out groups of people and restrict their freedom. The rejection and persecution of minorities, including gay people, and people with emotional problems belong here. The denial of greater autonomy to people as a smoke screen of hiding one's own perception of creative expression belongs here, such as the denial of equality to women and to blacks, the denial of choice whether a couple wants their sexual expressions to result in conception or not, and the denial of choice to a pregnant woman whether or not she wants to have the baby. A final addition to this list is the uncritical acceptance of irrational ideas such as the one that one should be perfect, or that one should be liked by everyone, or that one should finish or succeed in everything. We have pointed out that the basic sense of autonomy is fueled by a positive self-image and by a previous development of inner security. It is further supported by a positive climate that also offers opportunities for expression. However, there are many who attempt to role-play autonomous behavior in order to compensate against inner insecurity. For instance, we have all met people who want to be rich or powerful in order to put a cap over a pervading sense of inadequacy. The macho orientation of the male is often cited as an expression of this reaction. We have to guard against short-circuiting reactions on the path to true self-actualization. We need more psychological research on the manifestation of inner security, and also studies that describe how compensation for autonomy can lead to crime and self-destruction of various forms. It is therefore not merely for reasons of intellectual curiosity that we have traced the inhibition of our knowledge of autonomy in history in Chapters II, III, and IV. It is here important to remind ourselves that the better the distribution of goods, the more widespread availability of physical security, the promotion of better health, and the development of adequate leisure are all important foundations for the stimulation of autonomous behavior. Also, we need a more widespread and more wide-eyed emancipation from the old religious ideas that made Man a slave of religion and its ministers, and prevented self-initiated thinking and behavior as sinful and heretic. Finally we need more research and more knowledge on the functioning of the human mind to give us a clear picture of development and a better understanding of how and why emotional and cognitive functioning can go wrong. Pockets of these pitfalls in the three chapters dealing with history are still around us and we have to be able to identify them and guard against them.

Finally, we need to say a word about the inevitable clashes that come about when different people on the move from a self-actualizing base encroach on each other or block each other for self-expression. In such instances arbitration again is called for. If we attribute such a clash of interest to two rather mature individuals we usually do not encounter much of a problem. They will arbitrate between themselves and arrive at a mutually satisfactory conclusion. For instance, suppose a large tree grows on the border of two people's gardens. One person wants to chop the tree down in order to grow some vegetables and flowers in the resulting sunshine. The other has been getting a lot of shade and coolness for his home and is also an ardent birdwatcher who has enjoyed the antics of birds on the tree. These neighbors may be quite able to compromise. The first person saws off some branches that give him more sunshine in the areas he wants to cultivate, and leaves many branches leaning toward the other person's home and still harboring some birds.

In the old days there was no problem between two self-initiating individuals. The person with the greatest number of resources and greatest power would win out. In the beginning of the age of autonomy we recognize that people have rights to their ideas and a right to fulfill themselves. So the use of raw power to muscle another person out of the way is less possible. We are beginning to contain selfish initiative on the political front, as the curtailment of the tycoon and of the exploiter on the economic front have shown. Our call for a more frequent use of arbitration is also based on a recognition that we have to safeguard everyone's autonomy and everyone's road toward development and the opportunities to act. It is not enough to promote an understanding of autonomy and a dissemination of the order of steps leading to it. We also have to foster an acceptance of the morality of autonomy. People have to develop a sense of responsibility for safeguarding opportunities for everyone's expression of self-actualizing behavior. Part of this sense of responsibility is the willingness to consider another person's moves when one collides with him or to submit to arbitration by a third party if one cannot settle the issue adequately with the other person. Other avenues to overcome some of the dangers of excessive autonomy experienced in economic and social areas have been cited by Erich Fromm in his latest book.

M. The dawn of the age of autonomy

It is the main thesis of this volume that we have arrived at a new stage in the development of human civilization. We have stumbled onto a number of bits and pieces that could be assembled into a more coordinated set of principles and into a plan for action. These bits and pieces were discovered either by social scientists trying to tackle and understand the human mind through empirical investigations rather than just speculating on it in an armchair, or they were flashed under our nose because we suddenly became aware of a greater availability of behavior that was previously much more rare. Thus the development of leisure and of a longer life span allowed people to develop further along the maturational ladder and display autonomous behavior much more often and more forcefully. The bits and pieces were also pushed forward in greater magnitude and with more forceful illumination through the social experiments in political democracy that were ushered in by the great revolutions after the Renaissance. The political organization and constitutions provided the banners with which Man rose up to experiment with his autonomy; they provided the fertile soil on which he could nourish and expand his experimentation.

Now that we have discovered a genuine autonomy stage and can see it reflected in personality development and supported by political democracy, we can also understand why it was not discovered and emphasized earlier. Few people were able to get as far because killer diseases annihilated many on the road to this goal. The hard work required by most people for their survival and also to feed the lust and greed of the ruling autocrats took strength and time away from self-contemplation and introspective planning. Religious dogma drove the final nail into the lid that kept the hopes and faith in self-development out of sight. As we have increased our age span and our leisure, we are developing stages and capacities that were "built into us" by our physiological and our psychological heritage as living systems. They have been further stabilized by our learning and from our heritage of intelligent beings with a long history. Before the 20th Century the recognition of these capacities came up so fleetingly that they could not be programmed for a whole nation or for the human race. Now we can pull the various strands together, put the spotlight on them, assemble them into a program, and use them.

The other reasons for making a concerted effort to assemble the bits and pieces into a workable program are in the demands of our age. Before today we were in the more luxurious position of middling along with different ideas about Man and his relation to the earth and to the other people on it. We had the privilege of making mistakes, even costly ones, like the Crusades and the many wars in history. These catastrophes occurred mostly at random, as Barbara Tuchman described in her account of the 14th Century. The mistakes may have cost hundreds or thousands of lives and may have left whole areas fallow and depleted for decades. However, neighboring groups were not affected. Even in the ravaged areas new sprouts eventually would begin another life. In those ages some philosophers, novelists, and poets would "discover" autonomy and play with it.

Thanks to the fruits of that autonomy, we have now created vast and complex societies. They have become dependent on each other. To support a complex society the people in it have become interdependent on each other. No longer does each family grow its own food, make its own clothing, build its own house, cater to its own little illnesses or problems, or fix the few tools that were once needed. Nowadays millions of people may suffer if the garbage collectors go on strike. A whole community of over 2,000 may have to move out for several days if a brakeman on a freight train has failed to do his duty and has caused a derailment of tank cars that have burst open and spilled their poisonous gas into the community.

We have been so busy spinning off inventions and ideas into the creation of more refined, secure, and easy living that we have not noticed we are also creating some terrible evils which endanger that living again. While we produce electrical energy to power all of our machines and labor-saving devices, we are also spewing clouds of poisonous sulfur and hydrocarbons into the atmosphere. The busy mass production of our marvelous automobiles also creates millions of little monsters that saturate the atmosphere with poisonous products of gasoline explosions. As we invent new machines and chemicals to grow more food on our fertilized soils fewer people are needed to feed the millions, but we are also flushing the by-products of these fertilizers into our rivers and wells. Finally our inventive genius has produced weapons of mass destruction that are beyond any person's imagination. Hence we have to stop playing around, because we might invite general disaster for all mankind or for a large and decisive part of our world. For the same reasons we also can no longer allow a random process of human experimentation and human expression in little bits and pieces. In addition, we have inherited a number of pesky by-products in our own back yard that have soured the secure and pleasant existence of yesterday. Problems like alienation, isolation, feelings of powerlessness, excessive narcissism, and even anarchy nag us to "do something".

Our illumination of the self-actualization stage of human functioning and its potent companions of rational problem-solving and of principled morality looms as one salvation for Man. It may therefore be much more than a fad of "doing your own thing" or a "western value". It may be the only driving power that really installs reason as the main governing force for Man's destiny. It will take an institutionalized form of reasoning to safeguard the autonomy and the existence of everyone. Other alternatives of relying on some dogma or an ideology invented and supported by a powerful, autocratic clique is like playing with fire. With such fingers on a trigger of devices for mass destruction we are only increasing the predominance of human irrationality and invite the possibility of panic reactions. We will have to learn to trust the morality and rationality of people who have reached a more autonomous stage in their normal development. This reliance on their mediation role may then solve a whole range of problems, whether the dispute is about a boundary or about the rights of seal hunters versus the demands of the preservers of the natural environment. Since rational thinking can be employed in the solution of an engineering problem, such as spanning an estuary with a large bridge, we can use this form of problem-solving in human and social dilemmas, once we have made sure that this rational judgment has been further refined in the vats of personality development.

This new use of autonomy requires a more thorough search into the developing selves of many of us and requires a study and diagnosis of individual development. Some people may yearn for the good old days where nobody thought of a self or felt a need to define it and watch for its growth. Some people may be bothered by having to take a new look at themselves. However, this process is more necessary now because the problems arising from a conflicting self-structure can pepper many more people in the vicinity with fall-out and even hit those far away. The negligent brake-man on a freight train loaded with explosives, or the truck driver hauling nuclear waste material come to mind. Nobody is disturbed any more if we test or probe the pilots of our planes, the drivers of our interstate buses, or our policemen and the officers in charge of a nuclear missile silo. We expect that they must be emotionally mature and free of incapacitating psychological conflicts. Why is it not equally feasible to ask the people who are chosen to be the mediators of important disputes and problems and to ask our leaders to introspect on their development and maturation and to check on which human level they are functioning? For this we need to place attention on this development and on the relevant behavior. We have to make it a program to find this out and share our knowledge, so that all of us know what to expect, including our representatives and those who want to become our leaders.

If Jaynes is right about the "invention" of consciousness as a more efficient psychological integration of our two brains there is no limit as to what we can still accomplish with the brain. We are suggesting that we use our brain even more consciously after having learned something from the recent findings in the laboratories of social scientists. We now have the possibility of using reason, democracy, and a training or preparation for autonomy.

We have therefore arrived at an exciting new age in the history of Man. We have stumbled on some facts about self-actualization as a legitimate form of functioning and as a stage in personality development. We understand its nature a little better and its prerequisites and its behavioral correlates. We also have produced a culture where we live to enjoy it and where many people have the opportunity to use it. In addition we also have been able to safeguard its legitimacy with a democratic ideology. Now the question is what we do with it. Do we acknowledge it as a valid human characteristic and as a tool to solve our pressing problems, or do we use it merely as a toy or as an ornament? The answer may lead us either into a Tower of Babel situation that will decrease communication and lead to mass murder or mass suicide. Or it can lead to a higher integration of human civilization for the mutual benefit of all. The question is whether we are inevitably headed for disaster with the evolutionary time bomb of our autonomy as a fragmentary force built into us, or are we -- by virtue of our evolution -- capable of integrating the products plus the energy from our autonomy thus enabling our survival.

Bibliography

CHAPTER I

The Bible. Old Testament. Genesis 1-3.

CHAPTER II

Aurelius, Marcus. <u>Meditations.</u> Book XII, Great Books of the Western World: Encyclopedia Britannica, Inc., Vol. XII, Chicago: William Benton, 1952.

Epictetus. <u>Discourses.</u> Book IV, Great Books of the Western World: Encyclopedia Britannica, Inc., Vol. XII, Chicago: William Benton, 1952.

Machiavelli, Nicolo. <u>The Prince.</u> Great Books of the Western World: Encyclopedia Britannica, Inc., Vol. XXIII, Chicago: William Benton, 1952.

Socrates. (reference not located).

CHAPTER III

Aquinas, Saint Thomas. <u>The Summa Theologica.</u> Great Books of the Western World: Encyclopedia Britannica, Inc., Vols, XIX, XX, Chicago: William Benton, 1952.

Aristotle, Nicomachean. <u>Metaphysics and Ethics.</u> Great Books of the Western World: Encyclopedia Britannica, Inc., Vols. VIII, IX, Chicago: William Benton, 1952.

Augustine, Saint. <u>On Christian Doctrine.</u> Great Books of the Western World: Encyclopedia Britannica, Inc., Vol. XVIII, Chicago: William Benton, 1952.

Aurelius, Marcus. <u>Meditations.</u> Book XII, Great Books of the Western World Encyclopedia, Britannica, Inc., Vol. XII, Chicago: William Benton, 1952.

Descartes, René. <u>Meditations III.</u> Great Books of the Western World: Encyclopedia Britannica, Inc., Vol. XXXI, Chicago: William Benton, 1952.

Epictetus. <u>Discourses.</u> Book IV, Great Books of the Western World: Encyclopedia Britannica, Inc., Vol. XII, Chicago: William Benton, 1952.

Freud, Sigmund. Great Books of the Western World: Encyclopedia Britannica, Inc., Vol. LIV, Chicago: William Benton, 1952.

Fromm, Erich. <u>Escape From Freedom.</u> (re: Martin Luther) New York: Holt, Rinehart and Winston, 1941.

Herbert, E. and Tindal, M. (reference not located).

Herodotus. <u>The History of Herodotus.</u> Great Books of the Western World: Encyclopedia Britannica, Inc., Vol. VI, Chicago: William Benton, 1952.

Kant, Immanuel. <u>The Critique of Pure Reason and the Critique of Practical Reason</u>. Great Books of the Western World: Encyclopedia Britannica, Inc., Vol. XLII, Chicago: William Benton, 1952.

Locke, John. <u>An Essay Concerning Human Understanding.</u> Great Books of the Western World: Encyclopedia Britannica, Inc., Vol. XXXV, Chicago: William Benton, 1952.

Mill, John Stuart. <u>On Liberty and Utilitarianism.</u> Great Books of the Western World: Encyclopedia Britannica, Inc., Vol. XLIII, Chicago: William Benton, 1952.

Montaigne, Michel Eyquem de. <u>The Essays.</u> Great Books of the Western World: Encyclopedia Britannica, Inc., Vol. XXV, Chicago: William Benton, 1952.

Plato. <u>The Dialogues of Plato.</u> Great Books of the Western World: Encyclopedia Britannica, Inc., Vol. VII, Chicago: William Benton, 1952.

Plotinus. <u>The Six Enneads.</u> Great Books of the Western World: Encyclopedia Britannica, Inc., Vol. XVII, Chicago & William Benton, 1952.

Smith, Adam. <u>An Inquiry into the Nature and Causes of the Wealth of Nations.</u> p.336, Great Books of the Western World: Encyclopedia Britannica, Inc., Vol. XXXIX, Chicago: William Benton, 1952.

Socrates. (reference not located).

Tacitus, P. Cornelius. <u>The Annals.</u> Great Books of the Western World: Encyclopedia Britannica, Inc., Vol. XV, Chicago: William Benton, 1952.

The Bible. Old Testament. Deuteronomy 30: 15 – 20.

The Bible. Old Testament. Genesis 3.

The Bible. Old Testament. Isaiah 40: 12 - 26, 64: 8.

The Bible. Matthew 6:10, 6:22 - 34, 7: 1.

The Bible. Old Testament. Psalms 89:6 - 8.

The Bible. Romans 9.

Tolstoy, Leo. <u>War and Peace.</u> Great Books of the Western World: Encyclopedia Britannica, Inc., Vol. LI, Chicago: William Benton, 1952.

Weill, Kurt. The Musical: <u>Johnny Johnson.</u> Staged: 11/19/36 in New York City.

CHAPTER IV

Aquinas, Saint Thomas. <u>The Summa Theologica.</u> Great Books of the Western World: Encyclopedia Britannica, Inc., Vols. XIX, XX, Chicago: William Benton, 1952.

Augustine, Saint. <u>The Confessions on Christian Doctrine.</u> Great Books of the Western World: Encyclopedia Britannica, Inc., Vol. XVIII, Chicago: William Benton, 1952.

Aurelius, Marcus. <u>Meditations.</u> Great Books of the Western World: Encyclopedia Britannica, Inc., Vol. XII, Chicago: William Benton, 1952.

Copernicus, Nicolaus. <u>On the Revolutions of the Heavenly Spheres.</u> Great Books of the Western World: Encyclopedia Britannica, Inc., Vol. XVI, Chicago: William Benton, 1952.

Darwin, Charles. The Descent of Man and Selection in Relation to Sex. Great Books of the Western World: Encyclopedia Britannica, Inc., Vol. XLIX, Chicago: William Benton, 1952.

Descartes, René. Rules for the Direction of Mind. Great Books of the Western World: Encyclopedia Britannica, Inc., Vol. XXXI, Chicago: William Benton, 1952.

Freud, Sigmund. Great Books of the Western World: Encyclopedia Britannica, Inc., Vol. LIV, Chicago: William Benton, 1952.

Fromm, Erich. Man for Himself: An Inquiry into the Psychology of Ethics.(regarding Kant), Holt, Rinehart, and Winston, 1947, pp. 121 - 123.

Galileo, Galilei. Dialogues Concerning the Two New Sciences. Great Books of the Western World: Encyclopedia Britannica, Inc., Vol. XXVIII, Chicago: William Benton, 1952.

Hegel, Georg Wilhelm Friedrich. The Philosophy of Right. Great Books of the Western World: Encyclopedia Britannica, Inc., Vol. XLVI, Chicago: William Benton, 1952.

Heisenberg, Werner. Physics and Philosophy. Harper Torchbooks, 1958.

Hobbes, Thomas. Leviathan, Or, Matter, Form, and Power of a Commonwealth Ecclesiastical and Civil. Great Books of the Western World: Encyclopedia Britannica, Inc., Vol. XXIII, Chicago: William Benton, 1952.

Hume, David. An Enquiry Concerning Human Understanding. Great Books of the Western World: Encyclopedia Britannica, Inc., Vol. XXXV, Chicago: William Benton, 1952.

Husserl, Edmund. (German philosopher 1859 - 1938) (reference not located).

Huxley, Aldous. Doors of Perception. Bound with: Heaven and Hell. Harper-Row, 1970.

James, William. The Principles of Psychology. Great Books of the Western World: Encyclopedia Britannica, Inc., Vol. LIII, Chicago: William Benton, 1952.

Kant, Immanuel, General Introduction to the Metaphysics of Morals. Great Books of the Western World: Encyclopedia Britannica, Inc., Vol. XLII, Chicago: William Benton, 1952.

Lifton, Robert Jay. <u>Towards a New Psychology.</u> New York: Simon and Schuster, 1976.

Locke, John. <u>An Essay Concerning Human Understanding.</u> Great Books of the Western World: Encyclopedia Britannica, Inc., Vol. XXXV, Chicago: William Benton, 1952.

Mill, John Stuart. <u>On Liberty and Utilitarianism.</u> Great Books of the Western World: Encyclopedia Britannica, Inc., Vol. XLIII, Chicago: William Benton, 1952.

Montaigne, Michel Eyquem de. <u>The Essays.</u> Great Books of the Western World: Encyclopedia Britannica, Inc., Vol. XXV, Chicago: William Benton, 1952.

Nunn, C. Z., Crockett, H. J. Jr. and Williams, J. A. Jr. <u>Tolerance for Non-Conformists: A National Survey of America's Changing Commitment to Civil Liberties.</u> San Francisco: Jossey-Bass, 1978.

Plato. <u>The Dialogues of Plato.</u> Great Books of the Western World: Encyclopedia Britannica, Inc., Vol. VII, Chicago: William Benton, 1952.

Reichenbach, (reference not located).

Rousseau, Jean Jacques. <u>On the Origin of Inequality.</u> Great Books of the Western World: Encyclopedia Britannica, Inc., Vol. XXXVIII, Chicago: William Benton, 1952.

Russell, Bertrand. (Mathematician and Philosopher, 1872) (reference not located).

Semmelweis, Phillip Ignez. (Hungarian Obstetrician: pioneer in prevention of puerperal fever, 1816 - 1965) (reference not located).

Socrates. (reference not located).

Spinoza, Benedict de. <u>Ethics.</u> Great Books of the Western World: Encyclopedia Britannica, Inc., Vol. XXXI, Chicago: William Benton, 1952.

CHAPTER V

Aquinas, Saint Thomas. <u>The Summa Theologica.</u> Great Books of the Western World: Encyclopedia Britannica, Inc., Vols. XIX, XX, Chicago: William Benton, 1952.

Aristotle. Metaphysics. Great Books of the Western World: Encyclopedia Britannica, Inc., Vol. VIII, Chicago: William Benton, 1952.

Augustine, Saint. The Confessions. Book VII, Great Books of the Western World: Encyclopedia Britannica, Inc., Vol. XVIII, Chicago: William Benton, 1952.

Aurelius, Marcus. Meditations. Book XII, Great Books of the Western World: Encyclopedia Britannica, Inc., Vol. XII, Chicago: William Benton, 1952.

Darwin, Charles. The Descent of Man and Selection in Relation to Sex. Great Books of the Western World: Encyclopedia Britannica, Inc., Vol. XLIX, Chicago: William Benton, 1952.

Descartes, René. Meditations on First Philosophy. Great Books of the Western World: Encyclopedia Britannica, Inc., Vol. XXXI, Chicago: William Benton, 1952.

Epictetus. Discourses. Book II, Chapter 16, Great Books of the Western World: Encyclopedia Britannica, Inc., Vol. XII, Chicago: William Benton, 1952.

Hegel, Georg Wilhelm Friedrich. The Philosophy of Right. Great Books of the Western World: Encyclopedia Britannica, Inc., Vol. XLVI, Chicago: William Benton, 1952.

Hus, John. (14th century religious leader, 1369 - 1475) (reference not located).

James, William. The Principles of Psychology. Great Books of the Western World: Encyclopedia Britannica, Inc., Vol. LIII, Chicago: William Benton, 1952.

Kant, Immanuel. (In an article referring to "will") Great Books of the Western World: Encyclopedia Britannica, Inc., Vol. XLII, Chicago: William Benton, 1952.

Locke, John. An Essay Concerning Human Understanding. Great Books of the Western World: Encyclopedia Britannica, Inc., Vol. XXXV, Chicago: William Benton, 1952.

Luther, Martin. (reference not located).

Montaigne, Michel Eyquem de. The Essays. Great Books of the Western World: Encyclopedia Britannica, Inc., Vol. XXV, Chicago: William Benton, 1952.

Plotinus. <u>The Six Enneads.</u> Great Books of the Western World: Encyclopedia Britannica, Inc., Vol. XVII, Chicago: William Benton, 1952.

Rapaport, David. The Theory of Ego-Autonomy, pp. 722 - 744 and The Autonomy or the Ego, pp. 357 - 367. In Merton M. Gill (Ed.) <u>The Collected Papers of David Rapaport.</u> New York: Basic Books, 1967.

Spinoza, Benedict de. <u>Ethics.</u> Great Books of the Western World: Encyclopedia Britannica, Inc., Vol. XXXI, Chicago: William Benton, 1952.

The Bible. Old Testament. Deuteronomy 32: 48 - 52 (Moses punishment).

The Bible. Old Testament. Exodus 8 - 16 (Egyptian plagues).

The Bible. Old Testament. Exodus 32 (golden calf).

The Bible. Old Testament. Genesis 6: 11 - 8: 16 (Noah and flood).

The Bible. Old Testament. Genesis 13: 10 (Sodom and Gomorrah).

The Bible. Old Testament. Genesis 22: 1 - 19 (Abraham and son).

The Bible. Old Testament. II Kings (punishment of Jews to the breakdown of morality of kings).

Tolstoy, Leon. <u>War and Peace.</u> Book XIV, Chapter 12, Great Books of the Western World: Encyclopedia Britannica, Inc., Vol. LI, Chicago: William Benton, 1952.

Wyclif, John. (1320 - 1382) (reference not located).

CHAPTER VI

Adler, Alfred. "Creative Self" and Striving for Superiority. In Ansbacher, Heinz and Ansbacher, Rowena R. (Eds.) <u>A Collection of Later Writings.</u> 2nd Edition, Northwestern University Press, 1935.

Adler, Alfred. <u>Superiority and Social Interest: A Collection of Later Writings.</u> Ansbacher, Heinz L. and Ansbacher, Rowena R., (Eds.), 1979.

Angyal, Andras. A Theoretical Model for Personality Studies. Journal of Personality, 1951, <u>20</u>: 131 - 135.

Buber, Martin. <u>I and Thou.</u> Scribner, 1970, p. 100.

Erikson, Erik H. <u>Childhood and Society.</u> New York: W. W. Norton, 1963.

Erikson, Erik H. <u>Insight and Responsibility.</u> New York: W. W. Norton, 1964.

Fromm, Erich. <u>Escape from Freedom.</u> New York: Holt, Rinehart and Winston, 1947.

Fromm, Erich. <u>Man for Himself: An Inquiry into the Psychology of Ethics.</u> New York: Holt, Rinehart and Winston, 1947.

Fromm, Erich. <u>To Have or to Be.</u> New York: Harper and Row, 1976, p. 110.

Freud, Sigmund. Points by Binswanger in talk at Freud's 80th birthday celebration of the Vienna Society of Medical Psychology, 1936.

Goldstein, Kurt. <u>Self Actualization.</u> 1940.

Jahoda, Marie. <u>Current Concepts of Positive Mental Health.</u> New York: Basic Books, 1958.

Levinson, Daniel. (regarding: enjoyment of life) (reference not located fully) Bio. Med., 1979, 71(?): 195.

Loevinger, Jane. <u>Ego Development: Concepts and Theories.</u> Jossey-Bass, 1976, p. 67.

Maslow, Abraham. <u>Motivation and Personality.</u> 2nd. Edition, New York: Harper and Row, 1970.

Maslow, Abraham. <u>Towards the Psychology of Being.</u> 2nd. Edition, New York: D. Van Nostrand Company, 1968, p. 25.

May, Rollo. <u>Man's Search for Himself.</u> New York: W. W. Norton, 1953.

May, Rollo. <u>Love and Will.</u> New York: W. W. Norton, 1969.

Riesman, David. <u>The Lonely Crowd: a study of the changing American Culture.</u> Yale University Press, 1950.

Rogers, Carl. A Theory of Psychotherapy, Personality and Interpersonal Relationships as Develops in the Client-centered Framework. In Koch, S. (Ed.) <u>Psychology: The Study of a Science.</u> Vol. 3, New York: McGraw Hill, 1959, pp. 184 - 246.

Rogers, Carl. <u>Self Actualization.</u> 1959.

Smith, Adam. <u>An Inquiry into the Nature and Causes of the Wealth of Nations: 1904 Edition.</u> Derived from the Edwin Cannan Edition by arrangement with Methuen and Co. Ltd., Vol. 39, London: Pergamon, 1981.

Smith, M. Brewster. Journal of Social Issues. 1978, 34 (4): 181 - 199.

Snygg, Donald and Combs, Arthur W. Individual Behavior. A New Frame of Reference for Psychology. New York: Harper and Brothers, 1949.

Tillich, Paul. The Courage to Be. New Haven: Yale University Press, 1952, pp. 81 - 82

CHAPTER VII

Bandura, Albert. Self-Efficacy: Toward a Unifying Theory of Behavior Change. Psychology Review, 1977, 84: 121 - 215.

Barber, Theodore X., et al. Hypnosis. Imagination and Human Potentialities. Pergamon, 1974.

Ellis, Albert. Humanistic Psychotherapy: The Rational-Emotive Approach. McGraw Hill, 1974.

Goldfried, Marvin R. and Merbaum, Michael (Eds.). Behavior Change Through Self-Control. New York: Holt, Rinehart and Winston, 1973.

Frank, Jerome D.; Hoehn-Saric, Rudolf; Imber, Stanley D.; Lieberman, Bernard L. and Stone, Anthony R. Effective Ingredients of Successful Psychotherapy. New York: Brunner Mazel, 1978.

Lieberman, Yalom and Miles, Matthew B. Encounter Groups: First Facts. New York: Basic Books, 1973.

Luborsky et al. Factors Influencing the Outcome of Psychotherapy: A Review of quantitative Research. Psychological Bulletin, 1971 (March),75 (3): 145 - 195.

Rogers, Carl H. Client-Centered Therapy: Its Current Practices. Implications and Theory. Boston: Houghton, 1951.

Rogers, Carl R. (book reference not located).

Rosenbaum. (regarding: Pygmalion effect) (reference not located).

Shostrom Everett. Actualizing Therapy: Foundations for a Scientific Ethic. Knapp, E.; Knapp, P. and Robert, R. (Eds.), Edits Pub.

Strupp, Hans H. Psychotherapy: Clinical Research and Theoretical Issues. Aronson, 1973.

CHAPTER VIII

Allport, Gordon. <u>Becoming: Basic Considerations for a Psychology of Personality.</u> New Haven: Yale University Press, 1955.

Angyal, Andras. <u>Neurosis and Treatment - A Holistic View.</u> New York: Viking Press, 1973.

Bertalanffy, Ludwig Von. Group Therapy System: Application to Psychology. Social Science Information, 1967, <u>6</u>: 125 - 136.

Buber, Martin. <u>I and Thou.</u> Scribner, 1970.

Durkin, James (Ed.). <u>Living Groups: Group Psychotherapy and General Systems Theory.</u> New York: Brunner-Mazel, 1981.

Grinker, R. R. Sr. <u>Toward a Unified Theory of Human Behavior.</u> (2nd. Edition), New York: Basic Books, 1967.

Husserl. (German philosopher, 1859 - 1938) (reference not located).

Jaynes, Julian. <u>The Origins of Consciousness in the Breakdown of the Bicameral Mind.</u> Boston: Houghton-Mifflin Co.,1976.

Lifton, Robert Jay. <u>The Life of the Self: Toward a New Psychology.</u> New York: Simon and Schuster, 1976.

Maslow, Abraham. <u>Religions, Values and Peak Experiences.</u> Penguin, 1976.

May, Rollo. <u>Love and Will.</u> New York: W. W. Norton, 1969.

May, Rollo. <u>Psychology and the Human Dilemma.</u> New York: W. W. Norton, 1980.

Miller, James. <u>Living Systems,</u> McGraw, 1977.

Watts, Alan W. <u>Psychology East and West.</u> Random, 1975.

Watts, Alan W. <u>Three: The Way of Zen: Nature. Man and Woman: Psychotherapy East and West.</u> Pantheon Books, 1961.

CHAPTER IX

Mead, George. <u>Mind, Self and Society.</u> Chicago: University of Chicago Press, 1934.

Mill, John Stuart. <u>Utilitarianism.</u> Great Books of the Western World: Encyclopedia Britannica, Inc., Vol. XLIII, Chicago: William Benton, 1952.

The Bill of Rights of the United States Constitution. First Congress of the United States, March 4, 1789.

The Declaration of Independence. The Thirteen United States of America's Continental Congress, 1776.

CHAPTER X

Aron, Raymond. In Defense of a Decadent Europe. Regnery-Gateway, 1979.

Gruen, Walter. Soviet Psychology's Concept of Personality as Represented at the 1966 Moscow Congress. Soviet Studies, 1969, 20 (4): 499 - 510.

Marx, Karl. Capital. Great Books of the Western World: Encyclopedia Britannica, Inc., Vol. L, Chicago: William Benton, 1952.

Marx, Karl and Engels, Friedrich. Manifesto of the Communist Party. Great Books of the Western World: Encyclopedia Britannica, Inc. Vol. L, Chicago: William Benton, 1952.

Tuchman, Barbara W. A Distant Mirror. the Calamitous 14th Century. New York: Alfred A. Knopf, 1979.

CHAPTER XI

Campbell, Donald T. On the Conflict Between Biological and Social Evolution and Between Psychological and Moral Tradition. American Psychologist, 1975. 30 (12): 1103 - 1126.

Coopersmith, Stanley. The Antecedents of Self Esteem. San Francisco: W. H. Freeman, 1967.

Easterbrook, James A. The Determinants of Free Will: A Psychological Analysis of Responsible. Adjustive Behavior. New York: Academic Press, 1978.

Girvetz, Harry. Beyond Right and Wrong. New York: Free Press, 1973.

Kohlberg, Lawrence. Development of Moral Character and Moral Ideology. Chapter in M. L. Hoffman and L. W. Hoffman (Eds.) Review of Child Development Research. Vol. I, pp. 383 - 431, New York: Russell Sage Foundation, 1964. (reference "A")

Kohlberg, Lawrence. Stage and Sequence: The Cognitive-Developmental Approach to Socialization. In David A. Goslin (Ed.) <u>Handbook of Socialization Theory and Research.</u> Chapter 6, pp. 347 - 480, Chicago: Rand McNally, 1969. (reference "B")

Kohlberg, Lawrence. Continuities in Childhood and Adult Moral Development Revisited. In P.B. Baltes and K. W. Schaie (Eds.) <u>Life Span Developmental Psychology: Personality and Socialization.</u> Chapter 8, pp. 179 - 204, New York: Academic Press, 1973. (reference "C")

Kohlberg, Lawrence. The Implications of Moral Stages for Adult Education. Religious Education, 1977, <u>72</u> (2): 183 - 201. (reference "D")

Kohlberg, Lawrence. Talk at Clark University, June, 1979. (reference "E")

Lasch, Christopher. <u>The Culture of Narcissism.</u> New York: W. W. Norton, 1979.

Loevinger, Jane. <u>Scientific Ways in the Study of Ego Development.</u> In. Vol. XII, 1978 Heinz Werner Lecture Series, Clark University Press, 1978.

Mead, George H. <u>Mind. Self and Society.</u> Chicago: University of Chicago Press, 1934.

Rawls, John. <u>A Theory of Justice.</u> Cambridge: Harvard University Press, 1971.

CHAPTER XII

Bach, Kurt W. <u>Beyond Words: The Story of Sensitivity Training and the Encounter Movement.</u> New York: Russell Sage Foundation, 1972.

Descartes, René. <u>Objections and Replies,</u> Great Books of the Western World: Encyclopedia Britannica, Inc., Vol. XXXI, Chicago: William Benton, 1952,

Dostoyevsky, Fyodor. <u>The Brothers Karamazov.</u> Signet Books, 1957.

Fromm, Erich. <u>Escape from Freedom.</u> New York: Holt, Rinehart and Winston, 1947.

Greening, Thomas C. The Gestalt Prayer: Final Version. Journal of Humanistic Psychology, 1977, <u>17</u> (3): 77 - 79.

Keniston, Kenneth. For him there is no Exit from the Cellar. New York Times, 1976 (Feb. 20).

Larch, Christopher. The Culture of Narcissism. New York: W. W. Norton, 1978.

May, Rollo. Love and Will. New York: W. W. Norton, 1969.

May, Rollo. Man's Search for Himself. New York: W. W. Norton, 1953.

May, Rollo. Psychology and the Human Dilemma. New York: Van Nostrand Reinhold Co., 1969.

Perls, Fritz S. Gestalt Therapy Verbatim. Utah: Real People Press, 1969.

Rogers, Carl R. Carl Rogers on Personal Power: Inner Strength and its Revolutionary Impact. New York: Delacorte Press, 1977.

Schrag, Peter. Mind Control. Dell, 1979.

Schutz, William. Joys Expanding Human Awareness. Grove, 1967.

Smith, Brewster K. Journal of Social Issues, 1978, 34: 182. (full reference not located)

Toffler, Alvin. Future Shock. New York: Random House, 1970.

Tuchman, Barbara W. A Distant Mirror. the Calamitous 14th Century. New York: Alfred A. Knopf, 1979.

CHAPTER XIII

Akhoj, Karen. Contact, Demands, and Love. Copenhagen: Forum Press, 1979.

Asch, Solomon E. Effects of Group Pressure Upon the Modification and Distortion of Judgements. In H. Guetzkow (Ed.), Groups. Leadership and Men. Pittsburgh: Carnegie Press, 1951.

Asch, Solomon E. Studies of Independence and Conformity: A Minority of one Against a Unanimous Majority. Psychology Monographs, 1956, 70 (9): 416.

Allport, Gordon. Becoming: Basic Considerations for a Psychology of Personality. New Haven: Yale University Press, 1955.

Bruner, Jerome. The Making of Myth. New York: Putnam, 1962.

Commoner, Barry. The Politics of Energy. New York: Alfred H. Knopf, 1979.

Crutchfield, Richard S. Conformity and Character. American Psychologist, 1955, 10: 191 - 198.

Ellis, Albert. (reference not located)

Fromm, Erich. Escape from Freedom. New York: Holt, Rinehart and Winston, 1941.

Fromm, Erich. Man for Himself: An Investigation into the Psychology of Ethics. New York: Holt, Rinehart and Winston, 1947.

Fromm, Erich. To Have or to Be. New York: Harper and Row, 1976, pp. 164 - 167.

Gordon, Mary. Final Payments. New York: Random House, 1978.

Heilbroner, Robert. Capitalism. New Yorker, 1978 (Aug. 28).

Hollander, Edwin P. Conformity. Status, and Idiosyncrasy Credit. Psychology Review, 1958, 65: 117 - 127.

James, Muriel and Jongeward, Dorothy. Born To Win. Addison-Wesley, 1971.

Jaynes, Julian. The Origins of Consciousness in the Breakdown of the Bicameral Mind. Boston: Houghton Mifflin Co., 1976.

Kohlberg, Lawrence. The Implications of Moral Stages for Adult Education. Religious Education, 1977, 72: 183 - 201.

May, Rollo. Man: Search for Himself. New York: W. W. Norton, 1953.

May, Rollo. Love and Will. New York: W. W. Norton, 1969.

Mead, George. Mind. Self and Society. Chicago: University of Chicago Press, 1934.

Milgram, Stanley. Behavioral Study of Obedience. Journal of Abnormal Social Psychology, 1963, 67 (4): 371 - 378.

Piaget, Jean. The Moral Judgment of the Child. New York: Harcourt, Brace and World, Inc., 1932.

Redl, Fritz. The Superego in Uniform. In Nevitt Sanford, Craig Comstock and Associates. Sanctions for Evil. San Francisco: Jossey-Bass, 1971.

Sampson, Edward E. Psychology and the American Ideal. Journal of Personality and Social Psychology, 1977, 35 (11): 767 - 782.

Sarason, Seymour. Nature of Problem Solving in Social Action. American Psychologist, 1979, 33 (4): 370 - 380.

Schumacher, E. F. <u>Small is Beautiful: Economics if People Mattered.</u> New York: Harper Row, 1973.

Sherif, Carolyn W.; Sherif, Muzafer and Nebergall, R. E. <u>Attitude and Attitude Change: The Social Judgment-Involvement.</u> Greenwood, 1965.

Sherif, Muzafer and Sherif, Carolyn W. <u>Groups Crossroads.</u> New York: Harper and Brothers, 1953.

Sherif, Muzafer and Sherif, Carolyn W. <u>Reference Groups: Exploration into Conformity and Deviation of Adolescents.</u> Regnery-Gateway, 1972.

Shostrom, Everett. <u>Actualizing Therapy: Foundations for a Scientific Ethic</u>. Knapp, E.; Knapp, P. and Robert, R., (Eds.) Edits Pub.

Toffler, Alvin. <u>Future Shock.</u> New York: Random House, 1970.

Tuchman, Barbara W. <u>A Distant Mirror. the Calamitous 14th Century.</u> New York: Alfred A. Knopf, 1979.

Tyler, Leona E. <u>Individuality: Human Possibilities and Personal Choices in the Psychological Development of Man and Woman.</u> San Francisco: Jossey-Bass, 1978.

Whitehead, Alfred North. <u>Adventure of Ideas.</u> New York: MacMillan, 1933.

Whitehead, Alfred North. <u>Process and Reality.</u> New York: Free Press, 1969.

CPSIA information can be obtained
at www.ICGtesting.com
Printed in the USA
FFOW04n2004030717
37451FF